Get Real

A Philosophical Adventure in Virtual Reality

Philip Zhai

ROWMAN & LITTLEFIELD PUBLISHERS, INC.
Lanham • Boulder • New York • Oxford

ROWMAN & LITTLEFIELD PUBLISHERS, INC.

Published in the United States of America
by Rowman & Littlefield Publishers, Inc.
4720 Boston Way, Lanham, Maryland 20706

12 Hid's Copse Road
Cummor Hill, Oxford OX2 9JJ, England

British Library Cataloguing in Publication Information Available

Library of Congress Cataloging-in-Publication Data

Zhai, Philip, 1957–
    Get real : a philosophical adventure in virtual reality / Philip Zhai.
        p.   cm.
    Includes bibliographical references and index.
    ISBN 0-8476-8983-2 (cloth : alk. paper)
    1. Human-computer interaction.   2. Virtual reality.   I. Title.
QA76.9.H85Z45   1998
110—dc21   97-44738
                                                          CIP

ISBN 0-8476-8983-2 (cloth : alk. paper)

Printed in the United States of America

∞ ™ The paper used in this publication meets the minimum requirements of
American National Standard for Information Sciences—Permanence of Paper for
Printed Library Materials, ANSI Z39.48–1984.

Contents

Preface

Technology has tremendously helped us make history. We make powerful tools for manipulating natural and social processes: hammers and screwdrivers, cars and airplanes, telephones and televisions, among others. These are "tools" because they are separated from us, and using any one of these tools does not usually affect the fundamental ways in which we perceive the world. Whether it is being used or not, a hammer remains a hammer in the objective world; when we pick it up and swing it, it does not disappear or become part of us. Of course, as a consequence of making and using these tools in the environment affected by tools, we, the master of tools, also transform our ways of self-perception and the perception of our fellow beings on the socio-psychological level; like a self-trapped bear hunter, we sometimes even become a victim of our own tools.

Thanks to the emergence of virtual reality, our relationship with technology is now taking a drastic turn. Contrary to all previous technologies, virtual reality reverses the logic of the whole process. As soon as we enter the world of virtual reality, virtual reality technology functions to reconfigure the framework of the whole empirical world, and our perception of the technology as a separate object—or "tool"—disappears. Such an immersive situation enables us first to re-constitute our own being directly on the ontological level. Only after that can we engage ourselves in the fascinating ways of making and using tools in this newly created world.

Whereas all previous technologies have pertained primarily to tool-making on the objective side, virtual reality technology pertains primarily to experience-constituting on the subjective side. In other words, virtual reality, combined with teleoperation, is the first technology since the beginning of civilization that allows us to create an alternative empirical world in totality. When we chose a new empirical world, we are also choosing a new system of empirical sciences. Philosophically speaking, few other events in the history could be viewed as similarly significant.

This revolution of worlds and sciences hinges, however, upon our given ways of sensory perception and internal time-consciousness. These are absolutes without which no technology can deliver any empirical version of reality: While the so-called "objective world" is only one among the unlimited number of possibilities, the so-called "subjective world" of perception and consciousness is the source of universal necessity. But this is not to claim that the empirical world is in our heads; our heads form part of the empirical world. We must therefore guard against two common naturalistic mistakes: (1) equating subjectivity with idiosyncratic opinion and (2) equating the mind with the head as a body part. Keeping this in mind, we can understand why actual reality and virtual reality are equally "real" or equally "illusory" insofar as they are equally contingent upon our given sensory framework. But if the virtual is equivalent to the actual, why should we bother to create the virtual? Of course, the obvious difference is that the actual is mandatory whereas the virtual is our own creation.

In this book, I will make and justify the following two claims: (1) There is no ontological difference between virtual reality and actual reality. (2) As co-creators of the virtual world, we—humankind as a whole—for the first time begin to live a systematically meaningful life.

This is not, then, a book of technological predictions about what will happen in the near future, nor one of speculative techno-fantasies: the fictional stories in the book serve to help us understand the implications of virtual reality in its logical extreme. While you are absorbed in them don't forget to determine how those stories support the conclusions that follow from them. Through analysis of these mind-stretching stories, we will be led to realize what will happen if the well-coordinated combination of digital simulation, sensory immersion, and functional teleoperation develops to its ultimate. Therefore, how well today's technology can do the job is not a real issue. At issue instead is that on the one hand, the invention of virtual reality is an occasion for us to gain deeper understanding of the nature of reality; and on the other hand, an adequate understanding of the nature of reality will open our eyes and empower us to see how the virtual reality technology, though still in its primitive form, is prompting us to make a fundamental choice.

In chapter 1, a series of thought experiments achieves two goals at the same time. The Principle of Reciprocity of Alternative Sensory Frameworks demonstrates that from a vantage point that goes beyond either actual or virtual reality, the sensory framework of a virtual world has a parallel, not derivative, relationship with that of the actual world. Our biological sense organs are no less signal-transmitters and -transformers than the goggles and bodysuit we wear for the immersive experience of virtual reality (VR). We will also see that no matter how the sensory framework changes from one to another, the self-identity of the person who witnesses such a change remains intact. Therefore the change of a person's sensory framework shatters only the coherence of an outside observer's sense of that person's identity, not the person's own self-identity. Only if we have an unchanging point of reference can we understand the change of sensory framework; this unchanging point of reference is anchored in the given structure of the person's unified perceptual experience.

In chapter 2, our understanding of reciprocity is reinforced by a demonstration of how all the functionality of the actual world can also be implemented in the virtual world. In such a context, we temporarily leave behind the idea of the person's unchanging self-identity. We thus find the concept of causal connection essential to understanding the fundamental part of VR experience that enables us to tele-operate the natural process in the actual world. This kind of inside-out control is necessary for our subsistence. The word "physical" is used to designate causal processes, which are prior to any sensory framework. Since a spatial relationship depends on a particular sensory framework, our concept of causality here is independent of such notions as distance, continuity, and locality. "Inside-out control" is, however, metaphoric in this case, since there is no "in" or "out" if these words are understood spatially. But if by "out" we mean the physical regularity "outside" the entirely space, then our metaphor acts more as concrete description.

In order to show that the virtual is *totally* equivalent to the actual in its functionality for human life, we will see how cybersex resulting in human reproduction is possible. Since we are still taking a standpoint from the actual world, we examine how interaction between two sex partners in the virtual world can bring about the sexual-reproductive process in the actual world.

If VR were merely able to serve our basic economy of production and reproduction, that is, if it only had the foundational part, then it would not have such significant implications for the entire civilization. It is the unlimited possibilities of the expansive part that will be able to make us creators of our own brand-new civilization. If by "ontological" we refer to what we call "real," then it is our ability to create our own meaningful experience in the expansive part *in addition to* our ability to alter our sensory connection to the natural process in the foundational part that entitles us to claim an ontological authorship.

Chapter 3 first ventures into a progressive formulation of tentative rules we would implicitly use to distinguish the "real" from the "illusory," then goes on to deconstruct them; we find that the virtual and the actual can be reversed with regard to which is "real" and which "illusory." Even the concepts of physicality and causality, which are shown in chapter 2 to belong to the realm of a higher-level causal connection, could be applied to the virtual world for its own regularity as much as they could to the actual world. That is, if we can understand physicality and causality in the ordinary sense as part of the actual world, we can equally take it as part of the virtual world. And if we are tempted to interpret the virtual as derived from the actual, then the actual has to be in turn derived from a world of still higher-order, and so on and so forth, ad infinitum. In so doing, we would again end up with some kind of transcendental determination free from any sensory framework, even from space and time.

Then we analyze how our ultimate concerns would be the same in both the actual and the virtual world; we would ask the same types of philosophical questions without changing their basic meaning, and thus all philosophical propositions contained in works from Plato's *Republic* to *Get Real* would, if they are purely philosophical, have the same validity or invalidity in either world.

Chapter 4 demonstrates that no matter how we shift from one sensory framework to another, and despite the possibility of multiple versions of the empirical self, the unity of the mind always maintains itself on the deepest level. John Searle, Daniel Dennett, and many others who advocate either a classical neurophysiological or computational model of the mind have committed a Fallacy of Unity Projection. If we adopt a theory like quantum mechanics, which does not depend on a specific sensory framework, then we can avoid such a fallacy and hopefully begin to establish a unified theory of mind-matter. Possibly, I suggest, the square root of -1 may be the psy-factor in both quantum theory and the Special Theory of Relativity, and a re-interpretation of it might lead to a true breakthrough in physics.

Chapter 5 discusses the basic normative concepts necessary for evaluating VR. Adopting concepts from my previous book, I lead the reader to make a comparison between two sets of ideas essential to understanding human life based on a basic contrast between reality and ideality. The concepts of humanitude and personhood are identified as the basis for normative principles that do not depend on the alleged materiality of the world. Since creativity is understood as the source of all values, VR—which enhances our creativity—will enable us to live a more meaningful life.

In chapter 6, the potential danger of VR is shown to be just a special case of the fragility of technological civilization. This comes from two sources: (1) the impossibility of our complete knowledge necessary for a total control of VR infrastructure in order to prevent a total breakdown of the system; and (2) the possibility of the command of a huge amount of energy through teleoperation by a few malicious human beings. Due to such a potential danger, we should always have the actual world as the backup system. But this does not provide a final guarantee of safety either, because the system of nature may betray us as well.

We have to die regardless. But we can achieve immortality in a mitigated sense: our personhood as composed of meaning-complexes goes beyond the experiential contents of our life. Since VR makes us more creative, it also enables us to project a richer personhood beyond our lifetime. Cyberspace is therefore a habitat of humanitude. It will allow us to participate in a process of the ultimate re-creation of our entire civilization.

Acknowledgments

This book could not have taken its final shape without the insightful comments and suggestions by Michael Heim. His intelligence and free spirit have always accompanied his grand vision. The encouragement from a brave and productive thinker like him has driven me to the completion of this exciting adventure.

Jennifer Ruark's initial response to my proposal led me to a total commitment to this project. Later, Kermit Hummel's enthusiastic support convinced me further of the worth of the book. Maureen MacGrogan's ability to understand the author's perspective made the process of cooperative effort a pleasant experience.

I am grateful to Guiyou Huang, Chenyang Li, and Laura Xu, who had, before anybody else, read chapters of my early version and given me helpful suggestions. Amy Lamke and Chris Basnage did an excellent job in helping me proofread the manuscript.

Finally, my gratitude to Thomas Olshewsky of University of Kentucky goes far beyond what can be expressed on this page.

Philip Z. Zhai

1

How to Go "behind" Physical Space

There is another world
wherein this world
is another world
There is another dream
wherein this dream
is another dream
There is not another me
wherein this me
is another me

"Me and World," Z. Zhai, 1997

Virtual reality is currently often publicized as a new kind of game for recreational purposes, but by accident or by necessity, the word "recreation" can be seen as a pun which uncovers a critical process that could change the very foundation of civilization on the ontological level: we are "re-creating" the whole perceived world and returning to the root of the universal meaning. We will, accordingly, re-interpret what is "real" and what is "unreal" from a higher vantage point. Virtual reality is our own creation by means of symbolic programming and immersion technology. But if we can immerse ourselves in it and continue the process of creation and re-creation while we are immersed, the momentary experiential boundary between the actual and the virtual will disappear.

Imagine we further combine the technology of robotics and the digital–perceptual interface. We will be able to manipulate all processes in the actual world from the virtual world. In such a situation, we can, if we choose to, live in the virtual world in our lifetime, and generation after generation. We can design our virtual world in such a way that each potential perceptual item in the actual world has a lawful corresponding item in the virtual world; in addition, we can play with pure digital simulations. If we can do this in principle, how can we make a final distinction

1

between the "virtual" and the "actual" even on the ontological level?
The cyberspace in which we are immersed would be as "real"—if we are
empiricists—or as "illusory"—if we are Platonists or Buddhists—as what
we usually call the actual physical space. To begin with, our visual system
connected to the physical world through eyes (the sensor), for example,
is no more than a sophisticated device for signal transmission and transformation. Now let us wear a helmet so as to let the signals undergo one
more phase of transformation. This might make our perception a little
bit more artificial but does it make it less real?

But "real" or not, isn't this just a digital version of Huxley's "brave
new world"? What does it mean to "live" in the virtual world? In order
to prepare for discussing questions such as these, I will in this chapter
establish the Principle of Reciprocity between Alternative Sensory Frameworks, which is: *All possible sensory frameworks that support a certain
degree of coherence and stability of perception have equal ontological
status for organizing our experiences.* This principle will be able to lead
us to go "behind" the alleged physical space and see why the spatial
configuration we are familiar with is just one among many possibilities
of sensory framework. If you wonder how a relatively small computer,
which is an object in the physical space, can hold "inside" it a space
that is literally comparable to the entire physical space, you have to get
"behind" the space to see the point. "Behind" the space, it will become
clear why this claim of "the big contained in the small" is not a paradox
and how it is possible.

1.1   Playing the Game: Get Wired to Go Weird

Shootout in Cyberspace

Let's prepare our philosophical adventure in the ultimate re-creation
by entering the wonderland of recreation to begin with. The following
description should be quite close to what you can expect to experience
through advanced virtual reality technologies in the immediate future.

Before you get started with a state-of-the-art virtual reality game, you
and your partner will each be instructed to wear a helmet (or goggles) so
that you won't be able to see anything except the animated video images
on two small screens right in front of your eyes; nor will you hear anything except sounds from two earphones next to your ears. You see 3-D
animation and hear stereo sound. You may also have to wear a bodysuit,
including a pair of gloves, that will both monitor your body's movement
and give you different amounts of pressure against different parts of your
body, in accordance with your changing visual and audio sensations in

the game. You are now situated in a motion-tracker so that you can move freely without leaving the place; in the meantime, your walking movement is detected and the signals are fed into the computer that will also process all visual and audio information. So you are totally wired to perceive the weird! Your partner is in another room, wired to the same computer, doing the same.

As soon as the game gets started, you begin to see with your eyes, hear with your ears, and feel with your hands and with your whole body, a self-contained environment separated from the actual environment. In other words, you are immersed in cyberspace. Let us assume that you are experiencing a typical type of game as follows: Your partner and you, each holding a shooting gun, are ready to fire at one another. The 3-D images are so realistic and your hand-movement and the whole body's movement are coordinated with your images in such a way that you can hardly tell the difference between the animated image and your original body. Your partner looks as real as yourself. There are perhaps a few trees or rocks between you and your partner. There may also be a house you can get into and out of, and so forth. You can touch the leaves of the tree, and feel the hardness of the wall. So you run, turn, hide; you get nervous, bumped, scared, or excited; you hear noises from different directions. When your partner shoots at you, you feel the hit on the right spot of your body. You hesitate and pull the trigger to fire back . . . back and forth, back and forth . . . until one of you takes a "fatal" shot, lies bleeding, and loses the game. The game stops, but you don't feel the sharp pain of dying even if you are the loser. Instead you will shortly get un-wired and back to the actual world, alive and amazed.

This is how the best virtual reality game may entertain you for your recreation at present or in the near future. But this is merely a beginning. In this book, I will try to show you how and in what sense this kind of recreation is sending us on the way to the ultimate re-creation: For the first time in human history, we are undertaking an ontological shift at the very bottom of our civilization. We may have started the most exciting journey of creating a brand new habitat for our future generations at the ontological level.

Immersed in the Game and Never to Return?

You say, "What? Are you implying that we will play that kind of game forever and never return to the real world? Don't be silly or pretentious! A game is just a game, and that's it!" My answer would be: True, it is just a game for now. But this is by no means an ordinary kind of game. As soon as we start to play it, we begin to destroy a "wall" we have built unknowingly that was supposed to separate the real from the unreal based on some kind of alleged sensory privilege. We will eventually realize that there is no ultimate distinction between the real and the virtual if the virtual world has a certain relatively stable structure. The central idea is simple: ontologically and functionally, *the goggles are equivalent to our natural eyes, and the bodysuit is equivalent to our natural skin; and in both worlds we can have equally legitimate physical science of elementary particles*—there is no relevant difference between them that makes the natural real and the artificial unreal. But the significant difference lies in their relationship to human creativity: we were given one world, but can make and possibly choose the other. Let us see how, step by step.

1.2   What If Now . . .

Imagination Gone Wild Yet Intellect Disciplined

In order to understand the essence of virtual reality from a privileged perspective, we may want to find a standpoint even further removed from the physicalistic assumption of reality we are accustomed to. We are not talking about virtual reality proper yet; we are instead looking for a principle that will guide our understanding of virtual reality later. For this purpose I will appeal to thought experiments or what Husserl calls "free fancy variations."

Any thought experiment designed to clarify relations among concepts or grasp the essence of a single concept, as we know, does not need to concern the practical difficulty of the experiment, so the validity of a thought experiment is not contingent upon the advancement of technology. For the unique purpose it is to serve, it only needs to be theoretically possible in principle.[1] We can depend on such a procedure because we are, in this chapter, trying to establish the principle that ties actual reality and virtual reality together, not the technological principle of virtual reality construction. Keeping in mind the nature and purpose of a thought experiment, we are now ready for such experiments. Following Michael Heim, we pose such a question: "Are not all worlds symbolic, including the one we naively refer to as the real world, which we read off with our physical senses?"[2]

Totally Lost in Disney's Deep-Space Odyssey

Descartes's *Meditations* has been understood as a milestone of modern philosophy. The following thought experiment can be interpreted as a new version of his first meditation, but we will go further to discuss scenarios that will lead us right to the critical point for understanding the relationship between the virtual and the actual reality.

Suppose that Disney World has opened a new amusement park, called Deep-Space Odyssey. It's vacation time so you decide to take your family (say, your spouse and a four-year-old daughter) there. Just a few hundred yards east of the Magic Kingdom you see an exotic new gate, like the opening of a bypass that would take you to a totally unknown world of fabulous adventure. You reach the gate but the security guard stops you and tells you that before you are allowed to enter you must undergo a test. He wraps one of your wrists with something like a pulse sensor, from which two wires run into a cabinet. After a minute or so the security guard tells you that you are fine and releases you from the sensor. Your whole family goes through the same process. Then you enter the park as a group with a sense of uncertainty. You ask yourself, "What makes this park so seriously different from other parks that we need to be tested in such an annoying manner before we even get started?"

All of a sudden, you hear a big blast and in no time you see a big flame swallowing up the last inch of the space in front of you and you hear your spouse and daughter screaming. At that moment you say to yourself, "My God, we are finished. . . ."

"That's the end of the rehearsal, sir," says the familiar voice of the security guard, "and it's time to get real now." To your utter surprise, you find yourself still at the gate without being burned, and your spouse and child still around you!

Being an intelligent person, you gather that the first "release" from the sensor was not real and thus there was no flame afterward that washed you away from existence. The "sensor" is actually a device that sends signals to your brain that cause you to experience events that are pre-programmed and do not have a counterpart in the actual world. That simulated explosion was, as the security guard called it, a mere rehearsal to prepare you for what has yet to happen in the park, or so you think.

Refraining from complaining, the three of you enter the park. You choose to try the Planetary Collision ride first. The three of you are seated one next to another, and are warned to fasten your seat belts because you are going to experience a violent collision between the earth and another planet. You do as instructed and try to anticipate what kind of shock your whole family are going to receive when the collision "actually" happens.

As the ride gets started, you realize that the earth is meant to fly off the track, because you see in the sky all kinds of unfamiliar objects and lights dashing through faster and faster. All of a sudden you see a bright object appearing larger and larger, rapidly heading directly toward you. You know that this is the alien planet that is supposed to collide with the earth. It looks and feels so realistic that your heart starts pounding! But you still remember that this is merely a game and nothing hurtful will happen. However, contrary to your expectation, right before the moment the alien object hits you, you see people in front of you get hit first and torn into pieces! You scream loudly, and then . . . nothing happens. You again find yourself at the gate with your family, safe and sound, and the security guard smiling.

At this moment, you first become really angry since you feel sort of duped, then the anger turns into a disquieting worry. You regret that you ever wanted to come to this place. So you say to your spouse: "Honey, I think we'd better go home." Your spouse agrees, and you get un-wired and stop a taxi. All three of you get right in, heading toward the airport. A few hours later you see your home, sweet home. You reach into your pocket and get out the key, insert it into the keyhole, turn it, and. . . . Instead of unlocking the door, you find yourself back at the gate of Deep-Space Odyssey, again! The experience of the whole process of going home was also pre-programmed—a fake!

Now you begin to wonder whether your "back to the gate" experiences were also just part of the pre-programmed dream injection. From now on, how can you ever know for sure if you are back in the real life or just having injected experiences? Probably you can never know, and certainly you will never know for certain.

If this sounds scary, as a reader of this book you may console yourself by thinking that this Disney World stuff is just hypothetical. It did not actually happen to you. But then, Descartes would like to ask you a new question: "Does this have to happen in the context of amusement park, or could that happen in a totally different context as well?" More specifically, do you know for sure right now that you are reading a book called *Get Real* written by somebody called Philip Zhai? Or are you just perceiving so? How do you know for sure that you are not right now hooked up to a signals-generating machine that makes you believe that you have not been hooked up to anything, but are reading this line of this book which does not physically exist?

Furthermore, if you are now (your now) not sure whether you are really reading this book, I am now (my now) not sure whether I am really writing this book either. I, Philip Zhai, who might be either your dream character or a dream character of someone dreaming himself or herself to be Philip Zhai, might be as fictional as anyone else. Or you can even wonder how that security guard, if he was real from your perspective, knew he was not himself just having an electronically induced experience of being a security guard. Was he in a better position to know about his own situation? Can anybody, God included, know for sure that there is no higher-level reality that generates his or her perceptions of reality if "reality" is understood as a self-sufficient entity? Descartes used to have the hypothesis of an all-powerful evil genius deceiving him all the time. What should we make of that idea right now?

Reality Unreal or What?

Am I suggesting that everything is unreal? Not necessarily, because in order for something to be unreal there has to be something real as a contrast. If the unreal is all there is, then the term "unreal" would be just a label for that which is, and thus negates the very meaning of the unreal as opposed to the real. In other words, in order to understand anything as a dream, you must assume there is a dreamer. Otherwise the "dream" is no dream at all, since by definition a dream belongs to a subject who is not part of the dream. It is nonsensical to say that everything in everybody's life is a dream.

Besides, even if you are not actually reading a book right now as you appear to be, and thus the words you perceive here in black ink are not actually written by a real author, the meanings you get from reading these sentences cannot be fictional because meaning itself does not, in a relevant sense, depend on physicality. More important, the consciousness that articulates meanings and perceptual experiences, be they from senses or induced by injection, must be genuine consciousness, no matter how or whether we can define it in terms of other things. This is so because, as we will see, its self-identity can never be shattered no matter which sensory framework is chosen.

An Assumption Suspended

On the phenomenological level, we need to suspend the assumption that for anything to be genuine it has to meet certain externally imposed criteria such as observability or measurability. Instead, we can separate the essential from the accidental, without imposing such criteria, by seeing which component always maintains its one-ness and self-sameness in all circumstances, and which loses its identity of one-ness or self-same-ness when the circumstances change. The former will be the essential, and the latter accidental.

This new version of Cartesian meditation has helped us recognize the relativity of our perception. But this need not lead to ontological relativism in general. The perceptual is just perceptual, but the concept of reality cannot be taken as the same, prima facie, as the perceptual, before we prove otherwise. As for virtual reality, it does not have to invade our neural system like that; or at least in this book, this kind of "dream injection" is *not* taken as a version of virtual reality. The lesson we learn from this recreational story is that if you are immersed in an alternative field of perception structurally similar to the original one, there are no grounds on which you can be sure that the one is real while the other is not, at least from the experiential point of view.

See the Sound and Hear the Color

But what if the alternative field of perception is structurally different from the original? Let's briefly consider a simpler case, one which we could easily implement with modern technology, and which I call "cross-sensory perception."

If the functions of two types of your sense-organs were to be altered in such a way that the first type received stimuli from the source that originally gave stimuli to the second type, and vice versa, then you would have cross-sensory perception. For example, suppose we made a spectacles-like device that you could wear on your eyes, and the function of this device was to transform sound into light with corresponding variables (actually such a sound–light transformer can be easily made in an average lab of electrical engineering). On the other hand, we also make a hearing-aid-like light–sound transformer. If we were to wear both, we would see what we usually hear and hear what we usually see.

In such a situation, we would be almost immobilized at first due to a paradigm shift from the familiar to the unfamiliar. Imagine: You would have to tell day from night by listening to the background noise to determine how noisy or quiet it is. If there was a fire alarm from a rushing fire truck, you would not hear it but would instead see it as a dazzling trace of light. Furthermore, you would visually see my spoken words and auditorially hear the words on this page. But after a period of getting used to it, it is very likely that you would begin to handle the situation pretty well, depending on each person's specific adaptability. If we let our children wear such devices from very early on, it might well be that if the devices were taken away after they grew up, they would have as much difficulty adjusting to what we call the "normal" as we would from the opposite side.

Certainly, such a transformation would result in some loss of information. But even before the transformation, the information we receive by seeing and listening with our natural organs is just a small portion of what is potentially available (we cannot see, for example, the ultraviolet and infrared). So the question is: Can we claim, with a valid ontological justification, that the "normal" is "real," whereas the transformed is "unreal"?

As we go on, we will see that there is no such an ontological justification. We will also see that there is a stable basis that unites all variations. That is, independent of any arbitrarily chosen sensory framework, there is a set of binding constants shared by all possible experiences. The following section will lead us one step further to see how this might work out. But first of all, let's bear in mind that what we have achieved so far in this section can be summarized as follows.

Summary: Equally Ignorant

Since we are all immersed in a self-coherent framework of sensory perceptions, we can never know whether there is a higher-level experiencing agent responsible for our perceptual experiences; and if there is one, that agent would be as ignorant of his/her/its own situation for the same reason.

1.3   Cross-Communication Situations

Mis-Located Bodies

Apart from the pure mechanical continuity, there are two functional parts of our neck that connect our head and the rest of the body. The first part keeps the circulation system going (maintaining blood flow, etc.), while the second part passes information back and forth between the brain and the lower parts of the body. Such a system enables us to have internal sensations and feelings of different body parts and thereby control their movement, and so on.

Now suppose there are two persons, who are *observationally* identified as Adam (*A*) and Bob (*B*). In their necks, while the first type of connection is kept intact so each circulation system works as usual, let's suppose that the second type of connection is rearranged through a wireless telecommunication mechanism as follows. *A*'s information channel in his neck is cut and thus disconnected, although the appearance of the neck, as the connection between the head and other parts of the body, does not change significantly. Each end of the cut (via a chain of adaptive transformations, perhaps) is respectively connected to one of two radio transmitter-receivers. *B*'s neck undergoes a similar treatment with similar radio devices. Now, suppose the transmission frequencies are set up so that all information from below that should originally have gone to *A*'s brain is now intercepted and broadcasted to *B*'s brain and does not reach *A*'s brain. *A*'s brain receives information from *B*'s non-head parts of the body plus the information from *A*'s own head, with all sense organs (eyes, ears, etc.) as usual. *B*'s brain's connection to his own head and to *A*'s body is of the same symmetrical type. From the other direction, *A*'s lower-than-neck part of the body receives commands from *B*'s brain, and *B*'s from *A*'s. Let us call such a setup between *A* and *B* a "cross-communication situation," or CCS for short. The setup of a CCS is shown in Figure 1.1.

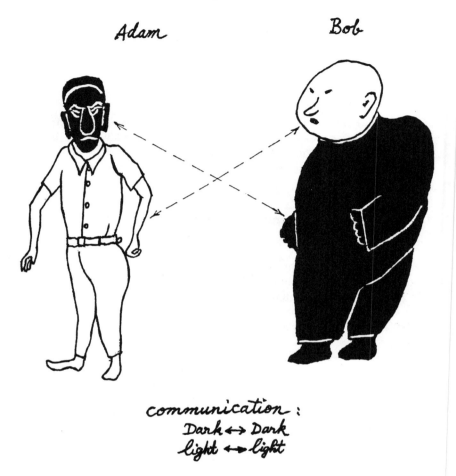

Figure 1.1 A cross-communication situation (CCS) between Adam and Bob.

In such a situation, *A* and *B* will each see, with the eyes sending information to the brain without telecommunication, his original body connected as before. But they are only able to feel and control one another's, instead of one's own, lower-than-neck parts of the body. This setting is illustrated in Table 1.1.

Adam and Bob Messed Up

In order to get a stronger sense of the situation, let us consider a few scenarios.

TABLE 1.1
Who Sees and Controls What in a CCS

	Adam (A)	Bob (B)
Can See (in a mirror)	A's Whole Body	B's Whole Body
Cannot See	B's Whole Body	A's Whole Body
Can Feel and Control	A's Head and B's Lower Body	B's Head and A's Lower Body
Cannot Feel and Control	A's Lower Body and B's Head	B's Lower Body and A's Head

Scenario 1: A and B are mutually visible and are in a CCS for the first time without knowing it. Suppose A and B are in the same room and each seated on a chair ten feet apart from one another. A sees B and B sees A as usual. Before either of them attempts to move himself in a sufficient magnitude, neither can discover much difference between a CCS and a normal situation. Now A tries to rise and walk toward the door, but he discovers that his body defies his effort and keeps him seated; at the same moment, he sees B rising and then B's body moving the way A intends to move his own body (walking). For B's part, B is surprised to find his body moving without his own effort while he feels still seated on a chair (because A is seated at the moment). Not knowing what is going on, B tries to stop his own body from moving. Since he feels seated kinesthetically, he needs first to rise before making an effort to assert a counter-movement. But when he does so, he sees no effect of his effort on his own body. Instead, he sees A rising and beginning to walk in the opposite direction, as B intended his own body to move. Of course, A is no less puzzled when he finds his body moving in the wrong direction against his own will. After a few rounds of mind-boggling inter-actions, A and B might begin to talk to one another and to a certain extent realize their peculiar connection in a CCS. Then they would per-haps learn to coordinate with one another.

Scenario 2: A and B are mutually invisible and unable to verbally or otherwise communicate with one another. Suppose that A and B are far apart from one another after their experience in Scenario 1. Let A be in an office in New York and B in an office in Tokyo, both seated on a chair. Now A hears the phone ring. He tries to stretch his arm and pick up the handset, but without B's cooperation, A will not be able to accomplish it, because his effort in New York can only move B's arm in Tokyo.

However, suppose that A and B had made an agreement beforehand that whenever B sees any part of his lower body begin to move, he will try to initiate exactly the same kind of movement. Then *B* (in Tokyo), seeing his arm moving, can move *A*'s arm to help *A* (in New York) reach the phone. If *B*'s cooperation is timely enough, the delay between *A*'s effort and *B*'s execution should be very short. In this case, *A* would not feel this situation was very different from moving his arm by himself before he entered into a CCS. But since *B* is following *A* passively, *B* will always know that he is serving the other. If *B* wants to break the agreement and begins to initiate his own lower-body movement, chaos will be created because in such a situation *A* and *B* may at any moment initiate different movements simultaneously, accomplishing neither. Very soon one or both of them will hit a wall or worse.

Suppose now that *A* has had an accident and one of his legs is bleeding. *A* sees his leg badly wounded but feels no pain. *B* felt the impact of the accident when *A*'s leg got hurt but cannot see anything wounded. *B* feels a sharp pain as if it were somewhere on the leg he is looking at, which is not at all physically wounded (due to the different posture and movement between *A* and *B*, the location of the pain, to *B*, might be confusingly floating).

Scenario 3: *A* and *B* cannot see each other but can communicate by using cordless phones. Now, if *A* and *B* are not hostile to one another, chances are that they can cooperate without running into big trouble even if they do not have a well-structured contract. Suppose that they are again seated on their chairs in New York and Tokyo, respectively, and that they both have, and know they have, cordless phones in their hands at this time. *A* wants now to go out for a soda. Of course he cannot just rise and walk because doing so will make *B* in Tokyo rise and walk. But *A* can attempt to direct his hand as internally felt to hold the phone in a speaking position, *in order that* *B*'s hand will hold the phone in a speaking position. In the meantime, as *B* sees his hand with the phone raised, he will try to do the same in response so that *A* raises his hand to the desired position (this will work only if *A* and *B* have sufficiently accurate knowledge of one another's height, size, etc.). After that, *A* can ask *B* to mobilize *A*'s body and follow *A*'s real-time verbal instructions over the phone until *A* gets to the vending machine and finishes the task and comes back. *B* can ask *A*'s cooperation in return as well.

A Fundamental Ambiguity

So far I have been using *A* and *B* to describe Adam and Bob involved in a CCS, and there is no troublesome ambiguity in doing so. This is so because we have been discussing the situation purely from a third person's point of view, using *A* and *B* as mere labels attached to two spatially separated bodies. But if we recall that *A* stands for Adam and *B* for

Bob—two personal names—we might see the inherent ambiguity immediately.

Let us designate Adam's original body (in New York) with two symbols: A1 for his head and A2 for the rest of his body; and Bob's (in Tokyo) with B1 and B2 in the same way. Now we ask, where are Adam and Bob, the two *persons* we just described in the CCS? To distinguish this type of question from the standard traditional question of personal identity, I will call it the problem of the locality-identity of the person. Since inherent in the idea of identity is one-ness, any belief that holds that A or B is in more than one place simultaneously would not count as a legitimate answer to the question of the locality-identity.

The first possible answer is that Adam is in New York and Bob in Tokyo, just as before, because none of their body parts has been transported from one place to the other. Such an answer is based on the spatial continuity assumption of locality-identity of the person. Insofar as A1 and A2 are in spatial contact, no matter what happens, according to this way of thinking, they belong to the same person, Adam, who is no more and no less than the combination of A1 and A2 as long as no spatial separation occurs between them. In order for A and B to switch parts of their bodies, their bodies have to be dismembered and then reassembled. The same applies to B as well.

If this answer is correct, a dead body would have as much to contribute to personal identity as a live body, insofar as the body has not come apart. But obviously the existence of a dead body does not entail the existence of the person because death is the termination of the person's existence by definition. Since the inadequacy of such a theory of identity has been discussed extensively in the philosophical literature, I don't have much more to say about it here.

The second possible answer is that Adam and Bob are both across New York and Tokyo, because they have traded one part of their bodies and are reconnected, regardless of the lack of transportation across a distance since the outset of the CCS. This answer is based on the communicability assumption of locality-identity. So now Adam has A1 and B2 combined as his body, and Bob has B1 and A2 combined as his. Adam and Bob are intertwined in the CCS. This is so because in order for two parts of the body to belong to the same person, they must be able to communicate with one another. Now that A and B both have body parts in two places at the same time in terms of communicability, according to this view, each person's spatial identity is not splintered but only ridiculously stretched, with the invisible radio waves maintaining the spatial continuity.

A third possible answer is superficially the same as the first in its conclusion, that is, Adam is in New York and Bob in Tokyo, but with a different attempt of justification. It claims that Adam is in New York and Bob in Tokyo because what Adam can see is only a place in New York and Bob a place in Tokyo. This is based on the assumption that a person can only see the place where he is located. But such an assumption will be shown to be problematic later when we discuss interpersonal-telepresence.

A fourth possible answer is also the same in its conclusion, but with a still different attempt of justification. It claims that Adam is in New York, and Bob in Tokyo, because their brains, which take control of all activities, are in New York and Tokyo respectively. This answer is, of course, based on the assumption that where the information is processed and commands originate is where the person is. Where the body's interaction with the environment takes place is regarded as irrelevant.

Both the third and the fourth answers, however, leave unclear to whom the two lower-than-neck parts of the body belong. In particular, since the second justification requires an A1–B2 and B1–A2 connection in order to make sense of information-processing and command-giving, they seem to have to endorse the second answer when pressed.

Of all the four, the second answer seems to be the most plausible. But this view is based on the belief that mutual communicability through radio waves makes two parts of body locally connected. This belief becomes problematic when we realize that radio waves do not spatially target any specific object. They rather have contact with everything in their way indiscriminately, so the contact alone does not single out B2 for A1, nor A2 for B1 as the target for connectivity. Moreover, radio waves do not travel over a medium (the so-called ether), so the physical connectivity does not exist in the classical sense when communication is not in progress. This view would imply that when Adam or Bob is in deep sleep, his locality-identity is almost suspended. Therefore this view is unstable with regard to the very concept of the locality-identity of a person. But the second answer does appear to be closer to a correct account of personal locality-identity. What is the catch?

What Is the Catch?

If we have an intuition that A1 and B2 still belong to a single person even when they are not actually communicating with one another (as in a coma) provided that they *are capable* of communicating with one another *exclusively*, then we are not basing personal locality-identity on spatial unity. The communicability between A1 and B2 (or B1 and A2) depends on a certain kind of synergy between the receiver and the transmitter on each end free of any spatially identifiable media. They are connected by nothing but the potential capacity of resonant *harmony*.

Therefore, there need not be spatial continuity in the usual sense for the unity of the person according to such an interpretation (Figure 1.2).[3]

A fifth possible answer to the question of location is that Adam and Bob as persons are nowhere, that is, that they do not occupy a spatial position, because space is the framework *by means of which* a person (characterized by consciousness) perceives the unity of objects. So the person is not itself an object in the space. For the moment we don't know whether this Kantian view is defensible or not, but it certainly brings up the question of what the person is if not spatially identifiable. In order to gain more insights on this puzzle, we now go further to expand our thought experiment based on CCS.

1.4   Interpersonal-Telepresence: I Am *Here*!

Teleportation with a Helmet

With the above discussion of the three scenarios and their possible interpretations pertaining to the problem of spatial locality, we can now bring in one more scenario, *Scenario 4*. Here, it does not matter where *A* and *B* are located. The significant difference is that they are blind from

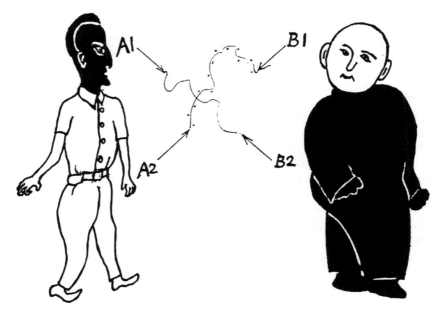

Figure 1.2 A1–B2 and B1–A2 as two separately unified persons connected by the potential capacity of resonance?

the very beginning. In such a case, their perception of the whole CCS will
not differ much from that of a normal pre-CCS situation because visually
they have never had a point of view anyway. But since the head and the
lower-than-neck part of the body are located in two different places, they
will now and then receive different stimuli from their respective environment. The lower part of the body might feel a high temperature, but the
head might feel relatively cold; the head might bump into a wall but the
hand can reach no wall, and so forth. But this kind of perceptual discrepancy will only disturb them occasionally. Usually, blind people would
not immediately perceive a dramatic change after a CCS arrangement:
they did not have a visual perception of the spatial locality before to
begin with,[4] so locality-identity is not an issue insofar as visual perception is concerned. For this reason mentioning such a scenario in passing
is a good transition to our discussion of interpersonal-telepresence.

Such a double-blind situation is not that of interpersonal-telepresence,
of course. In order to know what the latter is, we have to return to the
idea of a helmet, though the helmet here needs a little modification and
need not be connected to a computer. Let's leave the two small video
screens and two earphones intact, and let them receive signals carried by
electromagnetic waves just like a regular TV and radio. Outside the helmet, on the spots of the two eyes are mounted two video cameras and on
the spots of the two ears, two microphones, which will pick up sounds
from outside and of the person's voice. The pictures and the sounds they
pick up will be, of course, broadcasted. In addition, we need to attach to
the helmet a speaker that will be activated by signals from the other
party. Furthermore, the cross-communication now includes the information that controls the head movement from one to the other.

NASA has reportedly worked on telepresence for many years using
robots and computers that allow a person to be wired to see what a
remote robot "sees" and in return control the robot's movement by moving his or her own body. Also, when the robot's "hand" touches something, the person will feel as if he or she were touching it. So if you are
in a lab on earth while the robot is on the moon, you could experience
walking on the moon and picking up a piece of rock just as if you were
actually on the moon. Since the coordination of movement requires computation, it uses a computer. As long as a robot is used on the remote
end, their telepresence is not interpersonal. But now Adam's and Bob's
brains are performing much better than a computer, and their bodies are
much more responsive than a robot. In place of robots, they use one
another's body. So they are now ready to experience interpersonal-telepresence.

Again we use symbols *A* (in New York) and *B* (in Tokyo) to refer to the observed bodies instead of Adam and Bob as persons. Also remember that they are still in a CCS, so as communication units they are A1—B2 and B1—A2. Now let A1 and B1 each wear the modified helmet and tune to one another's wavelength (Figure 1.3).

What will happen to Adam and Bob? Now the discrepancy created by CCS is totally *compensated!* Adam will immediately see himself in Tokyo, not in New York, and Bob will see himself in New York, not in Tokyo—each feeling internally and seeing externally his own body there, even though altered. Before wearing the helmet, only the sense of touch between A2 and B2 was switched, but now the senses of vision and hearing are also switched: Adam's brain is still carried by his old body in New York, which is now controlled by Bob's brain—which is carried by Bob's old body, now controlled by Adam, and vice versa. Confusing, indeed. Where is Adam and where is Bob now? There is no more ambiguity: Before philosophical reflection, Adam and Bob will each claim, "I am here!"—the claims being made respectively from Tokyo (Adam) and New York (Bob), even though each's brain remains in the other place. What do they mean when they make such a claim?

Figure 1.3 Interpersonal telepresence between Adam and Bob.

A Smart Brain That Knows Not

One thing is sure: the two brains cannot possibly perceive their own locality without sense organs sensing their locality from outside. Internally, a brain cannot make sense of its own locality. For that reason, a brain cannot match a spatially observed brain with itself because its self-identity has nothing to do with spatiality. Suppose the two brains were detached from the heads. Could Adam and Bob, whose brains work for them through telecommunication, tell which one is their own? No, they could not (Figure 1.4). No matter where their brains are kept and how they are moved, as long as they keep functioning, Adam and Bob will keep perceiving but neither of them can perceive any change of spatial

which brain is mine ?

Figure 1.4 Not knowing which one is his own brain.

locality. Their self-identity is, however, all along unified, and their integrity of consciousness remains unshattered, as shown in Table 1.2.

Brain Switch without Surgery

The above situation is equivalent to a brain switch in its function of information-processing but not in physiological process. In the case of a brain switch, the brain would be carried by the body it controls, but here the brain is carried by the body whose whereabouts is under the other's control. So the self-identified Adam has no way to physically protect his own brain and has to rely on Bob's self-interest in maintaining a healthy body, and the opposite is true for the self-identified Bob. If the body controlled by Bob gets fatally shot (in New York, which is Adam's previous body), the brain responsible for the self-claimed Adam's life will be destroyed. What are left are the pre-shooting self-claimed Adam's functioning body (previously Bob's) now disconnected with any brain, and the pre-shooting self-claimed Bob's functioning brain now connected to no body (feeling as if in a state of total paralysis).

So the following is clear about the situation: from the normal situation before CCS through CCS to interpersonal-telepresence, neither Adam nor Bob has ever lost his self-identity from his first-person perspective. That is, neither of them has ever had to ask himself: Am I Adam or Bob? Adam has always been sure that he is Adam, and Bob that he is Bob, despite the locality-changes of their bodies. But from the pure outside observer's point of view, there is no way to identify which is Adam and which is Bob without tracing back the history of their connectivity or trusting reports from the self-claimed Adam and Bob. Therefore, Adam and Bob's self-identities are the primordial mode of personal-identity that does not depend on the locality-identity by an outside observer.

The problem now is that Adam and Bob also try to identify themselves

TABLE 1.2
Adam and Bob Are No Longer Confused About Their Whereabouts, Because Each Sees, Feels and Controls a Unified Body Separately, Even Though Swapped

	Adam (A)	Bob (B)
Can See (in a mirror)	B's Whole Body with Helmet	A's Whole Body with Helmet
Cannot See	A's Whole Body	B's Whole Body
Can Feel and Control	B's Whole Body	A's Whole Body
Cannot Feel and Control	A's Whole Body	B's Whole Body

locally when they each claim, "I am here." If we assume the self-claimed Adam, as a person, is the real Adam and the self-claimed Bob real Bob, are they correct about where they are? For other observers, there is no way to tell that Adam and Bob have switched their locality by observation alone. So all others would tell a story about Adam and Bob's identity different from what Adam and Bob themselves have to tell if we all stick to our own point of view. Adam and Bob must have something new when they each claim: "I am here."

Self-Identity versus Other-Identity

This leads us to the traditional controversy in the philosophy of mind on the distinction between the first-person and third-person standpoints, or between the subjective and objective perspectives. When Adam and Bob claim where they are, they cannot possibly just take a third-person perspective, because they certainly do not see themselves as one of the objects in front of them either in CCS or in interpersonal-telepresence. So maybe Adam and Bob are making their locality-identity claim from the first-person point of view? Not really, for such a point of view is totally internal, and thus cannot allow them to perceive spatial locality, which is external. Then, what is the catch, again?

After being in a CCS before the interpersonal-presence, Adam and Bob have suspended the belief that the body connected to their head has to be theirs. So the re-established sense of body ownership must be based on something new. This new basis is the correspondence between their will and feeling on the one hand, and the externally observed body's movement on the other.

As we recall, in a CCS, Adam and Bob progressed to recognize the switch when they saw their effort making the other's body move in the way they intended their own body to move. So conversely, the external connectedness now in the interpersonal-telepresence only re-establishes the practical convenience and the original "naturalness" of the sense of ownership, not the ownership itself. The connectivity they observe externally, which is used by other observers to establish locality-identity, does not help them eliminate the ambiguity of locality-identity created by CCS. Therefore, Adam and Bob cannot possibly observe in the objective realm that the body and their personhood get reconnected, since their personhood does not appear in the objective realm and thus cannot be observed as connected to the observable body. Consequently, Adam's and Bob's alleged self-identity of locality is not the same kind as the locality-identity we think of when we ask, "Where is . . . ?" which is exclusively from a third-person point of view.

But at least we know that interpersonal-telepresence not only keeps the person's self-identity unified but also re-establishes the confused locality-identity witnessed earlier in a cross-communication situation, and this cannot be understood from the third-person point of view alone. We must further examine the possibility of the first-person perspective in hope of gaining more insights into the situation.

Despite the inadequacy of the external observation, when Adam and Bob claim that they know that they are now in a new location, they must have made their judgment by observation since spatial locality, if perceived at all, has to be perceived as external. But an observation has two ends: the observed and the observer that performs the observing act. So while Adam and Bob do not identify themselves in the realm of the observed, they do so here as the center of the *observing* acts from the first-person perspective. In the objective realm, they each actually see an unfamiliar body similar to what a third-person sees. But they definitely know that the unfamiliar body is theirs, regardless of the unfitness they might feel. They know it by matching their own attempt to move a body with observed movement of the body in a certain way. An external observer, on the contrary, only sees the two bodies as before, and has no ground to judge, by observation alone, to whom the bodies belong, because he or she does not have access to Adam and Bob's first-person point of view.

Therefore, when Adam and Bob claim, "I am here," they are not making a claim of locality-identity in the usual sense of being "in" a place. They rather mean that they are the definite center of the observing acts that identify things as located around that center. The first-person perspective is a perspective we identify ourselves with our observing (and other types of) acts and all mental phenomena that contribute to these acts, not with the observed locality of our own body. So when Adam and Bob or any of us claim, "I am here," that "here" does not contain an objectified "in" in it (Figure 1.5).

Figure 1.5 Adam is not "in" the space but is the center of reference of the space.

Now that the third-person point of view is inadequate for establishing the putative locality-identity of a person, and the first-person point of view does not pertain directly to the locality-identity as exemplified in the question of where Adam and Bob are, we must conclude that, after analysis, Adam and Bob as two self-identified persons are nowhere in the space. Because persons are not spatially identifiable entities that are in the objective realm. This, therefore, confirms the fifth interpretation of Adam's and Bob's whereabouts, as discussed in the previous section, that is, they are, as persons, neither in New York nor in Tokyo. Rather, they are the reference centers for their observing acts, which establish the locality-identity of the observed objects in Tokyo and New York, respectively.

John Locke Is Locked Out

It's worth noticing that this is not the same as the Lockean theory of memory-identity. In Locke's empiricalistic philosophy, memory is understood as an attribute of the brain, which must be identified in the space first. According to such a theory, the person is always in the same place as the memory-carrier, usually the brain, is. So even when Adam and Bob have no way to know which brain among others they see is theirs, as illustrated in Figure 1.4, they are still in the place where their brain is. In such a case, the first-person perspective is totally eliminated. But *apart from* any theory, our CCS and interpersonal-telepresence thought experiments showed that the first-person self-identity always holds itself firmly and unambiguously no matter how the locality-identity from the third-person perspective has been fundamentally shattered in the process. In other words, our analysis of the first-person self-identity is phenomenological; it does not depend on an assumption of the causal dependence of consciousness on the brain, which must first be understood as an object *in* the space. At the same time, we have shown that the first-person perspective cannot be eliminated. It rather occupies a central role in personal identity.

Summary: A Person Is Nowhere

The splintered spatial locality-identity in a CCS can be compensated by, without transportation of any part of the body across a distance, a simultaneous cross-communication of sensory information that results in a re-established unity of self-perception; as a center of observing acts, the self-identifed person always maintains an unambiguous unity. Such a space compensation leads to the insight that one's alleged first-person locality-identity is not the same as identifying one's personhood in a locality in the space. The person as self-identified unity does not occupy a position in the space.

1.5   The Community of Interpersonal-Telepresence

Go Places at Will

Interpersonal-telepresence does not have to be of a fixed one-to-one correspondence. We can have a whole community of shared brains and bodies, matching them by selecting different channels of telecommunication, in the same way our regular TV and radio operate. The communication between the head and the lower part of the body, the video, and the audio should all be tuned simultaneously to connect the same brain and body at the two ends. And no one brain should be connected to more than one body at the same time, nor can one body to more than one brain. But as we can choose different wavelengths for connecting to different counterparts, we can potentially be "present" in any scene wherein there is already a community member (Figure 1.6). Imagine, if we lived in such an interpersonal-telepresence community, how drastically the meaning of individuality, privacy, publicity, ownership, and so on, would be changed.

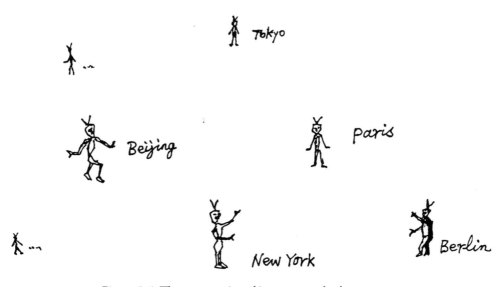

Figure 1.6 The community of interpersonal-telepresence.

The Body Goes Public

Suppose now I decide to join such a community by attaching necessary devices to my body as described above. This community has, say, five thousand members spread all over the world. What should I expect to accept as a consequence of my own decision?

In a normal situation, there are three basic states of connectivity among the members: (1) an active whole with the head and body well connected between two locations; (2) an open head with the device (OH for short) temporarily not connected to the lower part of a body; and (3) an open body (OB) temporarily not connected to a natural head. The latter two are necessary in order to make an immediate connection-switch possible.

In order to have a sensible communal life, a minimum set of rules must be stipulated to begin with: (1) no person should have a privilege to prevent anyone from choosing any available OB (all OBs are by definition available); (2) any person should be allowed to send a signal to anyone else to request him or her to release the occupied body under certain conditions; (3) the recipient of the request should respond under certain circumstances and does not have to respond under other circumstances according to another set of rules; (4) the two parties should agree, if possible, on the condition under which, and on the place in which, the takeover should be made, otherwise the takeover should be done in an official station in a standard manner; (5) if, say, two hours, before the time one is to release a body as planned, no request for a takeover has been received, one should report via a public bulletin board the availability of the OB, the information of which can be reached by anyone's scanner; (6) no person owns a private body unless one exits from such a community after negotiating back to one's original body according to a certain procedure, and therefore there is another set of rules that stipulate how to use the body legally.

In joining such a community, I give up my body as my own, and allow it to enter into the public domain. Now I need to find a body in a remote place, leaving my original body disconnected as an OB so that someone else can pick it up. I begin by uttering a few words as a voice command (a voice command allows an open head to operate), and my automatic scanner finds fifty OBs available, scattered over the Americas, Europe, Asia, and Africa. I have long dreamed of visiting Paris, the city of romance and the arts, so I pick an OB there in a public switch station in the downtown area. When I utter another voice command, boom, I feel an unfamiliar flash in my mind and in no time I find myself in Paris with a new body! I feel kind of awkward, because internally I feel somewhat distorted and can no longer properly control my body's movement. But

I was told beforehand that I would get used to it soon and I would feel comfortable with more frequent switches later on.

I manage to visit Paris for two days before I receive a request from Hong Kong for release. However, I don't want to switch with the requester directly, because I have visited Hong Kong many times. My scanner tells me that there will be an OB available five minutes from now in Sicily, that boot-shaped Italian island. "I would rather go there and I don't even have to send a request to anyone," I say to myself. So I respond to the Hong Kong request and agree to release the body for him to take over in three minutes in my hotel room while I am sitting on a chair. Three minutes later I utter the command and I leave the body in Paris. But the OB in Sicily is not immediately available. There is a two-minute time gap in between. During these two minutes I can see nothing but darkness and feel a total absence of body below my neck. I know my natural head is still carried by my original body. I can even feel vaguely that my head is in motion due to the movement of my original body controlled by an unknown person in an unknown place. My goodness, this is totally a perception-blackout! Two minutes pass, and I finally become connected again and all of a sudden find myself in, I guess, Sicily! So the story continues. . . .

The Survivor of a Fatal Accident

But the story does not go on smoothly forever. The second evening after I arrive, I have a terrible accident: the car I am in is hit by a drunk driver and the body I am associated with is fatally injured. I feel tremendous pain all over my body at first, but after a few minutes the pain is gone, along with the feeling of the whole body. I can hear nothing but can still perceive darkness. My whole feeling is exactly the same as the blackout during the two minutes right after I left Paris! Why? Obviously, the body in Sicily is now dead. Why am I not dead? Because my original head with my brain in it is *not* in Sicily. It is instead still with my original body in an unknown place controlled by someone else whose identity I do not know. What am I going to do right now? Nothing complicated: just utter the command to scan for another OB and get connected again. So I do and end up in Moscow, and. . . .

Do I mean that no one died in that accident? No, I definitely don't mean that. There was a brain in that body, which was very likely just having perceptual experience received from another unknown place (or, less probably, waiting for an OB, or sleeping) at the moment of the accident. That brain's function terminated in that accident. But whose brain was it? I don't know, except that it must be the one (let's call him or her *m*) who had contributed the body I was connected to before the accident.

But who was *m*? There are two possible sources of information about *m*'s identity: those who care to check the public record (if there is a system that traces who gets connected to which body); and those (either members or non-members of this community) who knew *m* personally or were in *m*'s company at the moment of the accident.

Now let's consider the second possibility only. *m*'s companions did not see the car accident, because they were not on the spot (Figure 1.7). *m* and *m*'s companions, who were in a certain unknown place, could not possibly see or feel anything unusual immediately before the accident. *m*'s original body was controlled by me and, although *m*'s brain was traveling with that body, the scene surrounding that body was *my* scene. So *m* died without any anticipation of the death, and *m*'s companions just saw *m* fall down all of a sudden without witnessing an apparent cause. Suppose they were informed enough to guess what was going on, they would perhaps feel great sorrow for *m*, and in the meantime, take care to protect the body (which became an OB) so that later, another person, whose brain was located somewhere else, might pick it up from afar. They would, of course, witness the body being resurrected by a new person when that happened. There was a great chance that I was that new person because the time I got disconnected in Sicily was the same time *m* died. If there were no other OB's available at that moment, my scanner might very well pick this one for me.

Figure 1.7 Me, *m* in the accident, and *m*'s companions.

Again I Am Nowhere

If I indeed end up in that body, how can they know that the body is resurrected by another person and not by *m*, who might have, for some odd but valid reason, just left temporarily? They either have to trust my statements or depend on their judgment based solely on my speech acts to gain certainty gradually. Here my self-identity is unmediated, that is, I know it by "acquaintance," in Bertrand Russell's language. But the outside observer does not have access to my "qualia," since this kind of qualia belongs exclusively to the first-person perspective.

The analysis of the concept of death in such a situation also helps to invalidate the view that personal identity is brain identity. If a brain is destroyed in one place, the person who dies of the brain destruction could be understood as being in another place pre-reflectively, or being nowhere strictly speaking at the moment of death. Therefore, the alleged "identity" between the person and the brain must not be there. This is so despite the causally necessary connection between the one and the other. So we can reiterate the following: the person as a person cannot be said to be anywhere, because personhood is not the right kind of thing (or not any "thing" at all) to have a spatial locality.

We might ask whether it is possible to undertake an inter-gender switch for telepresence. I would assume that the younger we are when we enter the interpersonal-telepresence community, the easier it would be for our brains to adapt to the potential diversity of the bodies. If we have been equipped with devices as integral parts of our bodies since we began to speak, for example, our brains would not have necessarily developed a special gender preference to hinder their adaptability later on. Of course, we can also ask what would happen if a three-year-old brain were connected to a fifty-year-old body, or vice versa. But all these difficult problems on the practical level would not affect our understanding of the situation on the theoretical level, that is, the splintered locality of the body does not have to break down the integrity of a person's self-identity.

What Is Colored but Shapeless?

Let's have a final test on the difference between what we perceive in the space and what is the *condition of* the spatiality inherent in one's personhood by doing the following.

Let's start with describing the colors of all objects in front of us. Say, there is a black tape recorder; a brown bag about 5 inches to the left of the recorder; a book with an orange cover about 3 inches to the right of a blue mug, which is close to the recorder; and so forth. Are there colors among those four objects in the background? Of course. There must be something else with colors to fill all gaps. You can describe these colors one next to another in greater detail if you wish, but you will notice that any color in your field of vision, viewed as two-dimensional, must be immediately next to another color which is in turn immediately next to still another, and so on. If you want to paint any part of the scene on canvas with exactly the same color distribution, you will be able to fill every small area with some color, as it is in the field of vision. You wouldn't leave a small patch of space in the middle of the canvas uncolored just because you don't see any in the scene, since it's impossible not to see some color in the middle. But if you can paint one part of the scene as it is, you can also paint the whole field of vision as it is, right? No, you cannot. Why? Because while any part of the field of vision you can clearly identify must have a boundary next to which there are other colored parts, the field of vision as a whole does not have an identifiable boundary. How do I know that? You may say, "If you cannot see the boundary, that is your own problem. How do you know that other people cannot see the boundary either?" I know that because I realize, a priori, that anything that can be viewed as next to one another must be an object *in* the field of vision, but the field of vision is the precondition for the visually perceived spatiality and thus is not itself an object in it. The field of vision as a whole cannot be put into itself just as a vessel cannot hold itself.

Suppose you come up with a painting smaller than your canvas so it shows a boundary between the painted part and the unpainted part. But no matter how close it is to the totality of what you actually see, you must either have left something out or added something to it. This is so because you have created a clear (or blurred) boundary of the field of vision, which you cannot possibly see. Wittgenstein's remark that thinking about a boundary must involve thinking about both sides of it also applies to visual perception. But the whole does not, by definition, have another side next to it. So whenever you seem to see a boundary of the "whole" and draw it, you have already gone beyond that boundary so the real whole must be bigger; so you have to redraw it, ad infinitum. Therefore, there is no way you can see the boundary of the whole and thus any alleged boundary in your painting must have been added to it by you.

Forget the painting. Let's ask ourselves: If there is a boundary of the field of vision, which must be fully colored, then what color surrounds the field? You might say "total darkness." But if you really see the darkness, the darkness must fall *within* the field—thus the answer is rendered invalid. If you think that the perception of total darkness is equivalent to perceiving nothing at all, then the question would be: does your forehead or your belly or anything, which is not a sense organ for visual perception and thus must perceive nothing visual, see the total darkness? Of course not. Otherwise we would always perceive more darkness than brightness no matter how much light is shed on the objective world, since our whole body except the eyes would always perceive the darkness. Therefore perceiving darkness is perceiving black color, which is different from perceiving nothing at all. The supposedly perceived boundary of the field of vision has to be formed between color and no color, which requires a total lack of perception. But only between two perceived colored areas can we see a boundary. Therefore no boundary of the whole field of vision can be perceived.

Now shut your eyes, and you will actually perceive the total darkness or a little bit of color. Can you now tell me the shape of that perceived darkness? Is it square, or round, or what? Again, I don't have to be you to know, a priori, that you only perceive unbounded shapeless darkness because that single darkness occupies your whole field of vision, which does not have a boundary or a shape. Only objects *in* the field have a shape. If you try, with your eyes open, to use your black ink to paint what appears to you when you close your eyes, you are going to fail by necessity. No matter how you shape your ink spot, as long as it falls in your field of vision as a bounded object so you can observe it, it won't resemble the darkness you "see" when you shut your eyes.

You Are Now "behind" the Space

What is the point of this final test? Of course, we are still making the same point, that is, the conscious self, of which the field of vision is a component, does not belong to the realm of objects in the space. But our body as externally observed does belong to that realm. Therefore, the unity of our personhood can be maintained regardless of the splintered spatial continuity of our body.

If we want to return to the situation of the person in the helmet again, we now can be sure that even if the person has never perceived, since his or her birth, the "actual" space as we perceive it without a helmet, he or she wouldn't have any special difficulty understanding the structure of the "actual" space. He or she would have exactly the same type (or types) of geometry as we do and prove its theorems following the same procedure. The person would ask the same types of question such as whether the space is finite or infinite, and be puzzled by these questions the same way as we are. Everything about the space here is the same for him or her as for us even though he or she has only "seen," from our pre-reflective naive point of view, two small "pieces" of space, that is, two small screens in front of his or her eyes!

We can conclude that questions about the limit of space, the geometrical structure of the space in general, and so forth, are not about the objectified space understood as separate from the field of vision. They are actually rooted in the field of vision as part of the basic structure of the conscious self. As long as you have the field of vision stimulated by light and have seen a variety of images,[5] you would have these same questions to ask, even if you have been locked up in a closet from the very beginning. So the Kantian view that space is the form of our intuition which makes objectivity possible seems to be vindicated.

Hollywood Challenged!

In order to verify the insurmountable division between the first- and the third-person perspectives, we can challenge any Hollywood filmmaker to visualize CCS or interpersonal-telepresence in a movie. All along, we have demonstrated conceptually how the self-identity of Adam and Bob, or of any member of an interpersonal-telepresence community, will be maintained without ambiguity from the first-person perspective, which is prior to any observation from the third-person perspective; in the meantime, the process of identity of others through sense organs from the third-person perspective becomes fundamentally ambiguous since the match between the observed body and a self-identified person can be switched without any observable change. In our illustrations, we had to use extra indicators such as A1—B2 and A2—B1 to present the match conceptually, or arrows to symbolize the connectivity of radio waves.

But a non-documentary filmmaker is supposed to use the audience's senses of vision and hearing to perceive the identity of each character. In such a case, a movie will not be, in principle, able to present Adam and Bob in a CCS or people in an interpersonal-telepresence. The only way this obstacle can be partially overcome will be using conversations between characters in a certain manner so that the audience can reach a certain degree of *conceptual* understanding of the story, in which Adam and Bob are in CCS or experiencing interpersonal-telepresence. That is, conceptual understanding, as what I hope will be happening while you are reading this book, does not always depend on a specific sensory framework; it can help us get "behind," so to speak, the empirical world, and our thought experiments here are designed precisely for such a purpose.

So I challenge any Hollywood filmmaker to prove me wrong in claiming that the first-person perspective is irreducible to the third-person one by showing me how to present Adam and Bob in CCS or anybody in an interpersonal-telepresence situation without conceptual explanation.

Summary: Personal Identity without Space

In the community of interpersonal-telepresence, an external observer cannot identify a body with a person by direct observation, due to the shifty nature of the telecommunication connection. Personal identity is not an identity of the body that occupies a definite spatial locality. A person can be self-identified without the knowledge of the supporting causal process related to his or her body.

1.6   The Principle of Reciprocity

From the One Seeing Many

Before we discussed CCS and interpersonal-telepresence, we might not have been very clear about the difference between objects (including one's own body as externally observed) identified locally *in* the space and the self that *opens up* the space and thus is not itself in the space. This could be due to our habit of taking the third-person perspective as the only possible perspective in terms of causal connection. After our habit-shattering thought experiments, however, we discovered that the personhood of the self need not and should not be spatially identified as being somewhere, because the self can open up a new field of spatiality anywhere without being transported (how can you transport the personhood?) in the three-dimensional space to a new place. Personhood does not, therefore, belong to the three-dimensional space. Consequently, we can take this position: our personal identity can maintain its own integrity across various sensory frameworks that organize our experiences in terms of spatiality. We have the constant of personal identity on the one hand, and the changeable framework of spatiality on the other.

But our earlier discussion of "dream injection" and cross-sensory perception has also established the position that all self-coherent sensory frameworks are equally legitimate for organizing our perceptual experiences. Put these two positions together, we arrive at the principle we wanted to come up with: the Principle of Reciprocity between Alternative Sensory Frameworks as stated at the beginning, or PR for short, which can also be stated negatively as follows: *Ontologically Speaking, There Is No Ultimately Privileged Sensory Framework for Organizing Our Experiences*. Here, there are multiple possible sensory frameworks for a single unified person across all of them.

Where Is Virtual Reality?

Virtual reality is not, as presently understood, necessarily the same as the kind of "dream injection" depicted in that hypothetical Disney adventure, or as the interpersonal-telepresence we discussed above. So we need now to see what the relevant differences are and how we can apply *PR* to virtual reality (and cyberspace) in order to understand its far-reaching consequences and implications.

As we recall, cross-sensory perception, cross-communication situations, and interpersonal-telepresence, just transduce or reconnect our senses in one way or another without anything being added by an agent in the process. But the "dream injection" is distinct from the others insofar as an agent (or agents) that *creates* perceptual experiences in the subject on a higher level is involved through programming. Virtual reality, thanks to its uniquely computerized interface, makes the combination of the two a natural option, except that *the agent who creates the perceptual experience and the agent who has the experience could be one and the same person.* Let us see what one of its inventors, Jaron Lanier, has to say about virtual reality as he originally expected it:

> We are speaking about a technology that uses computerized clothing to synthesize shared reality. It recreates our relationship with the physical world in a new plane, no more, no less. It doesn't affect the subjective world; it doesn't have anything to do directly with what's going on inside your brain. It only has to do with what your sense organs perceive. The physical world, the thing on the other side of your sense organs, is received through these five holes, the eyes, and the ears, and the nose, and the mouth, and the skin. . . . A minimal kind of Virtual Reality outfit would have a pair of glasses and a glove that you put on. The glasses allow you to perceive the visual world of Virtual Reality.[6]

Lanier's description is succinct and illuminating in terms of the setup of virtual reality and its amazing immediate effect. Now to put it back in the context of discussion, we realize that the computer cannot function as a transformer of our sensory input from the physical world like what we have in cross-sensory perception, CCS, and interpersonal-telepresence; it does no more than process all information and coordinate signals for all senses. Nor can it function as an intelligent agent's generator of artificial sensory input similar to what we see in our "dream injection" thought experiment. But the crucial and exciting difference is that the program that runs the system is digital and can be modified or restructured by us again and again as we wish, and this "us" can be the same person who receives the input! In such a case, autonomy replaces heteronomy. Therefore such a self-governed ultimate re-creation can be carried out by us either collectively or individually at different levels of operation. According to PR, such a switch from one framework to another does not change the integrity of the agent's personality on the ontological level.

Jaron Calls It an Illusion

Obviously, virtual reality (VR for short hereafter) as Lanier conceived of it does not involve anything like our "dream injection," despite some other speculators' inclusion of what they call the "neural-direct" version as a respectable option. The cyberspace we have here is not as William Gibson, who coined the word in his celebrated science-fiction book *Neuromancer*, imagined it such that we can be "jacked into a custom cyberspace deck" that projects our disembodied consciousness into the "consensual hallucination." The interesting thing is that whereas Gibson uses the word "hallucination," Lanier calls images of the virtual world an "illusion" without hesitation as he continues:

> Instead of having transparent lenses, they have visual displays that are rather like small three-dimensional televisions. They're much more sophisticated than small televisions, of course, because they have to present a three-dimensional world to you that's convincing, and there's some technology involved in accomplishing that, but that's a good metaphor. When you put them on you suddenly see a world that surrounds you—you see the virtual world. It's fully three-dimensional and it surrounds you, and as you move your head to look around, the images that you see inside the eye glasses are shifted in such a way that an *illusion* is created that while you're moving around the virtual world is standing still. The images come from a very powerful special computer which I like to call the Home Reality Engine.[7] (italics mine)

What I am showing in this chapter is, however, exactly the opposite, that is, the virtual is no more illusory than the actual, since they are *reciprocal* in their relation to the core of personhood as the center of sensory perception.

As we are immersed in virtual reality, we are enclosed by the cyberspace. If we recall, this cyberspace would have the same types of geometry as what we now call the physical space. If a person never sees the actual space as we see it, but has been immersed in the virtual world from the outset, he would be able to understand our geometry like anyone else. The significance of this understanding cannot be overemphasized and will be discussed further in chapter 3.

Natural versus Artificial

Some people might think that since devices of VR are additions to the natural makeup of our sense organs, so they intervene in the normal passage of the information from the physical to the brain, such intervention leads to distortion. But our sense organs and the connected nerves are

devices of transformation to begin with. Adding one more phase of transformation with devices of VR cannot possibly turn something "real" into
"illusory." If you think that the fewer phases of transformation the signals undergo, the more real the sensory perception will be, then a subtraction would make the perception more "real" than the real. But would
taking away the lenses in your eyes, which is clearly a case of subtraction,
make your perception more real? After such a subtraction, insofar as
the light can still stimulate your retina, you will very likely still perceive
something. But no matter what that something would be like, it certainly
would not be a clear picture. Would that fuzzy perception be more "real"
than the real? Of course not. Therefore, whether the perception is real
does not have a well-defined relation to how many phases of transformation the optic signals have gone through.

Our tentative conclusion is that the "natural" and the "virtual" are
either equally real if you anchor your notion of reality in the sensory, or
equally illusory if you preserve the notion of reality (as in Sartre's
"human reality" as Being-for-itself) for the core of personhood that preconditions the possibility of the sensory perception.

If we take the first option, there appears to be an affinity to Hilary
Putnam's "internal realism" here. When Putnam claims that realism is
not incompatible with conceptual relativity,[8] he assumes that there is an
ontological pole in our experience that lies beyond our conceptual framework. As I understand it, no matter how many possible options there are
for our different conceptualizations, and thus how relative our way of
using language is, the real need not vary accordingly. We can go one step
further along the path of Putnam and extend his internal realism from
the realm of concepts to that of sensory perception. That is, we do not
have the Reality on the objective side that runs across different sensory
frameworks, but we do have realities inside a chosen, once chosen,
framework: realities are internally real, no more and no less. As for how
our *sense* of reality originates, which is a separate question, we will discuss it later.

Therefore, a digital virtual world that has a corresponding regularity
to the actual world with an arbitrary sensory framework of organizing
our experiences is ontologically as solid as the actual world. After we
immerse ourselves in this virtual world, we can begin to augment it by
creating virtual items purely out of our unlimited imagination to penetrate the limit of our experience.

Don't Worry But Watch Out

With VR, we don't have to worry about the evasive spatially defined
causal connections with which modern physics has tremendous difficul-

ties. The digital connection takes over. With the technology of robotics, it is possible that from inside the virtual world we can do everything necessary to mobilize the actual objects outside the virtual world, including the hardware of our Home Reality Engine, and so forth. We can choose to program the known laws of physics into the structure of our virtual world so we can have a greatly expanded world that is operationally equivalent to the actual one; or we can choose different ones as we wish by making up new laws. Such a world is, as we continue to demonstrate in the following chapters, as real as the actual one except that it is our own creation, and can be re-created at will: Gods 'R Us.

To conclude this chapter, I want to remind the reader that we have not discussed virtual reality itself in a systematic way yet. None of the thought experiments we have had is part of VR proper. These thought experiments have, however, helped to establish the *Principle of Reciprocity between Alternative Sensory Frameworks* as the basis on which we will understand how VR and cyberspace will possibly re-lay the foundation of the entire civilization.

2

The Causal and the Digital under the Virtual

Having caressed the world
with a burning stroke
Leave it with no despair
but a growing hope
Allow her now to wear
the darkening wardrobe
She will climb
the invisible up-running slope

"Sunset," Z. Zhai, 1997

Having established the Principle of Reciprocity, or PR, we are now ready to focus on VR itself. We want to see how a combination between the manipulation of causal connection and that of digital connection can be facilitated in the infrastructure of VR, and how the interface between human agents and the physical world will enable us to re-establish the necessary cycle for a sustainable life within cyberspace. If we can demonstrate how the virtual world can function as well as the actual world in manipulating the physical world to maintain the subsistence of human life, the reciprocity between the virtual and the actual will show itself in a concrete process in terms of practical functionality. So what follows does not imply that we need to do everything in cyberspace; it will only show that in cyberspace we *can* do everything we do in the actual world to control the physical causal process.

In this chapter we will use the words actual, virtual, and physical in such a way that the actual or the virtual depends on a particular sensory framework, whereas the physical does not have anything to do with a sensory framework, not even a general spatio-temporal structure; the physical is therefore understood as the source of the given causal regularity that puts predetermined constraints on human creativity. In this sense, PR holds between the actual and the virtual worlds, which depend on

37

a certain sensory framework. Since the physical causality is beyond the contingency of any sensory framework, it is not governed by PR. (See Figure 2.1.)

Being clear about the meaning of, and the structural relation among, these key words, we can proceed to undertake more discussions as follows.

2.1   The Four Sources of Virtual Reality Input

Get Immersed

When we talk about "input" in the context of computation, we usually match it with "output" as a pair. The reference center for this "in" or "out" is the computer itself. When we feed in data by typing on the keyboard, for example, the computer receives input. Why do we give input to the computer? It is because we want to get output from it when we read the text or view the diagram on the screen, for example. In this sense of input and output, the human operator and the computer are clearly separated, and the interface between the human agent and the computer is mediated by symbols on the same level of interface.

As soon as we start to play computerized video games using joysticks, such an input/output model is already transcended because the players need not symbolize their intent when playing. They are interacting with the computer in a way similar to that in which we interact with our natural environment. The symbolic process goes hidden beneath the human–machine interaction. So this is no longer operated in the input/output model.

VR, understood as immersive, however, further surpasses such an interactive model, because human agents are cut off from actual contact with the natural environment and thus do not generally single out any particular objects or events with which to interact. Everything in one's sphere of perception, in which the visual, acoustic, tactile, kinesthetic,

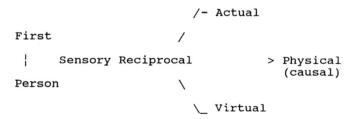

Figure 2.1 PR, actual, virtual, and physical.

and the whole haptic are all harmoniously coordinated, is equally part of the ongoing transaction. In such a case, we are no longer feeding data to a computer as input; we are simply *acting* in cyberspace, and being involved in the process of the virtual events.

Input in the Opposite Direction

In such a VR situation, is there still a sense in which we can talk about input? Yes, we can if we shift from the center of computation to the center of perception and action as the point of reference. From each individual person's point of view, we can discuss from what sources each of us receives input. That is, we are receivers instead of data-feeders in this case. In this sense, there are four possible sources that initiate input for our perceptual experience at each moment in a virtual world that has a stabilized infrastructure.

1) Input from oneself. As in the actual world, one can bring about all kinds of experience to oneself in the virtual world in a variety of ways. You can run, throw a ball, drive a car, cut a tree, and so on. When you do any of these, your sense organs receive stimuli from your VR outfit as well as from your own body internally.

2) Input from others. When VR is combined with a global network like the Internet we have now, there will be many persons that can interact with each other and thus form a virtual community. In such a case, everyone will be able to receive input from everyone else and send input to everyone else in the community. Actually, what happens currently in the text-based chat rooms already indicates how far VR may lead us along the way of mutual stimulation among participants of a virtual community: the extreme kind of stimulation will be erotic, as the word "cybersex" indicates. But we don't have to live in the extreme all the time or even most of the time. We can have a partner for tennis, another for chess, still another for boxing, for example, besides sex partners. The most spectacular cooperation among participants would be projects-oriented, and the goal and the outcome of the cooperation could be as grandiose as a total reconstruction of cyberspace itself.

3) Input from the natural process of the virtual world. If we want to design our virtual world in such a way that it resembles our actual world, then entities in VR must be able to send us input independently of our desires. If you do not take care to protect yourself, you might get hit by a rock, or even blown away by a tornado, for example. The nature of the virtual world evolves just as the nature of the actual world does. Since these "natural" events can only give

us stimuli through the outfits we wear, and the maximum strength of the stimuli depends on our own design, these "accidents" cannot actually harm us if we do not allow them to. But on the negative side, this virtual nature cannot provide us with materials necessary for our survival for the same reason. Therefore, if we choose to live in this virtual world, we must be able to interact with the physical world where the hardware of VR operates, with causal connections to other physical processes, on which our physiological sustenance depends. Hence the next source.

4) Input from the natural process of the physical world. This type of input is now mediated by a digital process, so what we perceive need not be the same type of stimuli as we perceived before we entered into the virtual world. All we need is a corresponding regularity. What we called in chapter 1 "cross-sensory perception," for example, is only one of many possibilities. Of course, at the beginning transitory stage, especially if we want to use this type of input as the cue to guide our action in controlling the physical process, we would like to adopt a reliable strategy of simple imitation. That is, we let things appear in cyberspace as they appear in actual space. After this stage, however, we might want to make things more interesting and exotic. This type of input can be made unambiguously distinguishable from the third type, which is not linked to the causal process in the physical world on the same level; thus we will be able to respond and interact with it effectively for the purpose of controlling the physical process. How we can do that will be discussed later in this chapter.

At this point, we are done with the discussion of the four sources of input from a single participant's point of view, viewing other participants as one of the sources (the second one as discussed above) of input, among the other three. But other participants are also at the receiving end. In order to see how we can have a community life as well in VR, we need to examine the mechanism of interaction among participants. Before we get to that, however, we need to know how we can survive in the virtual world while we are totally separated from the actual world.

2.2   Manipulation of the Physical Process from Cyberspace

You Are an Agent

For the sake of convenience, a human participant, understood abstractly only as an initiator of interactions, is here called an agent. A cause-and-effect physical process that is run for the sole purpose of trans-mitting information from the digital processor to the agent or vice versa, is called a subcausal process (the electric/mechanical process that takes place in the helmet is an example of a subcausal process). A cause-and-effect physical process that is run for its physical effects or for the purpose of leading to other physical processes is called a causal process, which is not a supportive process for the computation (shipping a computer or a cat to another place by train in the actual world, for example).

If we cannot do anything productive and, literally, reproductive, as understood in the actual world, from within the virtual world, then VR would remain a game, fascinating as it may be. In order that we can migrate into cyberspace as our new habitat, we need to take care of our basic economy that provides us with materials to meet our biological needs, either as individuals or as a species, while we are immersed in VR.

Survive and Prosper in Cyberspace

Despite the tremendous technical difficulties we can think of that would be involved in such a super-project, we have no theoretical difficulty in understanding such a possibility. If we can interact with a Home Reality Engine, and the engine as a supercomputer can function as the control center of any mechanical movements in the actual world, we can certainly mobilize any objects via interface in lieu of actual contact. Tele-presence as NASA has it is a prototype of such an inside-out control. When we discussed interpersonal-telepresence in chapter 1, we substi-tuted the bodies of other humans for robots in order to show how the first-person perspective differs from the third-person. But now that we are assuming that all humans are immersed in VR, robots, instead of human bodies, must be utilized to carry out whatever tasks we want to accomplish on the physical level. But how?

Fortunately, before we consider migrating into cyberspace, we human beings in the actual world need to apply, almost exclusively, only me-chanical contact to natural objects to make things happen. Chemical processes that generate medicine, for example, are initiated by our mov-ing things around mechanically—transporting, mixing, and so forth. Amazingly, we build dams, railroads, super-colliders, space shuttles, bombs, and other large artifacts; refine oil; blow up rocks; start a nuclear chain reaction and so on—all by initially moving our own body and as-serting our very limited physical force to something in a certain way, and not doing much of anything else (what else can we do?). Of course this is made possible largely by our ability to use sense organs to receive stim-uli from the environment and to turn these stimuli into meaningful infor-mation on the intellectual level. The good news is that when we are immersed in VR, our sense organs and intellect are no less connected to the physical world, though in a modified manner. Therefore, it is obvious that nothing can, in principle, prevent us from using robots as a substitute for our bodies in fulfilling necessary tasks for the basic economy of subsistence. Figure 2.2 shows the chain of modalities that underlies the loop of such a process: a process of inside-out manipulation.

This kind of manipulation would first, of course, lead to a series of parallel processes in the actual world, including mining, constructing, manufacturing, transporting, farming, fishing, cooking, cleaning, recycling, and so on—that is, all the things we now do in the world of the natural and manmade objects.

Second, the system would also need to take an alternative way to transport us humans in the actual world (actual travel), and give us the power to fulfill, with virtual contact, the tasks now fulfilled by our actual contact with each other or with ourselves. In such a system, if we want to travel to another place actually to avoid a hurricane, for example, we will not have to abandon our VR outfit if we don't want to, because the interface between the virtual and the physical world will enable us to mobilize things such as robots, cars, and airplanes in such a way that we will be taken to wherever we want to be. Probably we can accomplish all of this in VR by simply pushing an emergency virtual button and pointing our virtual finger to a location-indicator on a map.

On the other hand, if we want to have a virtual contact with another person for the purpose of actual effect in order to, say, feed a baby or feed ourselves, we can also simply do it in the virtual world. We may do it in a way similar or dissimilar to the actual act of feeding; in the meantime, the robot will perform the actual feeding accordingly.

As for the contact between a doctor and a patient, since a lot of instruments already function between the doctor and the patient in an actual hospital, we can easily imagine how to turn these instruments into digitally controlled ones. Moreover, the research on the application of VR to telesurgery is currently more advanced than many other possible VR applications, and the beloved Jaron Lanier himself has been involved in

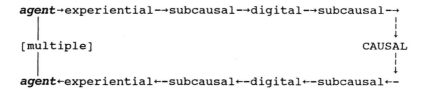

Figure 2.2 Manipulating the physical from the virtual.

it since the very beginning. But keep in mind that, since this kind of inter-personal actual contact is operated by persons immersed in VR, it re-quires a paralleled interactive process in the virtual world, that is, a process of interpersonal transaction as we will discuss in section 5.

Efficiency Matters and . . .

It is worth mentioning that in our design of the robotic system in the actual world, we can be concerned exclusively with the problem of effi-ciency. Other concerns such as the aesthetics of the appearance and con-venience (or sometimes safety) of human–machine interaction can be totally put aside, because humans are not supposed to be in actual con-tact with these machines. So the way of transporting human beings may be standardized and personal vehicles such as cars and motorcycles will be totally eliminated. The variation of things as a means of satisfying personal tastes will be taken care of in the virtual world. Even though you may be in a train in the actual world, you can choose to perceive driving your own convertible across cyberspace.

Apart from material production and ordinary interpersonal contact, a more serious problem arises: how can the production of ourselves, that is, human *reproduction*, be conducted from cyberspace? We may create some virtual babies in our virtual world by means of digital program-ming, but they certainly do not have self-identified personality apart from what they appear to be. According to our thesis established in chapter 1, the personal identity from the first-person perspective is the necessary precondition for any perceptual experience. So a virtual baby generated by our Engine is not a potential center of perceptual experience; it be-longs instead to the expansive part of our virtual experience that does not enjoy the same ontological status, and why this is so will become clearer later.

Therefore, if our reproductive function must still be of a biological nature as we know of so far, we still need to find out how such a biologi-cal process of sexuality can be carried out from within the virtual world. In other words, is human sexuality for the reproductive purpose replace-able by cybersex?

2.3   Cybersex and Reproduction

The Explosive Paul and the Implosive Mary

Fortunately, the sexual contact between male and female human be-ings still falls under the category characterized by the loop shown in Figure 2.2. Combined with an interactive VR process, two persons of the opposite sex will be able to finish, aided by manmade apparatus, the physiological process on the actual level, and be sensually and emotionally fulfilled on the virtual level.

Let us see how a sophisticated cybersex arrangement might work. On the female side, there will be an artificial male mouth (lips, teeth, tongue, saliva, etc.) and artificial male genitalia, both imitating male flesh as closely as possible, but planted with microsensors all over the surface, and moved by motors connected to the computer (the Engine). The penis should be able to be in states of arousal and non-arousal and somewhere in between, and ejaculate semen-like stuff at the right moment.

On the male side, there will be an artificial female mouth and artificial female genitalia, both planted with highly sensitive microsensors and moved by motors connected to his computer. As for the sense of touch from other parts of the body such as breasts and hands, the regular VR clothing will do its job there as usual.

Now what would happen when a sexual encounter occurs between a female and a male partner? We can, if we choose to, describe the process separately on two levels, the virtual/experiential and the actual. But in order to see the immediate correspondence between the two, I will choose a mixed discourse of the virtual and the actual in my description as follows.

Let's call the female Mary and the male Paul. In the virtual world they meet for the first time in a concert hall. Jaron Lanier, the Lord of VR, is to play his "Music of Changes." Mary and Paul are seated next to each other, mutually unknown. As soon as Jaron begins to play, Mary and Paul immediately feel a sort of synergy going on between them in the way they respond to the music. At the intermission, they strike up a conversation about the music and Lanier, and very soon romance develops: during the second half of the concert, they hold and squeeze each other's hand following the ups and downs of the music. When the concert is over and as they step out of the concert hall, their passion bursts out like a storm.

They manage to set up a private room on the spot (assuming they can do that in the virtual world), and their lips and tongues begin to explore and search each other passionately and their naked bodies intertwine and struggle like a hurricane. As their mutual stimulation escalates to the peak, they are ready for the intercourse. "Mary, you are my dream," Paul gasps; "You are my reality, Paul," Mary murmurs in return, as their bodies move back and forth in a harmonious rhythm. Finally, as Paul pours his passion with an explosive ejaculation, Mary screams with an implosive contraction.

Copulating and Procreating

For all the alleged physical and emotional intensity, we should not forget the fact that Mary and Paul are only having intercourse in the virtual world. On the actual level, the lips, tongues, saliva, and genitalia are all artificial surrogates for the receiver of the opposite sex. How, on the one hand, can the artificial organs expand and contract and move in exact correspondence with the actual in a remote place? And how, on the other hand, can the biological process of procreation be carried out in addition to the fulfillment of the sexual desire and emotional needs of both partners?

Keep in mind that, like all other parts of the VR outfit, these artificial sex organs are not only stimulators, but also sensors at the same time. So when Paul inserts his erect penis into the artificial vagina, for example, the opening of the artificial vagina immediately responds and measures the size and shape of the penis. The information will be transformed and transmitted to Mary's facility and the artificial penis will be, guided by the information, inserted into her vagina almost at the same moment, and its size be adjusted accordingly to imitate Paul's as precisely as possible. At the same time, the artificial penis will measure Mary's vagina in a similar way, and the information will be transmitted and used to adjust the artificial vagina Paul is dealing with. Of course, the back and forth movement will be controlled in a similar fashion. Because this is a real-time dynamic process that keeps going from the beginning to the end of the sexual encounter, the described rhythmic coordination will be felt just like an actual encounter in the actual world.

Now we have to deal with a tough and critical issue, that is, how Paul's sperm can be ejaculated into Mary's vagina in such a process if they want to have a child. As we know, since Paul and Mary are far apart actually, what Mary feels ejaculated into her vagina cannot possibly be the same thing that Paul ejaculates actually at that moment. Therefore, their first affair after the concert cannot lead to Mary's pregnancy by Paul's sperm. But Paul's semen is nevertheless ejaculated into the artificial vagina. We also know another fact: sperm can be kept alive outside the human body as has been done for many years in a sperm bank. So now if Mary and Paul decide to have a child after their first intercourse, they can, through the control mechanism discussed in the last section, have Paul's sperm transported to Mary's actual place and ejaculated from the artificial penis next time they make love, and so on and so forth. Or, if they prefer, they can utilize the technique of artificial insemination so as to totally separate the reproductive process from sexual intercourse. In such a case, Mary may choose any semen-like milky liquid or whatever she likes as the substitute for the semen to be ejaculated into her vagina during the inter-

course. She can even choose to use another man's semen to get herself
pregnant when she has cybersex with Paul, if Paul has no legitimate objection to that. The last option is that they actually travel to meet and
have intercourse actually. They can put away the artificial sex organs,
while still being totally immersed in VR perceptually in the whole process. Therefore, reproduction through cybersex is just a special case of
the combination of the process of interaction between participants to be
analyzed in section 5 on the one hand, and that of manipulation of the
physical process from cyberspace as analyzed in section 2 on the other.[1]

The Erotic Ontology

After the baby is born, what can Mary and Paul do for her if they want
her to be a member of the virtual world? They can let her wear the VR
outfit as soon as she begins to have meaningful perceptual experience.
How are they going to do it? They will do it again, of course, by that
inside-out control process using robots.

Michael Heim in his *The Metaphysics of Virtual Reality*[2] offers a very
stimulating discussion of what he calls "the erotic ontology of cyberspace." As he understands Eros as a drive to extend our finite being, he
can indeed do justice to his sensational presentation of virtual reality as
fundamentally erotic. Here, we have also seen how our love affair with
VR must reach its pinnacle when cybersex becomes a necessary part of
our virtual engagement.

A Dangerous Idea

Some people have the idea that teleoperation is unnecessary for human
procreation. They think the virtual world is a totally self-sufficient world
wherein human memes can replace genes. According to them, there is no
need for conscious perceivers behind the scene in order for anything to
be perceived: programming can do it all. If a simulated female image in
VR gets pregnant, and after that there is a simulated baby coming out
between her legs, and afterwards the simulated baby grows and finally
mates and procreates, then the life cycle will be maintained no less than
in the actual world. They have such a belief because they think a perceiving mind behind the scene is a fiction to begin with even in the actual
world. According to this view, even after the first-generation VR players
die, and thus no one wears the VR bodysuit and helmet anymore, cyberspace will still keep evolving and the avatars in them continue to live.

But such an idea is not only totally wrong but also extremely dangerous. It is wrong, because if it were right, VR would make no sense in the
first place. We would not need to wear the helmet and bodysuit to create

cyberspace, since VR had nothing to do with our sense organs. We could just write a VR program and run it in a computer without worrying about generating and coordinating different modalities of sensation. In that case, running a VR program would be no different from running a word processor. This is almost like saying that writing a history book is literally the same as creating the whole history, or that, by writing his plays, Shakespeare literally gave birth to King Lear, Hamlet, and the others. This immediately shows why such an idea is extremely dangerous: if we believed it, killing human beings would be understood as no different than burning a storybook or destroying a floppy disk![3]

But you may ask, if virtual reality depends on actual reality for the basic function of human procreation, but not the other way around, doesn't it mean that the actual is more fundamental than the virtual? No, because, as indicated in Figure 2.1, it is the physical or causal connection that determines the operational process of human reproduction, not the connection as empirically observed in the actual world. But since we already know the natural way of making things happen on the causal level in the actual world, we make use of that knowledge to design a virtual world from which we can make the same kinds of things happen on the same causal level. How? We will do it by inside-out control through teleoperation, as we have discussed. In the case of human reproduction, we need to make sure that man's sperm and woman's ovum make contact in the actual world even though in the virtual world such a contact need not be represented as a contact. In order for us to survive in cyberspace, we must do this as a matter of necessity.

2.4   The Expansion beyond Necessity

Get Rich by Doing the Impossible

Now that we can do all necessary work, including production and reproduction, from within the virtual world, should we say that VR is just another way of normal life? The answer is that the virtual world is much richer than the actual world because we can expand and diversify our experience creatively with a huge potential; so much so that the only limit is the limit of our imagination. Theoretically, we can understand VR at the bottom in terms of the following two basic components: (1) the foundational operation of the inside-out control of the physical process necessary for our survival, and (2) the expansive operation *within* cyberspace, free from the concern of any practical results, as the artistic fulfillment of our creative impulse. So far in the previous sections, we have only considered the foundational part. And it is this foundational part that corresponds to the actual world with an equal ontological status.

For the foundational part, VR has already shown its promising prospect today. By replicating our sensory perception as it was in the actual world, we might at first feel more comfortable adapting to the virtual world. But VR can do much better than that. One of the most amazing applications of VR we can now hope to see implemented in our lifetime is the combination of telepresence and visual magnification. Using such a combination, a medical doctor can "enter" into a patient's stomach, for example, to inspect his or her internal organs, just as a pest-control specialist inspects a house. After the inspection, the doctor can perform surgery on the organ while immersed in VR aided by a microrobotic surgical hand. About the present state of the art, read Michael Heim's report:

> Telepresence medicine places doctors inside the patient's body without major incisions. Medical doctors like Colonel Richard Satava and Dr. Joseph Rosen routinely use telepresence surgery to remove gall bladders without the traditional scalpel incisions. The patient who heals from surgery leaves the body nearly intact. Only two tiny incisions are needed to introduce the laparoscopic tools. Telepresence allows surgeons to perform specialist operations at distant sites where no specialist is physically [or "actually" in our word] present.[4]

It is nice to know the state of the art, but our philosophical reflections have to go far beyond the technological contingency. In fact, unless we can effectively control all relevant physical processes from within cyberspace with the help of robots, we cannot make any strong claims about how VR can change the entire civilization at its very bottom. Therefore, our vision should not be constrained by what technology can do for us in the near future in understanding the implications of VR. The point is that no matter how enormous the practical difficulties seem to be, if we can accomplish a small portion of the tasks of our basic economy that already involves every required aspect of an overall operation, then we can do the whole thing *in principle*.

The foundational operation is necessary for our sustenance, to be sure, and it is settled in principle through our discussion so far. But the most fascinating thing about virtual reality is not the fact that we can manage to survive there but rather the more far-reaching prospect: it will enable us to expand our experience in a way that nothing else could even come close to before. To understand that, let us see first how an *Omni* interviewer put it in an impressionistic tone:

> . . . On the living room wall of Jaron Lanier's disheveled bungalow in Palo Alto, California, hangs a poster of the four-armed Hindu goddess Kali. Her

16 fingers and 4 thumbs dexterously play a sitar. Most Westerners would find the image an exotic one, but in the context of virtual reality, the emerging field of which Lanier is the unquestioned guru, Kali looks as normal as Betty Crocker.

Virtual (or artificial) reality is the hot new computer technology that lets you do the impossible—from swimming through the heart's aorta to walking the dog on Saturn's rings. . . . [VR] enables people to create their own dreams in Technicolor and then let their friends jump in.[5]

It is by virtue of this kind of ability to let us "do the impossible" that VR strikes us as a generator of the pure meaning that is finally free from the supposed materiality. This is exactly the kind of *meaning* people refer to when, as we will see more clearly later, they ask the allegedly meaning-*less* question: "What is the meaning of life?"

Simulations Don't Count

This expansive part does not have the same ontological status as the foundational part since, first of all, virtual objects in it do not have their counterparts in the actual world through the connection of physical causality. They are produced on the digital and subcausal levels, and are disengaged on the causal level. In this expansive part, we may encounter all kinds of virtual objects as a result of digital programming. We can perceive virtual rocks with or without weight, virtual stars that can disappear anytime, virtual wind that produces music, and so on. We can also have virtual animals like or unlike animals we have seen before in the actual world. Second, we can "meet" virtual "human beings" whose behavior is totally determined by the program; they are not agents, do not have a first-person perspective, and do not perceive or experience anything. Therefore, in this expansive part, events are neither related to the causal process nor initiated by an outside conscious agent. This is a world of pure simulation.

Interestingly, Lanier is, on the one hand, one of the most practical VR pioneers insofar as he was the first person to make VR commercially available. On the other hand, as a musician and visual artist, he is also one of the most outlandish dream-pursuers in the field. Listen to what he has to say about what happens in his company:

At VPL we've often played with becoming different creatures—lobsters, gazelles, winged angels. Taking on a different body in virtual reality is more profound than merely putting on a costume, because you're actually changing your body's dynamics. . . . The emotional character of virtual reality is completely different from that of the physical [actual in our word] world. . . . What's exciting are the frontiers of imagination, the waves of creativity

as people make up new things. . . . I want to make tools for VR that are like
musical instruments. You could pick them up and gracefully "play" reality.
You might "blow" a distant mountain range with an imaginary saxophone.[6]

Because in VR we are empowered to make "realities" as we intended
them to be, Lanier suggests, in the same interview, that a better name for
it might be "intentional" reality. This is indeed a good suggestion. But
intentionality does not have to lead to arbitrariness. On the contrary, if
we want to create an expanded virtual world comparable to the actual
world, we'd better look into how our creativity can be used to reconnect
ourselves to the physical world. In doing so, we can validate our ability
to alter the basic structure of what we call "reality," instead of just having flashy fun and thrills. This is an area in which we draw in both the
foundational and the expansive parts of our VR operation to test our
ontological authorship.

Optional Local Continuity and David Hume

Contrary to what we illustrated in Figure 2.1, the common sense takes
spatio-temporal structure as the bottom line of physicality. Postponing
the discussion of our perception of temporality for the moment, we can
see how we may change our perception of spatial locality by furnishing
a different sensory framework. Suppose we recoordinate the light signals
from the actual world to the small screens of our helmet such that in
cyberspace we will see a different but regularly corresponding sequence
of signals as shown in Figure 2.3 (for simplicity's sake I show only one
dimension of such a recoordination). After such a recoordination, what
is perceived as continuous in the actual world is now seen as discontinuous in the virtual world. A bullet flying through from the left to the right
will, for example, cause a sequence of images in the field of vision of
those in the actual world continuously from 0 through 9. But in VR thus
programmed, the image of the bullet will first show up at the right edge
before suddenly jumping to the left edge and then back to the right (but
not as far) and then back to the left, and so on, and finally end up vanish-
ing in the middle at the point of 9. Thus in VR the spatial locality as

```
The actual sequence          The virtual sequence


0 1 2 3 4 5 6 7 8 9    ---→   1 3 5 7 9 8 6 4 2 0
```

Figure 2.3 The altered sequence of light signals.

perceived in the actual world is splintered, and the causal connection becomes indistinguishable from pure mathematical co-relativity.

Of course, when we move from one reference point of observation to another, the resultant visual effect of such a reconfiguration will become very complicated. For example, in the actual world, suppose the sequence ABCDEFGHIJKLMNOP is written on the board. Because the sequence is too long to be seen in its entirety under the given condition, only the first part of it, ABCDEFGH, would fall within your field of vision. In the virtual world, due to the spatial reconfiguration, this part will be turned into DCBAHGFE; that is, the two letters originally at two ends, A and H, now are in the middle; and the two letters originally in the middle, D and E, are now at two ends, and so forth.

Now if you moved your head to the right in the actual world, your frame of vision would be changed. Suppose the new frame would let you see CDEFGHIJ section of the long sequence, if were you in the actual world. But you are still immersed in the virtual world when you move your head. What are you going to witness? You will see DCBAHGFE changing into FEDCJIHG, given the relationship between the actual and the virtual spatial configuration described in the last paragraph.

Therefore, in the actual world, your head movement just allows you to see different portions of the same long sequence continuously; but in the virtual world, you will see DCBAHGFE turned into FEDCJIHG with no fixed ordering of those letters. Such a transition from the first to the second frame would seem to be chaotic, because the static images in the actual world now appear to be jumping around in the virtual world. That is, things that are motionless in the actual world will appear in motion in the virtual world when we change our reference point of observation. This certainly will require us to reformulate laws of physics according to our new perception of locality. But as long as there is a regular correspondence between the virtual and actual spatial configuration, these reformulated laws will represent the same causal regularity, which is independent of either the virtually or actually observed world.

Thus physicality and causality do not have to take a given spatial framework and must be understood as independent of either the actuality or the virtuality. In such a case, Hume's problem of conjunction versus necessary connection seems to be resolved.

Considering our Principle of Reciprocity, we may also see this as a way of dissolving the experiential difficulty of the quantum non-locality: any so-called local events can also be perceived as non-local and vice versa to begin with, insofar as the distance between two spatial points is contingent upon the sensory framework we happen to be trapped in.

A Hypothesis to Be Tested by Psychologists

To go one step further, I would assume that if we begin our recoordinated virtual experience, as exemplified by the altered pattern of the bullet's movement, from our early childhood, our mind would be adapted to perceive it as continuous in the virtual world. Conversely, if our VR outfit were then taken away, we would perceive the bullet's movement as discontinuous. That is, our perception of (not merely the way we use the words) continuity and discontinuity would be totally reversed. This is so because there is nothing inherently "gappy" between the signals that cause us to perceive spatial discontinuity, nor anything inherently "smooth" between the signals that cause us to perceive spatial continuity. Spatial continuity is merely the repeated pattern of coordination perceptualized in our constitutive consciousness.[7]

Space Further Reconfigured

We can see more possible variations as results of the combination of the foundational and the expansive parts of virtual experience. Actually, I will describe some of them later in the form of a concept design for a VR science museum. Here we will discuss two that are especially relevant in this context.

If digital intervention allows us to return to the starting perceptual point (360 degrees) in cyberspace after we turn our head 180 degrees (or any number of degrees) in the actual world, then it is legitimate to claim that we have turned 360 degrees at that point of returning, according to the Principle of Reciprocity (PR) we established in chapter 1. After all, there is no absolute reference that determines how many degrees our head has turned according to Einstein's Theory of General Relativity.

The cross-sensory perception without a computational process as discussed in chapter 1 can now also be facilitated via the computer in place of the soundlight transformers. The sound signals from the actual world picked up by microphones, and the light signals picked up by video cameras, will now be fed to the computer. The computer software is written in such a way that the person immersed in VR receives visual messages that vary in accordance with the variation of the sound signals the microphones pick up from the actual world, and audio messages the other way around. Obviously, such a process will result in the same effect as the one using transformers, insofar as the relationship between the physical input and the participant's experience is concerned, that is, seeing what we usually hear and hearing what we usually see.

The Economy of Inside-Out Control

These variations help us gain insights about the nature of causal connection, but do not necessarily expedite our inside-out foundational operation. A more practical way of combining the foundational and the expansive operation can follow a path illustrated by Lanier as follows:

> An architect can make a building real before it exists and bring people through it. In a demo with Pacific Bell recently, two architects got together over the phone and explored a proposed day-care center in VR. One showed proposed features to the other; they could see each other moving around in the room and could make design changes. By holding the glove a certain way, they could change their bodies to take on characteristics of children's bodies. So they were able to run around and test features like a water fountain from a child's perspective.[8]

As for the psychological aspect of VR, Nicole Stenger perceives with high sensitivity how the way our minds understand "reality" may be affected, and she interprets it as a psychological *consequence* of the VR experience:

> Our minds were softly leaking rainbows of colored imagination, soon to be joined by innumerable rainbows that would embrace the earth and change the climate of the human psyche. Perception would change, and with it, the sense of reality, of time, of life and death.[9]

Her picture is poetic, but her attitude is a little bit too submissive. In fact, before we enter the virtual world, our contemplation of the possibility of VR on the philosophical level will have already begun to obliterate our preconceived demarcation between the real and the virtual. As we have seen, the distinction between the real and the foundational part of the virtual is ontologically untenable because they are reciprocal according to PR.

If we are concerned only with the immediate experience, we can even erase the distinction between the foundational and the expansive. After we enter into the virtual world, we can integrate the foundational and the expansive operation in such a way that we understand the necessary distinction only on the teleological level. That is, we will get to know what kinds of things we have to do in order to survive, not in terms of what is real or unreal, but in terms of what goals we need to achieve. In so doing, we will in effect erase the ontological distinction at the moment of our pre-reflective perception.

What I mean by "teleological distinction" can be shown by a simple example in the actual world: travel for business and travel for pleasure are teleologically different in terms of their respective purpose but ontologically the same in their properties relevant to the operational process. In our ultimate programming of VR, we can certainly reduce the functional differences between the foundational and expansive parts of the operation into teleological ones if we want to. In such a case, the upper-level causality and the regularity of the purely virtual events will not be experienced as distinct by themselves, but as different in their expected consequences. This is just like what we often face before we enter the virtual world: when we push a button on a cassette player, for instance, we don't anticipate a disastrous consequence; but when we push a similar button on a board in the Pentagon, we know that it may start a nuclear war. In this case, the experience of pushing two buttons on the ontological level is practically the same if we don't know on the teleological level what different consequences they might each have. Similarly, the distinction between the foundational and the expansive operation in the virtual world can be made in such a manner as well.

Gods 'R Us

We can also confirm our ontological authorship by re-creating the whole infrastructure of cyberspace as the most challenging collective effort based on a consensus. This is done inside VR, of course. Lanier tells us how programming becomes more fun and more convenient in VR:

> Computer programmers could look at a whole program at once. A large program might look like a giant Christmas tree, and you could be a hummingbird flying around it. Landing on any one branch, you could see in great detail the structure of that part of the program. From a distance, you could learn to plan a very large program spatially.[10]

No doubt, we can do such programming back to VR itself while we are immersed in the same VR that is to undergo a radical change in its infrastructure. This will bring us much closer to the theme of this book, that is, the ultimate ontological Re-Creation: Gods 'R Us.

2.5   Interaction among Participants

Jump and Get Real

If all of us are immersed in cyberspace and surrounded by VR, interactions among us need not involve *causal* process as we defined it earlier. All that is involved is either subcausal or digital. Nevertheless, the stimuli from the VR outfit will feed us with rich experiences that are as real or illusory as before, according to PR. Thus, we will have the loop of interaction among participants shown in Figure 2.4, in which the arrows indicate the direction of a transaction.

When a participant comes up with an idea to initiate an action, she

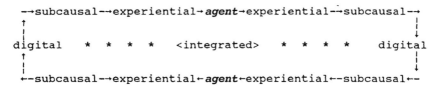

```
-→subcausal-→experiential→ agent→experiential--→subcausal-→
  ↑                                                      ¦
  ¦                                                      ↓
digital    *  *  *  *   <integrated>   *  *  *  *   digital
  ↑                                                      ¦
  ¦                                                      ↓
←-subcausal-→experiential←agent←experiential←--subcausal←--
```

Figure 2.4 Interaction among participants.

functions as an agent. As soon as she begins to act she first of all experiences herself acting and from the experience she gets immediate feedback that directs her operation toward a goal. In the virtual world, her action might be similar to or different from the action in the actual world in detail, but the basic pattern remains the same.

Suppose she begins to jump onto a roof. Her effort to jump causes her body to interact with her VR outfit so that the corresponding signals are generated and sent to the computer, or to the Home Reality Engine as Lanier calls it. Such a process is subcausal by our definition because its sole purpose is to generate digital information. As soon as the signals are converted into binary code that the computer can process through certain software, the subcausal process ends, while the digital process begins. In a truly interactive situation, the newly obtained code is now integrated into a computational process that also deals with code initiated by other possible agents. This process will involve code generated by many participants on the one hand, and the database responsible for the formation and behavior of the entities in the virtual world on the other. This is done according to commands written by the programmer in a totally digital manner, with any specific underlying physical process rendered unessential.

After that, however, the digital outcome of the computation has to be translated back into signals that can give the involved participants, now as recipients instead of agents, new stimuli (visual, pressure on the skin, etc.) via the VR outfit. This is again a subcausal process. The participant who jumped will, of course, experience something new in her virtual world as a consequence of her own action. If the program being run in the Home Reality Engine is intended to generate experiences for the participant similar to what we would experience in the actual world, then her jump will, if no intervention results from other participants or by an unexpected "natural" event, produce adequate visual, audio, and other relevant sensory stimuli for a successful jump. If the experiences are intended to be altered, then they will be altered. Such experiences will lead to further actions from the same participant who is now an agent again. The first cycle is finished and the second begins, and so on and so forth.

. . . At the same time, other participants might see her jump and thus try to stop her, or want also to jump at the same moment onto the same roof and clash with her. Then her jump will be unsuccessful and the Engine will feed her with a different set of stimuli accordingly.

Let Your Partner Paint Your Body or Whatever

Michael Benedikt puts forth a systematic suggestion about the architecture of cyberspace in which humans do not lose a sense of the "real" while benefiting from the possible empowerment in their interaction with each other.[11] But before anybody puts that kind of architecture into practice, we can see its precursor in the currently booming World Wide Web. Based on Virtual Reality Modeling Language (VRML), some Web sites can already give us a glimpse of what a 3-D "cybertown" would look like, even though not in an immersive mode. You can also conduct an online interactive conference over the Internet using these sites. As soon as the many chat sites in the Web merge with these pre-VR sites and provide us with an immersive environment, and one's self-descriptive textual profile is replaced by a so-called avatar, the Web will begin to turn into a virtual habitat. We will then be able to interact with each other in the way envisioned here. Then we can begin to call it a "cyberspace" in a more pregnant sense. As for the frontier of the interpersonal VR game outside the World Wide Web, Michael Heim's presentation of Myron Krueger's achievement is worth citing:

> In Krueger's Videoplace, people in the separate rooms relate interactively by mutual body painting, free-fall gymnastics, and tickling. Krueger's Glowflow, a light-and-sound room, responds to people's movements by lighting phosphorescent tubes and issuing synthetic sounds.[12]

Back to CCS

If we still care about the cross-communication situation discussed in chapter 1, we can think of a VR version of it here. We can easily, in the virtual world, swap our field of vision with another participant's without switching the body controlled by our action. If that happens between you and me, then your movement determines what I can see, and I can only see the body controlled by me as an object in the space separate from me; and vice versa for you. Can we also trade our bodies but keep the original field of vision intact? Certainly, but this is no different from what we just described: switching the field of vision. They are functionally equivalent and the only difference is our choice of reference in making sense of the word switching or the like.

It is clear that cybersex, undertaken either for its own sake or as a means for reproduction, must involve a *causal* process of the physical nature. It has to activate a process of inside-out control. But interaction among participants for the sake of communication or entertainment does not need causal mediation. The whole business can be taken care of on the digital and subcausal levels. Here, the foundational part and the expansive part converge and thus cannot be distinguished from one another.

But does it follow that the physical or causal is outside the mind as Figure 2.1 seems to show? No. There is no inside or outside before the introduction of a sensory framework. What Figure 2.1 shows is a logical relation that does not signify a spatial relation of inside or outside. Ultimately, physicality and causal determination are equivalent. That is, the mind has to follow a predetermined regulation in opening up the field of perception. That mandatory constraint on how the world can be constituted gives rise to our sense of physicality and objectivity, and thus to our sense of the opposition between the self and the world. This is also the final ground for the distinction between correct and incorrect thinking, and for the refutation of epistemological relativism.

2.6 The Final Decision That Is Irreversible: Alert!

VR for Today

In order to see how the limited recreational VR may irreversibly venture into the Ultimate Re-Creation, the best thing I can do here is present a concept design of a version of VR in a science museum, which we are almost able to build right now.

Compared to industrial VR, the science museum VR has the advantage of functioning as a metaphysical laboratory. It is free from considerations of practical payoff apart from its attraction of visitors who come for the sole purpose of recreation and education. So what kind of messages should we intend to convey and what kind of experiences should we let the visitors have when they are hooked up to our VR facility?

The same unique type of messages and experiences derived from the museum VR should continue to be significant no matter how far the specific applications could in the future have been developed in the industry. This is possible only if we are *not* concerned about what VR can *do* for our economy. Instead, our only concern would be how VR can help us understand the *nature* of reality. We want our visitors to pose and contemplate, during and after their visit, the deepest questions such as: "To what extent can we distinguish the illusory from the real?" "Is it possible that we had already been immersed in a sophisticated virtual world long before we ever heard of virtual reality?" or "Is it possible for us to live in the virtual world in our lifetime as if it were the only world we know of?"

Build a VR Museum Right Now, Please

What follows can be viewed as a real proposal for a concept design of a science museum VR to be submitted to a museum director. In order to distinguish the discourse of the events on the virtual level from that on the actual level, all italicized words hereafter in this section will pertain only to *events in VR*. Different processes are meant to implement different ideas as presented at the beginning of each passage, and the described concrete process is just one of many possible ways to exemplify the principle.

1. **The evasive boundary between the actual and the virtual at the entrance and exit of VR.** After the visitor puts on the outfit (helmet, gloves, etc.), *she sees the same surrounding* as she saw before (the VR facility in the hall with other furniture, the wall, etc.) and she *also sees herself wearing the outfit. So the VR outfit she is wearing does not seem to change her vision of anything, and the helmet does not seem to block her eyesight.*

She is now instructed by a "curator" to exit from the VR room and walk to the street outside the museum. But as soon as she reaches the street, she sees a totally unfamiliar scene and the "curator" tells her that she is already in the virtual world. Toward the end of her VR experience, she sees a sign at an exit saying "Back to the Real World." She takes that exit. Then she again sees the "curator," who tells her to take off her VR outfit by following specific instructions. She takes them off and suddenly she sees the familiar scene of the VR room as she saw before she started the game. But in reality the "taking off" was merely her virtual experience as programmed, and she actually remains in the suit; the strict instructions made her unable to see through the trick directly. *She is now possibly believing that she is back in the real world.*

As she walks toward the "exit" of the VR room, she is offered a cookie which the museum has prepared for visitors. She tries to take a bite but fails! At the same moment, the whole field of vision turns suddenly to a total darkness. This final strike makes her realize that she is still in the virtual world. After a few seconds, she is released from the VR outfit and back to the real world. How can she know for sure that she is not tricked once again? Take it easy. She will be offered another chance to taste cookies. This time she will take a real bite and . . .

2. **The real and the illusory.** The principles behind this distinction will

be a topic of the next chapter. Here we are trying to see how the visitor's experience will influence her distinction on the perceptual level.

After the visitor passes the initial stage of entrance, everything she perceives can be seen, touched, and heard (when stricken) at the same time. A baseball bounces back from the wall and as she catches it her hand hurts a little bit; when she holds it, she feels its heaviness just like an actual baseball. Everything obeys the same laws of physics as in the actual world. Cars run according to the same traffic rules and the wind blows and bends the trees as usual. Things such as houses and mountains stand still, undergoing no obvious changes. Other things such as water and traffic evolve independently from her observation. She sees a BMW waiting for the light to turn green. Then she turns around seeing a dog trying to bite his own tail. Seconds later when she turns back to see what has happened to that BMW she sees it running, about 20 meters away from where it was, accelerating. Thus, in the time lapse between her two looks at the car, the events related to the car evolve by themselves in a lawful manner as we see in the actual world.

But eventually she starts seeing things that don't seem as real. Whereas these objects may still evolve independently from her wishes, the process is not as lawful and predictable as the behavior of the BMW she saw earlier. A bird suddenly appears and then changes to a model airplane; then it vanishes into the thin air. Her own body changes from her normal slim size to a bulky one.

Later, things simply become "illusory" because when she sees a strange object heading toward her and tries to push it away, her hand does not meet any resistance. She catches a baseball but the ball is weightless. She finds she can order these objects to change into something else by giving a verbal command. Finally she can give commands so as to teleport herself instantly to any place she wants and rebuild the whole environment at will, and let all kinds of fantastic objects come and go in caprice. After all variations as described in items 3, 4, 5, 6, and 7 below, *she will take a backward path, that is, from the "illusory" to the "real" before she returns to* the actual world.

3. Possibility of alternative sensory frameworks. According to our discussion of PR in chapter 1, our perceptual experience of the actual world is contingent upon what sense organs we happen to possess. But we tend to be conditioned to believe that the world as we perceive it is as it is by itself. Immersed in VR, the visitor can be led to realize that other possible sensory frameworks might work as well as, or better than, the one she actually has without the VR outfit.

The visitor steps out of a room and sees the scene directly imported by an outdoor video camera without modification. *She also hears the same sound directly picked up by microphones. She sees and hears everything the same as* we see and hear it in the actual world. *But when she turns her head, the scene changes twice as fast as* it does in the actual world because the camera is designed to be controlled by her turn at a doubled speed, so after her head has turned only 180 degrees, *she returns visually to the point at which she began.*

Now it's time, she is told, for her to have cross-sensory perception: suddenly, the sound signals are transformed to light signals and light signals to sound signals with corresponding variables by the computer, and *she begins to see things that we hear, and hear things* that we see. When a fire-truck rushes by, *she sees a trace of brilliant light dashing through,* which is a result of the sound of the sirens. When we see a sharp lightning flash followed by deafening thunder, *she hears the sound caused by the light first and then sees the bright light* caused by the sound of the thunder.

After cross-sensory perception, she now sees and hears things with an expanded bracket of wavelengths: she will see things emitting only ultraviolet or infrared rays, which we cannot see, and *hear* ultrasound transformed into regular sound.

Recast again, she will experience things of shifted scale: she can, with the help of a microscope linked to the computer, *"zoom in" to see and touch the hills and bumps on the surface of the glass* that is completely smooth to those not in VR. *She can also "zoom out" to have a bird's eye view of the earth* by flying away from the earth with the help of a transmitter that receives signals from a satellite. All these variations should be arranged *in the middle of the transition from the illusory to the real.*

4. Finite yet unbounded space. Common sense makes us believe that the infinitely large and the infinitely small are infinitely apart from each other. We can break things downward into smaller and smaller and still smaller pieces infinitely on the one hand, and travel upward further and further and still further infinitely on the other. But this picture of the infinite unbounded space has long been jeopardized. Instead, Einstein's understanding of space as finite yet unbounded has prevailed. But before VR we have not been able to experience any one of the possible models of such a space. Here in VR we can provide an opportunity for the visitor to experience at least two of these models. The first model is a space whose edge on the largest end meets with its smallest possible unit. *The visitor zooms in downward to see smaller and smaller details of an object, but at some point she passes through the threshold of the smallest unit. At that point, she is brought to see the same view as she would have seen if she started with continuous zooming out upward. Now, if she continues to zoom in she will return to the scene of her starting point.*

Conversely, she can start by zooming out upward until she reaches the same threshold, passes through it, and returns to the same place she departed from. Here space is perceived as curled up with the largest "outer edge" and the smallest "inner edge" joined together. The trick is that the program is written in such a way that the loop is actually there to permit *things to evolve by themselves while not eliminating the necessary sense of continuity during the visitor's adventure.*

The second model is simpler: *The visitor travels straight ahead and eventually returns to the point of her departure. Her visual, audio, and tactile perception all verify her return.*

5. **Interaction among participants.** In the actual world, since our body is subject to others' attack, we have to be very protective in dealing with strangers. But in the virtual world, nobody can physically affect us in a way our self-managed program does not allow. We set the limit in the infrastructure to prevent any serious injury. Except for some minimum privacy as an added flavor, we can be maximally open to all other participants insofar as our psychological makeup allows.

After meeting the "curator" at the entrance, the museum visitor will meet other participants. (For the sake of convenience, images of real participants should be visually distinguishable from images of mere digital animation.) The visitor steps into a bar and sees a few people there playing billiards. She starts a conversation with a man and shakes hands with him, and then joins the group. Perhaps she gets a few erotic touches from the man and feels stimulated sexually. Maybe she came to the museum with her sex partner and *now meets him in cyberspace. They can try a session of mutual flirting, caressing. . . Or knowing that nobody can get hurt physically, they may try hitting each other with fist and stones for fun, both sensing the slight attack on the surface of their body from the other. Finally, they leave each other and continue their own journeys.*

6. **A second-level virtual world within the virtual world.** *The visitor sees in the virtual world a museum exactly like* the museum she saw in the actual world: the one she is actually in. *She is instructed by the same "curator" to enter the museum and put on the VR outfit as she did before* she actually entered VR. *She starts the process of an allegedly new virtual-virtual experience entirely comparable to the earlier VR experience . . . After a while, she exits from the alleged virtual-virtual world by "taking off" the outfit and comes "back" to the first-level virtual world.*

7. **Possibility of the inside-out control.** As we discussed earlier, if we cannot control the physical process from the virtual world, the VR game remains merely a game. But if through robots we can affect the physical process from *inside the virtual world*, VR and cyberspace might begin to become a habitat of the human race when developed to the extreme.

In order to convey such a message, a robot is placed in a separate room. The robot is there ready to be manipulated by the *visitor* as a virtual–actual interface, picking up a few objects and rearranging them in accordance with the visitor's pattern of *conduct in the virtual world. The visitor is instructed to enter a room that is an exact copy of the room with the robot. She is told that she can move those objects in whatever way she wants and must remember how those objects end up when she leaves the room.* After she returns to the actual world, she sees that the objects in the room with the robot are arranged exactly the same way as *she placed them in the virtual world. She was having a telepresence experience from the virtual to the actual and conducting teleoperation.*

After such a journey, the visitor would be easily alerted to such critical and legitimate questions: "If the inside-out control as experienced in the last scenario is extended to the whole system of agricultural, industrial production, and also to human reproduction, and the confusing boundary between the actual and the virtual as exemplified in the first process is finally erased, would there still be a 'real' difference between the actual and the virtual?" and "If there could be a second level VR as described above, would many more levels of virtual world also be possible, and is our so-called actual world only one level of these multilevel virtual worlds?"

But Should We Do It?

Putting the second question aside for the time being, let us assume that we are now living in a "real" world at least in a relative sense to the virtual world we have only had a glimpse of so far. Then the question would become: "Should we strive to eliminate the experiential distinction irreversibly between the real and the virtual once and for all?" Before we can answer such a normative question, we need to understand the nature of such a possible shift from the actual to the virtual, and this leads us now to engage in a systematic reflection on the meaning of the "real" in the next chapter.

3

The Parallelism between the Virtual and the Actual

Mating here are Yin and Yang
Flirting here are the momentary and the eternity
Negotiating here are the high and the low
Wrestling here are the full and the empty
The nothingness is kissing the plentitude
The limited plural is wooing the infinite singularity

"Horizon," Z. Zhai, 1992

3.1   Deconstructing Rules for the "Real" and the "Illusory"

Cookies Are Served

In my concept design of the museum VR, the visitor was supposed to experience the evasiveness of the boundary between the actual and the virtual. But finally the visitor could still manage to know that she was back to the "actual" world by tasting the cookies offered by the museum. If, however, the inside-out control through teleoperation is extended fully to all aspects of human life as we discussed in chapter 2, the trick of tasting cookies won't work anymore, because the robot will feed the visitor with cookies in the actual world when she acts to feed herself in the virtual world. In such a case, is there an ultimate experiential boundary that can not be erased in any circumstances? If the Principle of Reciprocity, or PR, is correct, there can be no such boundary. But we are accustomed to the idea that the actual is real and the virtual is illusory. In order to know that such a distinction is groundless, we need to analyze what kind of structures of our perception is responsible for our sense of reality.

For the sake of convenience, let us continue in this section to use the contrast between the actual and the virtual as the basis for our discussions. On that basis, we will try to see how those conditions that make things in the actual world real also have a counterpart in the virtual world, and thus the virtual and actual are ontologically parallel in the sense of being real or illusory. We will realize the following symmetry: if we call the actual world real and the virtual world illusory when we are in the actual world, we can also call the actual world illusory and the virtual world real when we are immersed in the virtual world.

The Gunman Wants My Rolex

Before we ever heard about VR, in the actual world we seemed to be able to distinguish between reality and perceptual imitations of reality in art, entertainment, and so forth. When we see a movie, we can be deeply moved or disturbed by the story or physically aroused by the graphic images or the language; but we always seem to know that it is just a show, not part of reality. Why? Let us look into it.

In order to undertake our analysis, let us now use, strategically, the words real and illusory as if they each had a well-defined and distinct reference. We will continue to do so until our descriptions become self-defeating because of such a usage of the words. This can be viewed as a "double gesture" in a process of deconstruction.

Suppose I am in an airplane flying to a place I have not visited. I am nearsighted, so I am wearing a pair of eyeglasses. It's a long trip in the air, and I fall asleep. While I am asleep, somebody replaces my eyeglasses with a similar-looking pair that lets me see a 3-D movie that is visually very realistic. Everything is arranged in such a way that as soon as I wake up and open my eyes, a 3-D movie will begin playing so that I will see a gunman threatening to kill me unless I give him my Rolex, which I always wear. I wake up and everything runs as planned. So I believe at first that I will either be killed or need to give up my Rolex. When will I begin to suspect that the gunman is just an illusion?

As I attempt to take my Rolex off my wrist, I first move my hands up to where I should be able to see them. But to my surprise, I cannot see my hands anywhere. In fact my whole body has disappeared from the scene. Since the image of my body is the least likely to disappear in the real world, its disappearance is a very good indication that the real scene of the world has been blocked from my vision and what I am seeing is not part of the real world.

At this point, I might begin to notice other abnormal signs: I may, for example, pay attention to what is outside the edge of my glasses and see a discrepancy between the gunman's surroundings and the background outside the frame of my glasses. But how can I know that the real is outside the frame and the illusory inside the frame? The answer cannot be that eyeglasses are a manmade device and a manmade device always distorts reality; this cannot be a valid answer because my original glasses for my nearsightedness are also manmade but they are supposed to *help* me see the real world, not to distort it. The reason why I believe that I know which part is real and which illusory is as follows. Outside the frame I can see my own body, the existence of which I know for certain; but inside the frame through my glasses my body does not show up. A real visual environment at least allows my body to appear in it; a visual environment that does not allow my body to appear is illusory. So I am applying a tentative rule (or T-Rule for short) implicitly as follows:

> *T-Rule 1*: The visual environment in which *my body image* resides can be real, and objects seen in that environment can also be real; the visual environment in which my body image does not reside cannot be real and thus is illusory, and objects seen in that environment are also illusory.

I call it a tentative rule because it is not a solidly established rule I can follow through without trouble. Suppose the 3-D movie incorporated my real-time body image into it interactively, in addition to the image of the gunman. So I have my avatar, as called by digiratis nowadays, representing me. Suppose my avatar is made to resemble me as much as possible. In such a case when I try to raise my hands I can see my hands raised as expected. Now I do not have a chance to apply T-Rule 1 anymore.

What would be the next clue I can make use of to tell the real from the illusory? I will take my Rolex off my wrist and place it on the table in front of me. But to my surprise, when I see my hand touching the table, I do not feel any resistance to my hand, a sense of texture, or anything else that should be part of my sense of touch. I cannot hear any noise either if I strike the table. Since I can feel the sense of touch with my Rolex, I know my hand is not numbed, and I can hear sounds from other sources, so I know I am not deaf. Therefore I would assume that the table as I see it visually is an optical illusion and thus is not real because it does not lead to an agreement between my sense of vision and my sense of touch. So I am now implicitly applying another T-Rule:

> *T-Rule 2*: A real object must give stimuli simultaneously to my different sense organs, agreeing with each other *in my perception*; any alleged object that does not satisfy this condition is illusory.

But now suppose when I try to place my Rolex on the illusory table, my hand does receive appropriate tactile stimuli at the right time from an independent but well-coordinated unknown source, and I also hear well-coordinated but independently generated sound, etc. In such a situation, T-Rules 1 and 2, taken as necessary but not sufficient conditions for the distinction between the real and the illusory, are both circumvented. What is the next clue that can lead me to see through the trick?

Suppose now the objects before me, such as the gunman and the table, disappear suddenly, and reappear later, and so on, at random; my sense of touch with the table also comes and goes in a ghostly fashion along the visual image. In such a situation, regardless of the agreement among my different modalities of sense, I would nevertheless begin to doubt the status of reality of these objects. Or, if the gunman acts like a cartoon character that defies laws of nature—say, flying without wings—I would also begin to think that it is no real gunman and I don't have to lose my Rolex. Here, I am applying another T-Rule implicitly:

> *T-Rule 3*: If the change of an apparent object, as seen, felt, etc., does not show a certain sort of regularity *as I expected*, then the object is illusory.

But T-Rule 3 cannot allow me to draw a final conclusion about what is real or illusory either. Events in a 3-D movie can certainly be made to follow the same laws of nature just as a regular movie if I don't attempt to participate in the story. So the gunman and the table do not have to behave in a ghostly manner. They can be made to appear just as lawful as I expected and thus circumvent T-Rule 3, while remaining illusory. Given this, what else can I appeal to in order to distinguish between the real and the illusory?

At this point of discussion, let us disregard the gunman temporarily and pay our full attention to the illusory table in order to avoid the more complicated philosophical question of other-mind for a while. How can I know that the table is not real? Instead of perceiving it passively, I now take action and try to carry the table with me to another place. Since the perceived table is only an image on the screen, and my senses of touch, hearing, and so forth, are only coordinated to that image, there is no way that it could be taken out of the screen. On the other hand, I—the real I—can go to many other places as I wish. Therefore, my attempt to take that perceived table with me must fail, and the failure will reveal the illusory nature of the putative table. Thus, we have the following T-Rule:

> *T-Rule 4*: If I cannot locate a perceived object and move it around in the real space wherein *my own body* is located, then the object is illusory.

We can apply T-Rule 4 only if we can tell the difference between the illusory space created through the 3-D images on the screen and the real space wherein my body is located. But suppose my attempt to move myself does not lead to my real movement in the real space; it moves instead only devices such as a treadmill that translate my action into corresponding signals. These signals enable the 3-D images and the stimuli to my senses of hearing, touch, motion, and so on, to cooperate in such a way that I have an immersive experience of taking a real table with me. In such a case (we are finally getting to VR again), how can I begin to realize that I am dealing with an illusory table?

Presumably, if I become skeptical, I can begin to examine the apparent table's primary qualities as defined classically by John Locke, which are supposed to be inherent in the object. Instead of indulging myself in sensory perception of the secondary qualities, I undertake an active study of the microstructure of the putative table. I will try to break it up into pieces, or do anything I can do to a real object from a simple strike to smashing its elementary particles such as neutrons and mesons in a supercollider. As soon as the table or its parts respond to my vandalism in an obviously un-physical manner (all parts disappearing suddenly, or broken pieces taking the size of the original unbroken piece, etc.), then I will begin to know that the supposed table is illusory. That is, I would follow such a T-Rule implicitly:

T-Rule 5: If *I do not witness* the supposed physical object obeying established mechanical laws of physicality as described by physical science and supported by common sense, then the object is illusory.

T-Rule 5 is very close to the assumption rooted implicitly in the mind of the majority of scientists who believe scientific realism. Naturalistic philosophers such as John Searle and Daniel Dennett would also tend to hold such a belief because it seems to them that mechanical laws of physics are the bedrock of causal connection, and causal efficacy is the final test of reality.

However, T-Rule 5 can also be circumvented in principle by our so-called ontology engineering in programming. With sufficient computational power, we can build all known laws of nature, and/or laws created by us, into the software. Since all empirical knowledge we have about objects in the world is acquired through our observation of the patterns of their behavior, the same sort of events will lead us to draw the same sort of conclusion about their ontology. That is, the alleged material solidity of the physical world is constructed solely out of the lawful *events* related to the perceived objects. When we talk about molecules, atoms, electrons, photons, down to quarks, we are merely using these concepts to organize phenomena we have observed as a result of our active participation; they are *derived from* events of which our activities are a component.

Therefore, there is nothing in principle that will prevent us from writing a program in the VR infrastructure to simulate the behavior of the actual world. Regularity is exactly what symbolic programming primarily aims at to begin with. In such a case, when I break my table into smaller and smaller pieces, I would be able to find molecules, atoms, electrons, and so on, as long as I encounter the same types of behavior of a table as in the actual world. Or, if I opened my virtual watch, I would see all the tiny and sophisticated virtual gears, working together, and it would be ticking!

This can be done only if, of course, we have mastered tremendous computational power at both hardware and software levels, which is difficult in practice (by now) but not impossible in principle. If VR pioneer Myron W. Krueger can program laws of his own creation into his "artificial reality" called VIDEOPLACE, why can we not just copy physical laws, as we read in a typical textbook of physics, and incorporate them into our ultimate programming? Let us see how Krueger describes his virtual world:

> In this VIDEOPLACE environment, students would be cast in the role of scientists landing on an alien planet. Their mission would be to study the local flora, fauna, and *physics*. The world would be deliberately unrealistic. It would operate by unfamiliar *physics* and would be designed to give children an advantage over their teachers. Their unique behavior, as well as their size and perhaps even what they were wearing, would allow them to discover different things about the environment.[1](italics mine)

Krueger uses the word "physics" here without hesitation even though the world is "unrealistic." We should be able to see his point now. As long as objects in his VIDEOPLACE environment show some kind of regularity, they will give us a sense of physicality, even though they follow a new set of laws.

In our case, the illusory table is made to follow the same set of physical laws that I am familiar with in the actual world and therefore is deliberately realistic rather than unrealistic. In the virtual environment, we can even find a super-collider in which virtual particles are smashed and elementary particles such as mesons, protons, and pions are observed through virtual bubble chambers. In such a situation, not knowing the sharp turn of my perceptual history at the moment I was placed into VR while I was asleep, what else can I do to find out that the table is illusory?

You might have already seen the catch: an actual super-collider consumes a tremendous amount of energy, whereas the virtual one does not consume energy in the same way. In fact, there is no way to write a VR program that makes any virtual event consume more energy necessarily than other events apart from the energy needed for the computational process. Therefore, the law of conservation of energy seems to be absent in the virtual world, and that seems to be the final ground on which we can distinguish the real from the illusory. But energy is not something we can see flowing separately from objects that undergo changes while consuming energy. So we need to appeal to the second law of thermodynamics, which tells us that energy does not accumulate itself to serve our intended process of transformation. We must at first intentionally channel energy in a certain way (running an electricity-generating power station, for example) into a specific process in order to use it for the intended result. Therefore, if I can break the apparent table into smaller and smaller pieces and finally run a super-collider without locating and operating, or intentionally connecting to, a more and more powerful generator of energy, then the table is illusory. Hence we have:

> *T-Rule* 6: If I can break an apparent object into smaller and smaller pieces or affect it in whatever way without *an intended effort* to bring in proportionate energy, then the object is illusory.

Does this T-Rule 6 finally save me from the confusion between the virtual and the actual? Not quite. The underlying program can again circumvent this T-Rule if it indeed incorporates *all* laws of physical science at the level of correlation of all events. Energy is no more than another concept used to organize the *mandatory regularity* of *events* as perceived by us. In modern physics, the traditional distinction between particles and energy carried by or transmitted among them already becomes an obstacle to a consistent understanding of the physical world in its entirety. Therefore, T-Rule 5 has already covered the content of T-Rule 6, if we understood the former literally.

Therefore, we can make the following events happen in VR. When I try to break my perceived table into pieces, I do need to assert my physical power increasingly as the size of the pieces gets smaller and smaller. When the work reaches a certain level I must find a knife or a hammer or a chisel in the virtual world in order to continue. Later, when those pieces reach the threshold of visibility, I need to take them to a lab and operate the lab exactly as I would in an actual lab: pushing buttons to start a motor, turning on lights, boosting the computer, and so on. Finally, I need to write a proposal that justifies my use of a super-collider. After I receive the approval of my proposal, I take my material to the site of the collider, which is operated by a group of engineers who appear in the virtual world and are supposed to know how to acquire the needed amount of energy. I will see, hear, touch, and smell whatever I would in an actual facility, including bubble chambers that show traces of elementary particles as expected. How can I now apply T-Rule 6 to distinguish the illusory from the real? I can't.

Now what am I supposed to do in order to tell the real from the illusory? I must use my own body as a tool for a final test. I must try to perceive whether the supposed destructive (or constructive as well?) process can bring about any perceived consequences to my body as it would in a natural world. If I dip my fingers into a sizzling frying pan but feel no damaging heat, or let a car run over me while I keep whistling "Yankee Doodle," or the gunman throws his gun against my head but I feel only a light touch, then I will conclude that the objects and the events are illusory. On the contrary, if in the perceived environment, a fire can burn me and the smoke chokes me, or a knife can cut me badly enough that I will collapse soon if the seen bleeding is not stopped, or electricity can shock me if I touch an open circuit, that is, all kinds of events with their energy affecting me as expected, then I will conclude that the objects and the events are real. In such a case, when the gunman pulls the trigger, I will be badly wounded, if not killed. If I am indeed killed, I am really killed, and gone with me is the issue of the real as opposed to the illusory table. Thus the T-Rule which I follow implicitly is:

T-Rule 7: If the putative energy in an event cannot *hurt me* proportionately as expected, and cannot finally threaten to terminate *my ability* to interact with the environment, then the event that seems to carry energy is illusory.

At this point, we have reached the crucial junction where the virtual and the actual meet and separate decisively. This is the junction at which the causal process is blocked at large from the subcausal on the one hand, and the corresponding stimuli for the foundational part of our VR experience are generated on the other, through the Home Reality Engine and the bodysuit in a subcausal process. Filtered by this kind of causal/subcausal exchanger, we can control the causally real process under the protection of the causal blockage so that the amount of energy won't exceed the maximum tolerance of our sense organs. Speaking of the virtual world from the perspective of the actual world, we can say that we are carrying out remote control of actual processes most of the time, while experiencing the directness in our sense perception within a preset energy threshold.

Insofar as T-Rule 7 gets to this bottom line in distinguishing the real from the illusory, it seems to be finally grounded on the foundation. So even though the ultimate programming might be able to incorporate all causal laws of nature into my VR environment, my existence does not belong to this level of causal interaction. I belong instead to the causal world of a higher order.

Since the cross-level interaction is intentionally set to the limit of the energy level tolerable to human sense perception, anything beyond that is dammed away from me. As a consequence, the coordination between my visual and auditory senses on the one hand, and my sense of touch and the whole haptic field of senses on the other, breaks down when I see and hear something fatally destructive but experience no threat to my well-being. This is so because the visual and the auditory sensations do not usually have a direct proportional impact on my safety, that is, my *existence*, whereas my haptic sensations (touch, penetration, balance, etc.) do. This is the final phenomenological origin of the Lockean distinction between the primary and secondary qualities. This is also the bedrock for the scientific realism that takes the priority of concepts based on the sense of touch (particles as penetration-resistant) over those based on senses of vision and hearing (colors and sounds as derivative from the motion of particles).

However, the sense of touch has a clear connection to the sense of vision. *Before* I touch, or am touched by, an object, I can already *see* that the touch is going to occur. So I can use my sense of vision to guide my hand, for example, to undertake an act of touching. How? Because the visually seen spatial proximity almost always accompanies a sense of touch. The impenetrability perceived by the sense of touch on the one hand, and the spatial continuity by the sense of vision on the other, cooperatively contribute to the formation of my conviction of the spatial properties of an object. Because on these properties at least two senses agree, they seem to occupy a primary ontological status. So Locke believes that these "primary qualities" cause "ideas" that "resemble" them exactly. The so-called "secondary qualities," on the contrary, are perceived only by one modality of sense. Colors, for example, as part of the sense of vision do not involve the sense of touch or any other senses. As a result, I can judge that two objects are in contact by seeing them, but I cannot judge that anything is colored by touching it. So there is no way to train a blind person to tell different colors by his or her sense of touch, but there is a way to train a person with paralyzed hand not to touch certain things by using his or her sense of vision. Similarly, sounds only pertain to auditory sense and are thus also secondary.

After our reflections on VR, however, we realize that such a coordination between senses alone does not entail anything more real behind the sensible; a well-authored program run in a sufficiently powerful computer will do the trick. In the expansive part of our VR experience, we can have pure simulations of any objects that appear to have primary qualities, as well as secondary qualities that appeal to merely one modality of the sense. This is the main reason why VR can venture into our ontology directly, unlike any other technologies we have known. The very idea of the total coordination of all senses cuts deep into our assumptions about the so-called primary qualities as inherent in the singularity of the alleged self-sufficient object.

There is no necessary limit to such a total coordination. Only when the system reaches the built-in ceiling of the strength of stimuli for the sake of our self-protection does the coordination need to be halted. When you use a virtual hammer to knock a virtual nail into a virtual wall, you may see, feel, and hear exactly what it is like to nail into an actual wall with an actual hammer. When you use the same virtual hammer to touch your own hand gently, you may also feel as if you're being touched by an actual hammer. But if you try to hammer your own virtual finger like knocking a nail, you will feel like, say, being hit with a light weight rubber hammer, no matter what you see visually. No matter how hard you try to hit yourself, you are not going to be injured or feel sharp pain. Your sense of vision and your sense of touch no longer correlate as before. Such a design does not raise a difficulty, because there was no pre-given correspondence between different senses to begin with in a virtual world. On the contrary, the perceived correspondence before the system reaches the ceiling is a deliberate design in programming.

In what way can I, when immersed in a virtual world, finally distinguish the real from the illusory then? There seems now to be a final rule: the real has predictable consequences to my well-being and existence, while the illusory does not. That is, whether the perceived causal events have a proportionally energized experiential consequence to the observer seems to be the final test for reality. This is what T-Rule 7 is all about.

Robots Are Taking Over!

If there were only the expansive part of VR, T-Rule 7 would indeed be the final rule that I could use to tell the illusory from the real. But we have not forgotten that there is also a foundational part of VR that uses robots as a means of the inside-out control. This part of VR renders T-Rule 7 futile.

As we recall, in this foundational part, whatever we see will have counterparts in the actual world, and whatever we do will affect the physical process and thus will have predictable causal consequences to us, physically and experientially.

Thus when I am threatened, from outside the virtual world, by a real force that is destructive to my body, the foundational part of my VR experience will show a corresponding series of events perceived as destructive. If I am doing something meant to correspond to an act of hammering a nail into a wall, then there is an actual nail being knocked hard, and the energy involved is proportional to my effort to swing the hammer. When I see an image that represents a bullet finally hitting me, the destructive force, either carried by an actual bullet or something equivalent, will penetrate my bodysuit and then my body; it will wound me badly if not kill me. I will feel the pain as expected and need to be taken to an emergency room as soon as possible. At the moment my bodysuit is destroyed, the division line between the causal and the sub-causal will be eliminated and I will be brought to the actual world from the virtual world. If I am in an actual building doing something that is meant to make the same building collapse, my bodysuit and my body will very likely be destroyed when the building collapses.

At this point, you might think that the Principle of Reciprocity (PR) is defeated. When we face the issue of life and death, you may argue, we must concede that the actual is real while the virtual is illusory. But such an argument is invalid. Before we enter the virtual world, we don't wear any special bodysuit but we do have the skin, eyes, and other sense organs. In a normal situation, these sense organs operate at the subcausal level to generate signals for the brain just as does the bodysuit. When a bullet penetrates my skin and destroys it, the division between the causal and the subcausal is also eliminated. The bullet inside my body stimulates my nerves directly, bypassing the skin, and causes an unbearable pain. Is my perception of the bullet inside my body more real than my perception of the bullet with my skin right before it penetrates? If not, that means that our skin as a medium of our perception of the bullet does not decrease the degree of reality. That is, to mediate between senses and perception is not to distort reality.

What if the bullet destroys my eyes? Our analysis will be similar. Now compare the bodysuit, the goggles, and the other equipment I wear, with my skin and my eyes, we will see how they are parallel. You realize that the actual is no more real than the virtual, and the virtual is no more illusory than the actual, because the only difference is the difference between the artificial and the natural. Why can we not have artificial reality and natural illusion instead of the opposite? Therefore PR remains valid.

Therefore, T-Rule 7 is also a tentative rule. Passing the test of this rule does not guarantee a final distinction between the illusory and the real. But what else can we appeal to for a final distinction? On the experiential level, we cannot go any further, because this test of T-Rule 7 is a test of life and death; it does not leave room for more experiential tests.

Of course I could recover from my injury and lose my goggles and bodysuit forever, that is, begin to live in the actual world rather than in the virtual world. But it has been made clear that such a switch is between two parallel worlds experientially, not between the illusion and reality ontologically.

I seem to have ordered the seven T-Rules arbitrarily. But the order is not arbitrary. A later T-Rule is needed only if all earlier T-Rules have already been circumvented in our attempt to distinguish the illusory from the real experientially. If you change the order between any two of them, such a sequence will be broken, and an earlier T-Rule would not be able to make sense. If, for example, you are damaged by a force which seems to testify T-Rule 7, but T-Rule 6 tells you that there is nothing "real" out there because you could affect the putative object in whatever way you choose without using a certain amount of energy, you wouldn't relate the damaging force to the putative object, which has been deemed to be illusory precisely because it could not possibly exert "real" effect on anything, including you. Therefore each following T-Rule cuts deeper into the question of the putative experiential demarcation between supposed reality and illusion.

Where Is Brenda Laurel?

In chapter 1, I challenged any Hollywood filmmaker to visualize the match or mismatch between the first-person and third-person perspectives, which is logically impossible. Therefore, any wise filmmaker should not try it at all. But now my theatrical VR heroine Brenda Laurel is invited to do something possible and extremely exciting.

VR differs radically from all other technologies precisely because it operates at the point where the first-person perspective objectifies itself through a reconfiguration of the sensory framework that makes the third-person perspective possible. Brenda has been a pioneer of the VR theatrical art, working at the metaphysical cutting edge, literally. Hey Brenda, since you are ahead of us, I don't have to challenge you. But I do hope you will help us understand the seven T-Rules by putting us in front of the threat by the gunman. If you do that, should I consider buying a real Rolex?

Summary: Seven T-Rules Gone in Order

Here is a summary about the seven T-Rules with regard to what is real. (1) The coherence within one (not necessarily visual) single modality[2] of sensation: something "real" happens at this moment; (2) the agreement among different modalities of sensation: there is an agreement that what is happening is "real"; (3) the regularity over temporal duration: there is a constant "it" that endures as the "real"; (4) the mobility in the space: that "it" is out there in the "real" space; (5) the mechanical lawfulness:

there is a conservation of spatial identity in "it" that undergoes a "real" change; (6) the correlativity between change and the known supply of energy: "it" has "real" effects on other things, and does not create or destroy itself by pure chance; (7) the proportional causal impact on the person's body: the conservation of energy is not fake but "real." But in the end, none of them survives a progressive process of deconstruction.

Rotating the Fork

At this point, we can imagine what would be the case if I started out in the foundational part of the VR instead of in the actual world, thus reversing the process as we suggested at the beginning. Suppose before I fell asleep I was in the virtual world. What would happen when my 3-D goggles were replaced with a pair of eyeglasses for nearsightedness without my knowledge? I could now as well call my experience in the foundational part of VR "real" and the experience in the actual world "illusory." Then I would ask the same type of question to start with and use T-Rule 1 through T-Rule 7 in the same manner, ending up with the same uncertainty. This shows exactly the parallelism between the virtual and the actual world. That is, the Principle of Reciprocity is reconfirmed.

3.2   Communicative Rationality as the Final Rule

Bishop Berkeley Says Thusly

There might be a more serious challenge. Since all T-Rules have a point of reference anchored in the first-person perspective, they do not seem to address the issue of intersubjective validation. Key words in these T-Rules are "my body image," "in my perception," "as I expected," "my own body," "I do not witness," "my intended effort," "hurt me," and "my ability." For a typical scientific realist, such a "subjective" language describes nothing inherent in objective realities that are governed by universal causation. Therefore, one may argue, the lack of final validity of all seven T-Rules pertains only to the phenomenology of perception, but not to the concept of physical reality as studied in the hard-core science.

But as many philosophers since antiquity (Berkeley being the best known, perhaps) have demonstrated, if we admit that what is real is behind the perceived, then that which is allegedly real must be a postulate or a product of inference. After the linguistic turn of this century, some even reduce the notion of reality to our syntactic necessity. In addition, material realism, which is supposed to support the objectivity of empirical studies, turns out to lead logically to its opposite: it finally degenerates into naturalistic relativism, which turns around to undermine the very idea of objective reality. This is inevitable because material realism only recognizes the validity of empirical science that leads to the naturalization of epistemology, which in turn leads to cultural relativism of knowledge and truth.

The Final Rule: Relativism Prevented

In such a situation, reformed rationalism that strips away the dogmatic assumption of transcendental items such as substance appeals to the notion of intersubjective consensus as the final bedrock of rationality. But here "consensus" is not just a simple case of agreement. Otherwise the question of validity or truth would become an issue of politics that can be settled by vote.

The most convincing form of such a reformed rationalism is the theory of communicative rationality originally proposed by Jurgen Habermas and Karl-Otto Apel. According to this theory, such a consensus is a rationally justified one reached through a counter-factual domination-free procedure. In such a procedure all participants make validity claims and redeem them by following a strict set of rules. These rules are formulated as the minimum precondition for the possibility of any validity claims, and the most crucial one is what I call "the Principle of Performative Consistency" in my book *The Radical Choice and Moral Theory: Through Communicative Argumentation to Phenomenological Subjectivity.*[3] As Habermas, Apel, and myself have argued, communicative rationality is more basic than any other types of rationality, and the concept of validity is more universal than that of truth. Thus, any claim for truth must be justified argumentatively, and the argument should be redeemed as valid. Therefore, intersubjectivity that operates on constitutive subjectivity of each individual is the final ground for the conviction of truth—in particular, the truth about whether there is a final distinction between reality and illusion. Therefore, we have the following rule.

> *The Final Rule*: If I can justify to all, or others can justify to me, in a process of communicative argumentation, that there is or there is no final line of demarcation between the real and the illusory, then I must hold such a justified claim as my rational belief.

Thus, through communicative argumentation, I can reach my justified belief about whether there is a final line of division between the real and the illusory. The central conception of communicative rationality is the Principle of Performative Consistency, which is as follows:

In the process of argumentation, a claim made by a participant must be consistent with the presupposition(s) to which he or she has already been committed in his or her *act* of making this claim.

So far in this chapter, I have put myself in an imagined communicative situation in which I tried to state seven T-Rules presupposed at each stage of my questioning. The members of the communication community are all potential thinkers, including myself. But if knowledge is justified *true* belief, do I now have knowledge? That is, is my justified belief "true"? According to the theory of communicative action, there is no question of truth separate from that of argumentative justification, because truth claims are just a subclass of validity claims, which are redeemed communicatively. So the "objectively true" is now reduced to "intersubjectively justified."

Foundational Part of VR No Less Real

What are the rationally justified beliefs I have reached? I used T-Rule 7 to justify finally that there is a line of division between the expansive part of VR on the one hand, and the foundational part of VR and actual reality on the other. But there is no final line of division between the foundational part of VR and actual reality. Therefore, I must take the following claim as valid or true: *the foundational part of VR is no more illusory and no less real than the actual reality.*

But Is the Gunman Real?

We have dropped the question of the ontological status of the gunman in the middle of the process because it involves a more sticky issue of other-minds. Now we can return to that issue and deal with it in the framework of communicative rationality. Communicative rationality is based on the conception of a counter-factual rational communication community, which already presupposes multiplicity of participants. Because it is counter-factual, it does not need to answer the question of how to tell observationally which object does and which does not have a mind. In chapter 1, we have already concluded that the absoluteness of a person's self-identity is acquired at the price of the absence of an observational criterion of the other's identity from the third-person perspective.

Epistemologically, only my sense perception and the empirical world I perceive can be illusory; my mind or the other's mind that makes sense perception possible but is not part of it cannot be illusory. This is so precisely because the identity of a mind cannot be vindicated from the third-person perspective. Because the identity of the mind does not change as the sensory framework changes, there is no way to verify that the mind is there by sense perception, which depends on a contingent sensory framework.

Communicative rationality must assume the existence of other minds, but it does not give us a procedure for identifying other minds. On the contrary, whether I can believe that a human-like object is a body of a subject that is a center of perception and thinking, that is, a mind, must depend on whether the validity of such a claim can be communicatively redeemed.

Now how can I know whether the gunman is real or illusory? Starting by assuming that he is "something," I will at first use the seven T-Rules to examine him on the physical level. If he does not pass one of these tests, then I don't need to raise the question of whether he has a mind, since that apparent "he" is deemed illusory. If he passes all tests under the seven T-Rules, then by communicative argumentation I will realize which alternative is more justifiable: to take him as a real gunman or just as an illusory gunman? Here the Principle of Performative Consistency will be the final criterion. Since T-Rule 7 already involves my action, the gunman's passing of this T-Rule compels me to take him as real performatively. Thus, even though I cannot have a total certainty, taking him as real is communicatively rational, and taking him as illusory irrational, until it proves communicatively the opposite later. This holds as well in the actual world. There is no way for me to tell a human-like robot from a real human being conclusively, but unless there is a strong counter-evidence, I will take you, the reader of this book, as a real human being if I see you appear to be human when I meet you. This is the only rational conviction compatible with my act of argumentative justification and writing a book for you to read.

3.3   How Phenomenological Descriptions Are the Same Throughout

Two Evaporating "Hard Facts"

Apart from the epistemological question of how to tell the real from the illusory in an immersive setting, the realist would claim that even though you don't know it since you are immersed, the ontological difference lies in the two hard facts: (1) For one single perceived object, the source of stimuli for each modality of sensation is separate from the source for any other modality in VR, whereas in the actual world all sensations responsible for the perception of one single object come from the same source. In VR, the sense of vision may have its physical source, for example, in a remote place, but the sense of touch has its source just in a nearby facility connected to the bodysuit. (2) All stimuli in VR are artificially produced and coordinated by certain human agents whereas those in the actual world are mandated by nature, which does not make them happen deliberately. Or if God created the natural world, He just made material entities stimulate our sense organs automatically by causal necessity and thus He does no coordination when we perceive a physical object.

But if we understand the essence of PR established in chapter 1 and our discussions that followed, we would know that the first so-called hard fact is not hard at all because it is formulated from the perspective of the actual world. Since the actual and the virtual are reciprocal and symmetrical, when we shift the perspective from the actual to the virtual, as evidenced by our examination so far, the description can be perfectly reversed. Terms such as "remote," "nearby," and "separate" are all space-dependent, but space is already shown, in Einstein's Special Theory of Relativity and in my analysis here, to depend in turn on the frame of reference. But at least, if we do have the same set of senses, we will have a sense of spatiality. Accordingly, if the space is perceived as three-dimensional, the status of validity of geometry will remain the same regardless of the reconfiguration of spatial locality. That is, the textbook of geometry might need additions as a result of our new study based on our new experience in VR, but the contents of an old textbook of geometry used in the actual world can be taught in a school of the virtual world without a single change.

But the objection may continue: in the actual world, we can do scientific research to discover laws of nature, and a sense of the unknown hidden behind the scene is a major reason why we perceive the natural world as real. But this objection does not have much logical power. First of all, the software in the VR infrastructure only specifies general rules that allow events in cyberspace to evolve by themselves. Continuous interactions among the first-order rules will generate second-order rules that even the original programmer does not know directly. Second, later people of later generations will be born into such a virtual world just as we are born into this actual world; they need to do a lot of science in order to know the laws of the virtual world. Finally, in the actual world, some people believe that there is a Creator, God, who knows all laws of nature; but these people do not feel the created world unreal. Thus, if in the virtual world Gods 'R Us, reality as our own creation can be as real. Therefore, we have equal reasons to call both the actual world and the virtual world either "real" or "illusory," as we wish.

There is another objection to the ontological status of VR. It says that sensory simulations can never acquire sufficient perceptual faithfulness to erase our experiential distinction between the virtual and the actual, because the required enormous computational power will be forever beyond the reach of human technology. This objection is, however, based on two mistakes. First, it assumes that from our present level of mastery of computational power we can foretell its theoretical limit. Such an assumption is obviously erroneous. Before the electronic computer was invented, who would have been able to predict even just the computational power of today's simple calculator? Second, the faithfulness of simulation is not even a real issue here. Our analysis of VR here is not trying to figure out how VR can fool our senses. We are trying to show why the virtual and the actual are ontologically equal, which means neither is the prototype of the other. Ultimately, there is no need to copy the actual to the virtual. If we do try to imitate the actual at the beginning stage of VR development, it will be only for the sake of practical convenience or the ease of our psychological adaption to the new environment. After we get used to the new environment, we need not consider how much our perception in VR resembles that in the actual world.

Even in the actual world, we have already witnessed a significant alteration of our sense of physical reality. Intuitively, for example, the weight of a physical object contributes a lot to our sense of reality. We are used to thinking that a real thing should be more or less heavy, and we measure the quantity of a thing by weighing it. When we go shopping we expect to pay for anything that weighs more than zero pounds (except for balloons). But now we know that everything in a space station like Mir becomes almost weightless due to the absence of gravity. Everything weighs zero pounds there. But even so, no one seriously claims that things in Mir become less real. That is, the weight of an object does not have a necessary connection with its status of reality. Therefore, in cyberspace, objects do not have to appear to have weight comparable to what we usually see in the actual world. But if we don't need to imitate gravity in cyberspace, why do we have to imitate anything else faithfully in order to make things "real" there? We surely don't.

The bottom-line question is: Does the digital-perceptual interface provide sufficient information for our teleoperation for an efficient inside-out control? If it does, we will then focus on the expansive part of VR as an arena of our artistic creativity. If it doesn't, let us work on it if we choose to. Therefore, to claim that the virtual environment needs to resemble the actual environment in order to be ontologically equivalent involves the fallacy of circular reasoning: assuming the secondary ontological status of VR in the premises and then pretending to derive it from the premises as a conclusion.

Optional Reality Is Fake

Thus when we claim that in the virtual world the sense of vision, the sense of hearing, and the sense of touch for a single virtual object are separately generated, we are adopting a frame of reference from the actual world. If we shift the point of reference from the actual to the virtual, then we can claim with an equal force of logic that in the actual world stimuli of different modality of sensations received from a single (single only from the actual point of view) object are separately generated if a different spatial configuration is adopted in the VR infrastructure as we discussed in chapter 2. The one-and-the-same-ness of the source is not inter-referentially identified but rather a convenient postulate by the immersed observer in a given sensory framework. If we want to accept a scientific realism in the actual world, there is no less reason that we accept the same in the foundational part of VR.

But inherent in the notion of realism is an exclusion of such a parallelism, since this parallelism entails that what is called real is merely optional. An optional reality is, however, no reality at all. Or if we agree with Berkeley that the assumption of a singular entity behind the scene is unfounded to begin with, and the division between primary and secondary qualities is thus also a fabrication, then the parallelism between the actual and the virtual goes without saying and the notion of reality as such is rejected to begin with. Either way, scientific realism that takes the actual frame of reference as the only possible one is invalid.

The only possible "realism" is the so-called instrumental realism, that is, taking the notion of reality as a convenient organizational tool for articulating the lawful regularity of events. But this is a fake realism because it takes away the basic meaning of the conception of reality. As we realized earlier, in the virtual world, we can study elementary particles in physics just as we do in the actual world. Here a phenomenology of experiential necessity precedes an instrumentalistic postulation of so-called reality as an item of organizational expediency.

The Myth of Singularity

The second objection is based on another unjustifiable assumption, which contends that the unity of senses from the mandate of nature must be based on the one-ness or singularity of an entity, from which stimuli for different modality of sensations are issued automatically without a deliberate process of coordination; an artificial environment like VR is, on the contrary, a result of deliberate coordination among different senses without anything singular and "solid" behind them.

But such an assumption is again based on reversed logic. The alleged singularity behind the scene is in fact derived from the regularity of phenomena. If the regularity of phenomena in VR can be understood without a singularity behind the scene, then we can infer that the comparable phenomena in the actual world can also be understood without such a singularity.

Consider the extremely organized process of human reproduction and the required complexity of genes. Clearly it is a case of coding and coordination. If nature can carry out such a complicated process of coordination like procreation of human life without an invisible agent behind, it can certainly do as well in coordinating our different modality of sensations. Or if there is an agent behind the scene responsible for the actual events in the world, who is God, then the so-called actual world is already a virtual world. Either way, everything would be equally virtual or actual, and equally physical or causal.

This Is No Collective Hallucination

Since William Gibson called the cyberspace of VR a "collective hallucination" in his *Neuromancer*, many people have followed that line of thought. The phrase "electronic LSD" has also aroused a great deal of enthusiasm in the media. By now, we should know why these labels do not do justice to VR.

Let us imagine a nation in which everyone is hooked up to a network of VR infrastructure. They have been so hooked up since they left their mother's wombs. Immersed in cyberspace and maintaining their life by teleoperation, they have never imagined that life could be any different from that. The first person who thinks of the possibility of an alternative world like ours would be ridiculed by the majority of these citizens, just like the few enlightened ones in Plato's allegory of the cave. They cook or dine out, sleep or stay up all night, date or mate, take showers, travel for business or pleasure, conduct scientific research, philosophize, go to movies, read romances and science fiction, win contests or lose, get married or stay single, have children or have none, grow old, and die of accidents or diseases or whatever: the same life cycle as ours.

Since they are totally immersed and everything necessary for their survival and prosperity is done by them while they are immersed, they don't know that they are leading a kind of life that could be viewed as illusory or synthetic from outsiders such as us. They would have no way of knowing that, unless they were told and shown the undeniable evidence. Or they would have to wait for their philosophers to help them stretch their minds by demonstrating such a possibility through reasoning.

A more interesting possibility is that their technology would lead to the invention of their own version of VR, which gives them an opportunity to reflect on the nature of "reality" in a tangible way, just as we are now doing at this moment. Then they would possibly ask the same type of questions as we are asking now.

If there were such a free kingdom, can we say they are in a state of "collective hallucination"? No, if by calling it a hallucination we mean to know that ours is not the same. What if I ask you: "How can you show me that this imagined nation is not the one we are in right now?" That is, how do we know that we are not exactly those citizens immersed in VR?

In order to separate ourselves from such a possibility, let us assume the basic laws of physics in that virtual world have been programmed to be different from ours. Suppose their gravity is twice as much as ours. So their "physical" objects of the same molecular structure as ours will accelerate, say, twice as fast when they are in free fall, and be twice as heavy when they try to lift them. At the same time, they can see lights such as infrared or ultraviolet, which we cannot see. Their scientists will formulate the law of gravity according to their observations. Due to a well-coordinated interface, they can teleoperate things in our actual world smoothly and thus run their basic economy well.

Knowing all of these from our "outside" point of view, can we thereby judge that their scientists are wrong while ours are right? Of course not, because they would have as strong a reason to tell us that our scientists are wrong. Moreover, from their point of view, they are not doing any teleoperation, but are controlling the physical processes directly; we are in fact doing teleoperation. If we tell them that their VR outfit gives them a distorted version of reality, they would tell us, by exactly the same logic, that our lack of such outfits disables us from seeing things as they are. They would ridicule us and say, "You don't even know what ultraviolet and infrared look like!"

When we described the above situation, we still used an asymmetrical language as if we had the privilege to know that they are hooked but they don't know that we are unhooked. But our discussions all along have shown there is no such asymmetry on the ontological level. They and we are just differently hooked in a parallel arrangement, because our use of sense organs are one way of being so "hooked" in the first place. This is not relativism. But from the vantage point of the constant mind, we realize the optional nature of our sensory framework.

Summary: Three Principles of Reflexivity

1) Whatever reasons we have for justifying the materiality of the actual world are equally valid or invalid for justifying the materiality of the virtual world.

2) Whatever reasons we have for calling the perceived objects in the virtual world illusory are equally applicable or inapplicable for calling those in the actual world illusory.

3) Whatever functions we need to perform in the actual world for our survival and prosperity we can also perform in the virtual world.

3.4   Fundamental Philosophical Questions Remain

Lao Tzu Debating Berkeley

The ancient Chinese Taoist Lao Tzu could be regarded as the first philosopher of VR. For him, any binary opposition is only provisional since it depends on concepts that are valid only from a particular sensory framework. Only Tao is absolute, across all possible conceptual and sensory frameworks. Tao is not to be found in a place or at a time. It cannot even be said to be inside or outside any particular person. It is everywhere and nowhere all the time and at no time. Any description of Tao will lead to a paradox. But Lao Tzu still attempts to say something about it. How? By constructing paradoxes that show how a description of Tao must fail: this is a "double gesture" in Derrida's term, a process of deconstruction.

Idealists in the empiricist tradition, such as Berkeley, argue that there is nothing "real" as implicitly supposed by common sense (actually, nowadays scientific realism is just a more articulated form of such a common-sense view). According to Berkeley, apart from the well-coordinated regularity of sensory perception, there is no permanent material entity out there behind the scene that bears primary qualities as Locke assumes. In chapter 1, our PR supports such a Berkeleyian position. But empiricists such as Berkeley do not allow us to take anything non-empirical as the ontological starting point for further understanding of the world. They have a simple dichotomy between empirical facts and the "relations of ideas," as Hume puts it.

The Quarrelsome Rationalists

Philosophers in the rationalist tradition from Descartes to Hegel, on the other side, reject such a dichotomy. Where traditional empiricists simply locate reality or objectivity in a putative realm of materiality, these rationalists find a world of tremendous complexity where objectivity can never be divorced from subjectivity. Descartes's talk about the "natural light" that reveals what he calls the "first principles," Leibniz's celebration of "pre-established harmony" among human "monads," Kant's formulation of the synthetic a priori "categories," and Hegel's interpretation of the self-evolving "shapes of consciousness" are all instances of the attempt to take account of the *given* structures of human cognition and/or experience as the *ontological* starting point of understanding all other "realities" as empirically observed.

There is a division between realism and idealism among Rationalist philosophers too, however. They disagree on whether there are substances separate from the givens in the mind insofar as objectivity is still understood as ontologically opposed to subjectivity. In fact, Kant's idea that space and time are forms of intuition of the mind that organize the manifold from the external world into meaningful experience came very close to our understanding of sensory framework. Or we can say, our discussion of VR here vindicates the Kantian view of space and time. But Kant did not give us an adequate account of the basic structure of the mind in terms of spatiality and temporality.

Leibniz's monadology might also be a relevant reference, and his notion of the pre-established harmony might be wiser than that of the material singularity. But Leibniz did not understand our given spacial configuration as optional. For him, this "best world among all possible worlds" leaves no room for a human-created cyberspace. Or would he consider cyberspace as a window within the window?

A New Turn of the Mind

The founding father of hardcore phenomenology, Edmund Husserl, takes a new turn of rationalism by tracing both objectivity and subjectivity back to the same origin in the given structure of consciousness. Insofar as the structure is *given*, it is ontologically determined and thus needs to be *discovered*, not invented. So, contrary to a widespread misunderstanding, Husserlian phenomenology excludes cognitive relativism from the very beginning. Starting from constitutive subjectivity, there is no room for cognitive subjectivism as usually understood in the empiricist tradition.

But in chapter 2, we did talk about our "ontological authorship" at the point when we discussed the shift from the given sensory framework to the virtual one, which can in turn be re-created over and over again by digital programming. In what sense could we say that we are an ontological "author"? On that occasion, we still assumed that ontology is about "realities" that are empirically observed material entities. Now that such a notion of reality has been put away, and we know the so-called ontological framework is changeable and thus we can re-create it as we wish, what else is left intact during such a process of paradigm shift?

Here, Husserlian phenomenology comes to the fore: besides empirical contents and the formal framework, there are phenomena, or essences, of perception which are "den Sachen" that cannot be altered no matter what we do. Historically, long before Husserl, Descartes already realized that certain truths such as those in geometry and arithmetics are valid either in the "real" world or in a dream, as shown in his first *Meditation*. Such a Cartesian position concords clearly with our PR and most of Husserl's theses in his *Logical Investigations* and *Ideas*.

On a deeper level, our internal time-consciousness remains the same regardless of the shift from one to another sensory framework. Therefore, Husserl's positions in his *Phenomenology of Internal Time-Consciousness*, if valid, will be valid in both the actual and the virtual worlds; or if invalid, invalid in both worlds. In the previous section, throughout the whole process of deconstructing all seven T-Rules, all experiential contents remain seated in temporality and spatiality. We can change from one spatio-temporal framework to another, but there is no way we can change the spatiality and temporality of our perception. In the following chapters, we will further demonstrate how the intentional structure of consciousness and its derivatives remain intact as long as our experience continues, no matter on what level of actual or virtual world.

No Expiration Date

In general, any valid phenomenological descriptions, along with pure mathematics and logic, which are not directed at empirical facts based on a particular sensory framework, must remain valid regardless of what sensory framework is chosen.

According to Husserl, all genuine philosophical propositions must be a priori valid or invalid, including all those made by Empiricists such as Hume and Mill (see Husserl's *Logical Investigations*, vol. 1), even though they themselves claim mistakenly that their positions are empirically grounded. I think this Husserlian position can be taken as a normative criterion for the demarcation between philosophical and empirical approaches. If so, all genuine philosophical questions will have the same significance in any given or chosen sensory framework, that is, in any actual or virtual world. Plato's allegory of the cave, for example, will be discussed in exactly the same way by those totally immersed in VR as by those outside VR; Descartes's *Meditations* will have the same intellectual appeal; Leibniz's question—Why is there something rather than nothing at all?—will be posed in VR as it was centuries ago; Kant's positions on human apperception, things-themselves, and so forth, will remain as significant; Hegel's "science of logic" will retain its speculative charm as always; Husserl's phenomenological descriptions of the intentional structure of consciousness, of the eidetic evidence of the validity of logic, etc., if valid, will remain valid, or if invalid, will remain invalid.

Finally, this book on virtual reality and cyberspace will have the same significance for those who have entered the virtual world as for those who are in the actual world right now. As all other genuine philosophical discussions, our discussions here are not contingent upon the sensory framework in which we now happen to be trapped. They all have a self-sliding capacity in the sense that all their primary references will be automatically slid to those in the newly entered world while preserving the same meaning. Due to the reciprocity between the virtual and the actual world, no matter which world we happen to be immersed in, we will pose philosophical questions about that world in exactly the same way we would pose them if we were immersed in any other world. Looking forward, if we migrate to a virtual world of our own creation and are immersed in it, the questions discussed here will have the same philosophical significance as they have when they are first published. Therefore, books like this one, whose intrinsic values will last for generations, will continue to make the same sense even if mankind has migrated into cyberspace (which is why it is not a good idea)! Remember the idea of the second-level VR in my concept design of the museum VR toward the end of the last chapter? That idea tells you that when we are immersed in an ultimate virtual world, we can still create VR from inside that world, and so on and so forth, ad infinitum, in principle.

New Creation Story?

This is to declare the end of empiricism, but not the end of the Ultimate. The Ultimate is the given lawfulness, which we cannot change, because none of the options we have been talking about can be taken without the mandatory constraint at the ultimate level. We are not materialists, neither are we idealists if by "ideas" we mean those items in our conscious mind. If we still choose the word "reality" by which to call the Ultimate, then we can say the Ultimate Reality is the mandatory lawfulness. But it is better to avoid the word "reality" in order to free us from its traditional connotations. So, if you like, you can call this position "transversal immaterialism" or "ontological transversalism."

Under such an ontological constraint, we could re-create the whole empirical world through VR. If so, could this book eventually be rewritten and presented to our later generations in a form of a Re-Creation story? If our children have actually abandoned the actual world and live in VR with a sense of safety and security, would they continue to create their own VR? If that happens, we would say, Gods 'R Us.

"Let there be binary code," then, "Let there be light," and still then, "Let us have a new body. . . ."

4

All Are Optional Except the Mind

At across around,
Into through up'n'down;
Behind below between,
Under onto within.

After among about,
Over upon or out;
Before beneath beyond,
Outside against alone.

Aback above abask,
Aslant asquint astrike;
Again afresh anew,
Astern aslope askew.

"At Beneath Askew," by Z. Zhai, 1987

4.1 John Searle's False Notion of Body Image in the Brain

Temporality Inherent in the Mind

Across all possible virtual or actual worlds, our perceptual experience has to take spatiality and temporality as the basic structure for any objects to appear and any events to happen. Does this mean that space and time are on the same level of ontological necessity? No. Spatiality stays there only because across all sensory frameworks the same set of our sense organs is utilized; and whether in the actual or the virtual world, all sense organs are activated by their same respective type of stimuli.

But it is certainly possible to remove one or more of our sense organs while we still have a spectrum of perceptual experience. If we don't have a sense of vision, for example, our sense of spatiality will become dramatically impoverished. If our sense of touch is further eliminated, it will be seriously questionable whether we still have a sense of spatiality. What if all modalities of sensation are eliminated except the sense of smell? It seems to be very reasonable to assume that, in such a case, our sense of space will have been diminished completely.[1] If we are not quite sure when our sense of spatiality will be totally lost, we are pretty sure that our sense of temporality will remain as long as we are still perceiving something at all, that is, as long as we are conscious. For that reason, temporality is absolutely inherent in the mind, whereas spatiality might just depend upon a particular characteristic of our sensory framework.

Therefore, everything else is optional except the mind. But temporality always stays with the mind; that is, the mind is essentially temporal. Thus in order to understand the essence of the mind, we must not skip temporality. Discussing the mind without discussing temporality is beating around the bush. Thus any explanation that *presupposes* temporality, or even worse, spatiality, will at the most only touch upon the manifestation of the mind, not the mind itself. Since the concept of the objectified space-time must have experienced spatiality and temporality as its content, anything that already presupposes such an objectified framework of space-time must not be used as the starting point for an adequate explanation of the mind. Otherwise it will necessarily lead to a self-referential pseudo-explanation or even a paradox. Since all causal explanations in a model of classical mechanics have presupposed such a framework, they are not able to shed light on the problem of the nature of the mind as such. Thus cognitive approaches such as John Searle's and Daniel Dennett's, based on neuroscience, which is in turn based on the classical model of causality, are not likely to have as much explanatory power as their proponents have claimed.

The Amputee and John Searle's Confusion

As we know, an amputee can have "phantom feelings" such as a pain in his foot after the foot has been amputated. Obviously it involves a discrepancy between the amputee's unsharable first-person somatic sense of spatial locality and the observed body image from the third-person's perspective, which he shares with other observers. Internally he feels a pain-in-the-foot, but externally there is no foot to be observed. Taking a neurophysiological starting point, however, Searle is led to a very interesting but mistaken claim about this phenomenon:

> Common sense tells us that our pains are located in physical place within our bodies, that for example, a pain in the foot is literally inside the area of the foot. But we now know that it is false. The brain forms a body image, and pains, like all bodily sensations, are parts of the body image. The pain-in-the-foot is literally in the physical space of the brain.[2]

Thus, according to Searle, all bodily sensations are parts of the body image. If so, we must also claim that when I soak my hands in hot water, my hands don't have the feeling of the warmth, while my brain does. But this kind of talk must lead to a paradox. Suppose I have a headache that spreads all over my head. According to Searle, my headache is "literally" in the brain. The truth is that when I shut my eyes, I also feel that my head, as internally sensed, is on my shoulder. How do I feel internally that my head is there? I feel it by having sensations of it, pleasant or unpleasant. My headache may make me aware of the presence of my head more than other sensations because it is conspicuously bothersome. So my internal sense of where my head is must be the same as where my headache is. Would Searle therefore tell me that my head is "literally" in the physical space of the brain because all my bodily sensations are parts of the body image?

If his answer is yes, then a paradox results immediately. My brain is contained in, and is thus a part of, my head, and at the same time, my internally felt head is "in" my brain: the brain is in the head and also the head is in the brain! Such an apparent paradox is due to a confused mixture of two perspectives. The term "brain" refers consistently to the object as observed in the space from the third-person perspective, while the term "head" at first means the observed object from the third-person perspective and then means, without acknowledgement, the first-person somatic differentiation. Since no first-person identity can be confined in a spatial locality, as shown in chapter 1, the claim that my internally identified head is "in" my objectively observed brain is a categorical mistake.

Searle might argue that a pain is different from the internal feeling of the head. It is so because a pain cannot be observed from outside and thus does not have an independent status from the third-person perspective, whereas a head is primarily an object of the third-person perspective and the internal feeling of it is derivative. But such a distinction is superficial and unfounded. A pain certainly has an observable counterpart, which a doctor always makes use of. It is no more than a linguistic fact that we don't call it a pain but a bruise or inflammation. The internal feeling of a pain is so acute that we need a special name for it for practical purposes, while the internal feeling of the head is not so conspicuous as to need a special name.

It might also be argued that the same feeling of pain has different observable symptoms so the pain is not the same as the symptom. But a different appearance of a head also gives you the same feeling of a head. So the relation of the internal feeling of a pain to its external symptom is parallel to the relation of the internal feeling of a head to its external appearance. If we cannot logically claim that one's head is in one's brain, we cannot claim that one's pain is in one's brain either.

Clearly, Searle's confusion on this matter is derived from the overall inconsistency of his methodology. He on the one hand insists correctly on the irreducible distinction between the first-person and the third-person perspective, but on the other hand maintains that the only possible way of understanding the first-person mind is neuroscience that, as an empirical science in the confinement of classical mechanics, is based exclusively on the third-person perspective. Such an overall inconsistency leads him to misinterpret the philosophical implications of some findings in experimental neuroscience.

When Searle claims that all bodily sensations are parts of the body image, what the term "bodily" or "body" refers to cannot, according to him, be understood from the first-person perspective, because he believes that from the first-person perspective there are only bodily "sensations" which are parts of the "image" of the body, not the body itself. So the "body" here must be defined from the third-person perspective in which the possessor of the body and other observers are on a par. Now how does Searle know that the pain-in-the-foot is "literally" in the physical space of the brain, which is part of the body, not merely part of the "body image"?

Certainly he cannot open the brain and see the pain there; he must take a functional approach to testify his claim. That is, the neuroscientist tells him that if we apply a pain-stimulus to a certain spot of the brain, the subject will experience exactly the same sensation of a pain-in-the-foot, which may or may not exist; if we can, conversely, prevent the pain-stimulus from reaching that spot, no matter what happens in the foot, no pain will be experienced. Such a finding in neuroscience should not surprise anybody. How could it be otherwise, given the established fact that the brain is the processing center of all perceptual information? But the conclusion Searle draws from this finding is misleading.

The Whole Universe in My Brain?

Such a functional correspondence tells us only that proper stimulation at that spot of the brain is the necessary and sufficient condition for the feeling of the pain-in-the-foot, but not that the pain occurs "in the physical space of the brain," as Searle claims. If I follow his logic, I would also be able to claim that the image of the computer screen now in front of me is not out there but in my brain, because if the optical signals are stopped anywhere before they reach my brain, I will not be able to see the screen; and if similar signals generated by any other source can reach the right spot of my brain, I will have the image of the screen in my mind. By the same token, this is true for all other modalities of sensation. As a result, we will end up claiming that the perceived properties of the whole world are not literally out there but only in my brain. But my brain is also part of the physical world. How can the whole world be physically in a small part of itself? Should we therefore claim that all properties of my brain are not in the physical space but are literally in a small spot of my brain?

Searle might try to find a way out of such a paradox by applying his distinction between the intrinsic and the non-intrinsic properties of the physical object. For him, what are literally in our brain are those non-intrinsic properties, and pain is one of these; intrinsic properties are indeed in the object. This is what he says:

> The expressions "mass," "gravitational attraction," and "molecule" name features of the world that are intrinsic. If all observers and users cease to exist, the world still contains mass, gravitational attraction, and molecules.[3]

Such a distinction is not very different from Locke's distinction between the primary and secondary qualities, which has been severely challenged by Berkeley. In chapter 3, we have already realized that such a distinction is *derived* from our experience of the coordination among different modalities of sensation. It is true that molecules will continue to exist after all of us have died *insofar as* "existence" is meant to be defined *within* the sensory framework we now happen to possess. But as we recall, in the virtual world, we would have a new type of particle physics comparable to the particle physics as we know it at present in the actual world. That is, in an alternative framework, what we now call "molecules," perceived as particles, could become not particles but only a certain kind of predetermined regularities, because the spatial locality could be radically reconfigured. This is comparable to what happens to mass when gravity is understood geometrically in Einstein's General Theory of Relativity.

Since the spatial locality itself is contingent upon a specific sensory framework, the only given necessity in the world is the lawful necessity of events, not any object understood as the building block of the physical world. This is the major insight we have acquired so far through our various thought experiments.

The Credit Searle Deserves

But on another level Searle is right that as soon as we start to speak of a physical object, we are already speaking *in* a given sensory framework, and have departed from the first-person perspective and initiated the third-person perspective. So any properties of the object that are rooted in the framework can be understood as intrinsic to the object. That is why the Lockean distinction still makes sense here, and why Descartes was so certain that extension is the essence of materiality. But it is also precisely at this point that Searle goes wrong: he mistakenly applies the third-person concept of locality to the first-person concept of pain. While a concept of the brain acquires its meaning only *in* a particular sensory framework and for that reason has intrinsic as well as non-intrinsic qualities, a concept of the pain is always first-personal and thus is unrelated to this intrinsic vs. non-intrinsic distinction which is made from the third-person perspective.

But More Disastrously . . .

More disastrous is that Searle's notion of "a body image in the brain" will lead him to a fallacy similar to what he calls the "homunculus fallacy," which he attributes to his cognitivist opponents.[4] Suppose there is a body image in the brain, then the-pain-in-the-foot must occur in the spot of that image that corresponds to the foot, and the-pain-in-the-hand must occur in the spot that corresponds to the hand, according to this doctrine. If so, the two spots must be spatially separate. But suppose a person has a pain-in-the-foot and a pain-in-the-hand at the same time and he feels both distinctly. In order for him to be able to contrast these two pains, there must be a higher-level information-processing center to receive stimuli from the two spots of the "body image" in the brain. Then this higher-level center would need a smaller body image, and so on and so forth, until the image is reduced to a single point which is no longer an image, or else the regression will go on ad infinitum. But if the final end of the process is that single point, then this point should be understood as the "place" where the-pain-in-the-foot and the-pain-in-the-hand and all other pains occur, not those alleged spots in the so-called intermediate "body images." This "place" cannot, however, possibly be a spatially identifiable "spot" because space as understood in classical mechanics must contain mutually separate points, instead of a single point, since a single point is physically nowhere. In sum, such a theory of a "body image" in the brain will need more and more smaller and smaller body images without an end, or if there is an end then that endpoint will be spaceless and not an image, and thus cannot be located anywhere. Following Searle's theory of the "body image," we will end up with no image or with an infinite regression.

A Pain with an Index

What is then the correct interpretation of the phenomenon of the phantom pain of an amputee? First, we need to understand our locality-reference of a normal pain correctly. Before I lose my foot, I feel a pain in my foot not because I see the pain there. Instead I realize that the pain is "in" my foot in an essentially modified sense: my pain with a *locality-index* accompanying it *corresponds* to my foot, which is externally observed. I don't at all intend to claim that an observable physical injury itself is the pain, or that a signal generated by the injury is the pain. My feeling of the pain is identified from the first-person perspective, from which the acting center of constitutive subjectivity constitutes, by necessity, the third-person perspective; and only with such a constitutive capability are we allowed to talk about the observable physical injury and the passage of the signal from the foot to the brain.

A Real Pain Which Is Nowhere

Since we attribute the third-person perspective to our sensory framework, we might be tempted to think that the spatiality associated with such a perspective is based on the biological and neurophysiological structure of our sense organs. But such a way of thinking is unjustified because biology and neurophysiology, like any other branches of science based on the classical model, already presuppose spatiality. But spatiality is, again, intelligible only *after* the third-person perspective is constituted.

Therefore, a phantom pain is phantom only because the correspondence between the first-person pain-identity and the third-person locality-identity previously established is now interrupted by the loss of the foot. Since a correspondence between two items is relational, there is no way to assign it to either item alone, so the phantom pain cannot be said to be "in" the brain after the foot is gone. Then where is the pain-in-the-foot "literally"? Before losing the foot, it was "in" the foot in an essentially modified sense of the word "in," as we have just clarified; after losing it, the pain is nowhere. The observed stimuli responsible for the pain end up in the brain before and after, but the pain has never been and will never be in the brain.

Since a person's internal sense of locality is completely a matter of the mind's somatic coordination with our sensations, we can now easily understand Lanier's following report:

> At VPL we've often played with becoming different creatures—lobsters, gazelles, winged angels. Taking on a different body in virtual reality is more profound than merely putting on a costume, because you're actually changing your body's dynamics.
>
> What surprised us is that people adapt almost instantly to manipulating radically different body images. They pick up virtual objects just as easily with a long, spindly arachnid arm as with a human one. You'd think your brain is hardwired to know your arm, and that if suddenly it grew three

feet, your brain wouldn't be able to control it, but that doesn't appear to be true.[5]

Therefore, if the size of my body grew ten times proportionately over-night while I was asleep, I would not have to feel internally that my finger tips were ten times farther from the center of my perception. I would feel the internal field of my body, before I opened my eyes and before any objects strained me against my huge body, approximately the same as yesterday.

Daniel Dennett Turned Outside-In

Daniel Dennett does a great job exposing the logical inconsistency of the idea of a "Cartesian Theater" in the brain, of which Searle's notion of body image in the brain seems to be a version. In fact, my analysis of Searle's confusion did the same thing. But overall, this book can be viewed as a counterpart of Dennett's *Consciousness Explained*. Dennett takes scientific materialism for granted from the third-person perspective, and understands causality within the given sensory framework of space. His concept of the brain is uncritically based on the classical notion of locality.

From such a starting point, Dennett successfully exposes the confusion of the notion of Cartesian Theater, but at the same time wrongly discards the ontological status of the mind altogether. Our discussion of VR so far, however, has shown the opposite: everything else is optional except the mind. That is, the first-person perspective has ontological priority over the third-person perspective. Therefore, if the brain is understood in neurophysiological terms that depend on an optional sensory frame-work, the discussion of it has already bypassed the key identifier of the mind. No wonder Dennett cannot find the mind in his neurophysiological approach.

Since a propositional attitude presupposes the division between the first-person and third-person perspectives, Dennett's attempt to explain consciousness solely from the third-person perspective will necessarily trap him in a more devastating performative inconsistency: while he claims that his explanation of consciousness is valid and his opponent's invalid, the explanation itself does not allow for the possibility of any validity claim. This is so because, as I have argued in my previous book,[6] this kind of radical reductionism entails that, apart from the causal be-havior of the speech act, there is no meaning to be understood in speech since meaning is essentially different from causality; but validity is a mat-ter of meaning, not of causality. Since his explanation of consciousness is just one among many cases of speech-behavior, his explanation of consciousness will become neither valid nor invalid according to the very same explanation. Dennett even wants us to follow him:

> And second, get rid of the Language of Thought; the content of the judgments doesn't have to be expressible in "propositional" form—that's a mistake, a case of mis-projecting the categories of language back onto the activities of the brain too enthusiastically.[7]

Thus, according to Dennett, the justification of the judgments made in his whole book can be translated into descriptions of his brain activities as a consequence of evolution. But anyone who believes exactly the opposite of his judgments also has his corresponding brain activities as a consequence of evolution. Why should we believe him? He would say that believing his explanation of consciousness will enable you to do better in the process of natural selection. But that is an empirical claim Dennett has yet to testify without using "the Language of Thought"! Dennett is hopelessly trapped in a self-defeating situation, as any naturalistic reductionist would be.

Blind Spot and "Filling-In"

After analyzing (correctly) why there is "filling-in" that makes us usually unaware of the blind spot, Dennett falls back to the trap of his misleadingly naive scientific materialism:

> The fundamental flaw in the idea of "filling-in" is that it suggests that the brain is providing something when in fact the brain is ignoring something. . . . The discontinuity of consciousness is striking because of the *apparent* continuity of consciousness.[8]

According to our analysis, however, the blind spot exists only from the third-person perspective under an optional spatial configuration. From the first-person perspective, the blind spot is not a "spot" at all. The brain, understood as a spatially confined object, does not see; only the pre-spatial mind uses the eye to see. Can the eye see the blind spot that is in itself? Of course not.

Suppose, counter-factually, the blind spot could appear in our field of vision. The color of the spot (presumably black?) would be different from the surrounding colors. But no matter what color it might be, insofar as we could see it, there would have to be retinal cells responding to it. But the blind spot is exactly the spot wherein there are no retinal cells. Could we possibly see the spot? Certainly not. By definition, our blind spot does not allow us to see anything, including the spot itself. Think about this. The optic nerve sends electrical signals, not the third-person spatiality, to the visual cortex. The electrical signals just carry a message. How can that message itself have a "spot" to be "filled-in" or "ignored"?

Suppose, again, our retinal cells were distributed, from the third-person point of view, around a circle at the back of the eye. Would our field of vision appear as a ring enclosing a black pie? No. If the absence of retinal cells in the middle could make us perceive something black, then, as we have discussed in chapter 1, every part of the body which is not part of the eye would let us see blackness; our field of vision would appear in the middle of boundless blackness. Evidently, such a way of thinking is incorrect.

If my retinal cells were scattered all over my body, I would still see a unified field of vision because my mind does not depend on a specific spatial configuration. The brain, empirically understood, need not "fill-in" or "ignore" anything either because there is no inner "spot" to be filled in or "ignored" to begin with in the electric signals.

But why can a blind spot be detected? Because when there is a relative movement between the observed object and the eye, the blind spot will cause a discrepancy: the object or part of it will appear and disappear abruptly. It appears, then disappears and re-appears later. That is, the discrepancy is perceived as a temporal one, which cannot be reduced to anything else. This is so because temporality is inherent in our consciousness. From the first-person perspective, spatial differentiation can, in principle, be reduced to the combination of temporal differentiation and somatic differentiation of motion. Temporal differentiation and somatic differentiation are the final irreducible elements of consciousness, and thus the preconditions for understanding the empirical world. Dennett's naive scientific materialism cannot hope to let us understand consciousness as such.

The Cart and the Horse

It is also a necessary consequence of Dennett's methodology that he fails terribly when he tries to explain the distinction between time and time-perception. According to him, time-perception is generated through temporal referral by the brain that "represents time" as if we could make sense of "real time" independently of our time-perception. When he interprets Libet's "backwards referral in time" experiment, he uses the concept of objective time in such a way that the measurement of objective time does not depend on our internal perception of temporality. But no matter how we objectify time, the final reference of time must be grounded on our time-perception, modified by the coordination of our spatially conditioned sensations as discussed in chapter 3.

Furthermore, according to Einstein's Special Theory of Relativity, time is defined *after* the concept of simultaneity *and* that of the speed of light, in which the concept of distance is inherent. Consequently, our previous discussion of the reciprocity between different sensory frameworks with different spatial configurations has a direct implication for the under-standing of time and temporality: if spatial distance depends on a specific sensory framework and thus on our spatial perception, the conceptual grasp of time must also depend on our time-perception. As for the fact that we use instruments, such as clocks, to measure time, it is merely a convenient stipulation for the purpose of practical coordination.

Either Zhai or Dennett

As we recall, in chapter 2 we came across a dangerous idea: some peo-ple claim that simulated agents in cyberspace are equivalent to conscious human beings hooked up to cyberspace. They hold such a belief because they think anything that cannot be observed from the third-person per-spective is nothing at all. They think they have something solid to cling to: the material singularity that gives us sense data.

Now that my discussion of VR has demonstrated how the alleged ma-teriality must come to an end while the mind with a predetermined struc-ture stays firm, Dennett's position and mine become totally incompatible. Dennett attempts to make the mind disappear and keep the material ob-jects, but such an attempt itself is already based on the priority of the mind over the material, even though he does not realize it. Starting from the first-person perspective of the mind, we can understand how the third-person perspective comes about. But starting from the third-person perspective, there is no way to understand the first-person perspective and its qualia, so the easiest way to get around it is to dismiss them altogether. But such a dismissal is like sawing off the branch you are sitting on—a total self-destruction.

Our analysis here so far has turned things around entirely. It is now clear that we can never re-create the human mind through artificial intel-ligence (AI), but we can re-create the whole empirical world through vir-tual reality (VR).

Summary: Back to the First Person

If we understand the contents of the mind as identical to the physical process in the brain, then space perception is generated through spatial referral by the brain just as the pain-in-the-foot is so generated. Given this, if we follow Searle's logic, we have to say that space is "literally in" the brain, and thus the whole universe is also "literally in" the brain; since a brain (in contrast to the mind) is by definition an object in this

universe, then the brain is *in* the same brain itself according to such a
logic. Obviously this is a self-contradiction. Such a self-contradiction is
due to a confusion between the first-person perspective (the mind) and
the third-person perspective (the brain) on the matter of spatiality. Dennett's explanation of the mind is even more detrimental simply because
he attempts to eliminate the first-person perspective totally, which has
been shown to be impossible in chapter 1.

4.2   The Fallacy of Unity Projection

No Dualism

Do we therefore have to support some kind of mind-body dualism?
No. Since the division between the first- and the third-person perspective
is contingent upon our sensory framework, if we can start our understanding from a vantage point that is logically prior to our sensory experience, we might be able to explain everything that comes after. If a
theory's concepts of space and time do not depend on a specific sensory
framework but are able to explain our perceived space and time with
logical consistency, such a theory will be on a level higher than the division between the first-person perspective and the third.

Of course, even though such a theory can explain all observed phenomena, the concepts in that theory will not designate any observable
objects. If we apply these theoretical concepts directly to any post-sen-
sory objects, we will be trapped in paradoxes. But is such a type of trans-
sensory theory possible?

Quantum Mechanics

Quantum mechanics is exactly such a theory; theories of relativity
seem to come close, and the recent Super-Strings Theory appears also to
belong in this category. Unfortunately, mainstream brain science has
been very slow to follow the footsteps of modern physics. This has been
so because the precondition of an adequate understanding of the human
mind has not been recognized, and thus the possibility that the new physics has provided that precondition has been largely ignored.

But there are exceptions. There are a few competent investigators who
dare to step over their own disciplinary confinement as conventionally
established. Henry P. Stapp and Roger Penrose are among these excep-
tional investigators who grounded their new adventure on physical/
mathematical science.[9] They argue that classical mechanics and computation theory cannot explain consciousness adequately, but quantum me-

chanics is a possible alternative framework for such an explanation. Even though some of their arguments might not be fully justified, at least their conviction that the new physics is extremely important in understanding the human mind is inspirational.

Don't Be Self-Defeating

Being so inspired, I am here to demonstrate how any theory based on the assumption of spatial locality in a classical framework of physics will be self-defeating when applied to the explanation of consciousness as such. If my position is correct, no approach in cognitive science to the human mind based on the structure of the brain, understood as a spatially identifiable object, will be able to explain consciousness as such despite its possible practical applications. It can at best help us understand some consciousness-related phenomena observed from the third-person perspective, not the consciousness itself as identified from the first-person perspective.

Stapp's distinction between the intrinsic description and an extrinsic one is interesting. Such a distinction is made in the context of a computer model of the evolving brain as assumed by many mainstream cognitive scientists. Such a distinction is interesting because it helps us uncover a fallacy prevalent among the conventional researchers engaged in the empirical studies of mental phenomena. This fallacy I call the "Fallacy of Unity Projection" (FUP hereafter), which is stated as follows:

> Engaged in an empirical study of the alleged mental phenomena of an object (say, a brain or a computer), one assumes that the perceived spatial unity of the data is inherent among the data themselves in the object, but in truth the unity is projected from one's own observing mind. In other words, the observer projects the perceived unity of the data, which is a *consequence* of the synthesis of his or her own constitutive consciousness in the background, erroneously onto the data themselves in assuming that, or in an attempt to explain how, the data *warrant* the unity of the perception, and thus of the consciousness, in the object to be explained in the foreground.

Hofstdater and Tipler Also Guilty

There are two groups of researchers who have committed this fallacy: (1) those who, like John Searle, believe that neurophysiology in the classical framework can completely explain consciousness as such causally, and (2) those more provocative Strong AI believers such as Douglas Hofstdater, Daniel Dennett, and Frank Tipler who regard intelligence and consciousness as no more than symbolic computation, and consider physical causality irrelevant. These two groups are opposed to one another with regard to the basis of the unity of consciousness: physical versus digital, or causal versus symbolic. But they all assume that the physical (brain) or the digital (computer) process classically understood as a locally discrete one does not prevent them from understanding the unity of consciousness as such.

Why is FUP indeed a fallacy? Or, why can't, a priori, the unity of consciousness be derived from a discrete process? I will first clarify how, by logical necessity, an attempt to explain the unity of consciousness in terms of locally discrete physiological process must lead to an infinite regression and only a final non-discrete explanation can stop the regression. Then I will discuss briefly how a symbolic explanation will lead to a total elimination of the distinction between conscious and non-conscious phenomena. After that, I will demonstrate why all alleged explanations in these two frameworks are invalid because they are a result of FUP.

Let me start with a slightly different, but more structured, account of the type of difficulty we witnessed when discussing Searle's notion of a "body image," because such an account is essential to our further understanding of why the type of theory like quantum mechanics is necessary in order to explain consciousness as such.

Brain Discredited

Brain physiology in a classical framework, regardless of its possible variety of the theoretical models, assumes that a brain is one object among many others as we see them in space. Let us see why such an assumption, while correct for other purposes, does not allow us to explain the mind as such. For the sake of simplicity, let us just analyze a case of one-eye two-dimensional visual perception.

How do we see objects in the space? Obviously space and objects do not enter into the eye and travel to the processing center in the brain. An eye only receives light as signals from the object and transmits these signals to the brain. Now suppose we see two objects, M and N, two inches apart in the space. How can we explain the fact that M and N are perceived simultaneously as separate objects in a unified field of vision?

As we know, the brain is not an optical device like an eye and the optic nerve does not transmit light, so there are no images cast upon the visual cortex or anywhere else in the brain.[10] So what the brain receives are transformed signals (electrical, chemical, or whatever). Now the question is: For objects M and N, does the brain register two separate signals from each on two separate spots, or just one single combined signal on one spot?

If the brain receives two separate signals, say m for M and n for N, then it would not be able to perceive the distance between M and N, which is two inches. It wouldn't help to assume that the distance between m and n is proportional to that between M and N, since in the classical framework, if m and n are not in contact, how far apart they are does not change the state of affairs in either m or n. In order for the difference of the distance to affect the perception, we must introduce a higher-order perceptual function that "measures" the distance between m and n. But in doing so, the higher-order function (say, the memory) would need to absorb the signals from m and n onto one single spot for simultaneous processing, according to the classical understanding of causal locality. So there is no way for the brain to have received two separate signals from M and N without a final synthesis of the two in order to perceive M and N in a unified field of vision. We must appeal to a spot that performs a higher-order function of synthesizing m and n. But if this spot remains a classically understood physiological site, we will ask the same type of question legitimately as we did earlier: Does that spot receive signals from m and n separately and thus form its corresponding m' and n', or just one single combined signal from m and n, before the measuring is done? So on and so forth and, eventually, we will have to consider the second alternative, that is, that somewhere in the brain there is one single spot that receives one single combined signal to form a final unified field of vision.

But if we assume that the second alternative actually depicts what happens in the brain, we need to see how that one single spot can do the trick of forming a unified field of vision in our perception. In the classical framework, by "one single spot" we mean an area in which each point is in direct contact with some other points continuously without interruption. Since any physical event must spread over a definite area that can be divided into many smaller areas, we can reduce the event in that area to the sum total of sub-events in those smaller areas, just as what happens at any moment in New York City is the sum total of what happens on every spot of the city at that moment. In Stapp's words, "The fundamental principle in classical mechanics is that any physical system can be decomposed into a collection of simple independent local elements each of which interacts only with its immediate neighbors."[11]

Given such a picture, can we understand the simultaneous one-ness of consciousness? The answer is no. The key is that the interaction among local elements takes time. If we take away the factor of time, interaction will not happen. When interaction becomes irrelevant, then the immediate contact among neighboring elements will be functionally equivalent to the separate-ness among elements far apart, just as two separate words printed on this page do not bother each other whether they are next to one another or two hundred words apart.

Therefore, at any moment, each separate smaller area in the spot will have its own separate state of affairs, independent of any other state of affairs outside that area. As a result, taking these neighboring elements apart and rearranging them arbitrarily would not affect the totality of states of affairs in the spot. We still don't know, and there is no way to know, where the final process of synthesizing takes place. The point is that insofar as a physical system is understood in terms of classical locality, any difficulty with multiple spots will also be a difficulty with the so-called "one single spot," because there is simply no one final single spot that cannot be divided into smaller spots according to the classical understanding of spatiality. One or many here is merely a matter of arbitrary division. Since the interaction between any two points must take time, no interaction is allowed in order to reach the momentary unity of consciousness, or here more specifically, the unified field of vision.

Dennett's Multiple Drafts Model does not work either, because the alleged "editor" (the memory?) of separate "Drafts" cannot lead to the apparent unity of the field of vision. Dennett's response would be that there is no real unity, and the perceived unity is merely apparent. But what we want to understand here is exactly the apparent unity, not any kind of unity from the third-person perspective. Therefore, as long as we stick to the classical concept of physical locality, we will be forced to take a hopeless path of infinite regression in our attempt to understand, vainly, the unity of consciousness.

Why the Mind Is Not a Computer

Let us turn now to the computation theory of consciousness as held by believers of Strong AI. Unlike believers of the physiological explanation of consciousness, Strong AI proponents take the physiological process of the brain as unessential to the phenomenon of consciousness (which is, according to them, on the same level as intelligence, a view which Weak AI believers do not share with them). They instead believe that any causal process that can support a reliable symbolic operation will do as well, because consciousness is a function of symbolic pattern, not of physical interaction. In their answers to the challenges raised by philosophers such as John Searle and Hubert Dreyfus, they usually argue that even though each symbol alone does not have consciousness, the totality of the whole symbolic system does.

Such a holistic symbolic interpretation of the mind is well presented by Dennett and Hofstdater in their anthology, *The Mind's Eye*. A typical argument in the book is analogical. Human intelligence or consciousness to symbols is like a painting to colored dots in Hofstdater's opinion. In a painting, each dot viewed separately is meaningless but many individually meaningless dots put together produce an emergent property on a higher level, and so we have a meaningful piece of artwork. Similarly, it is argued, human intelligence or consciousness is just such an emergent property out of the lower-level symbols.

On this score, Searle has a perfectly valid objection: the so-called emergent properties on a higher level are actually only in the eye of the beholder. They are meanings instead of properties. Where is the beholder? If it's in the brain, then that tiny beholder would be the source of consciousness, not the symbols encountered on the lower level. Then we would need another beholder in the beholder, ad infinitum. That beholder is actually Hofstdater himself: he projects his own interpretation to the object.

Is a Stone Also Conscious?

Searle is also correct when he claims that in the eye of a possible beholder, any possible physical structure can be interpreted as a symbolic system. Thus understood, everything could be interpreted as conscious, that is, there is no distinction between a conscious being and an unconscious being. Such an alleged explanation of consciousness turns out to be no explanation at all.

But why do advocates of either theory believe that they have explained the one-ness of consciousness? Because when they interpret their own theory, they are using their *own* mind extrinsically, so they project the one-ness of their interpretive mind onto the data to be interpreted, and then believe the one-ness is a logical consequence of their theory. That is, they commit the Fallacy of Unity Projection, or FUP.

Stapp does an excellent job of distinguishing between intrinsic description and extrinsic description. But he does not seem to realize that the possibility of intrinsic description depends on the unifying function of the describer's consciousness on the extrinsic level. Actually, such a dependence is the direct reason why it is so easy for a researcher to commit FUP.

Cut the Root

Ontologically, FUP is based on a deep-rooted but erroneous assumption of common sense and Newtonian mechanics: spatial locality is totally separate from sensory perception, and everything, including mental phenomena, takes *place* in a specific locality. Since the unity of consciousness first of all takes the form of spatial unity, such a unity is immediately projected onto the observed object. In a regular case, such a projection does not cause a problem insofar as the mechanism of consciousness is not the subject matter. But as soon as the unity of consciousness becomes thematic itself, such a projection leads immediately to a fundamental misinterpretation. It is so because now the consciousness being discussed and the consciousness undertaking the discussion are fundamentally confused by such a projection; but a clear separation between the object and the subject is assumed to be maintained, according to the researcher guided by such a classical model.

Conversely, due to such an erroneous assumption, some psychologists seem to see mental "projections" in cases where there are no projections. For example, they claim that the-pain-in-the-foot is "projected" to the foot while it is "in fact" in the brain. What they mean by "in fact" is that the spatial localities of the brain and the foot are mind-independent facts, whereas the felt pain from the first-person perspective is mind-dependent. But when you ask them whether the projection is a fact or not, they would have a difficult time responding. They certainly do not mean the brain needs to send a signal back to the feet in order to feel the pain-in-the-foot. Since the brain only takes in electric signals but not the space itself, how can it know a mind-independent space if such a space exists "out there" at all? So the brain understood as an object "in" space does not deal with space as such, and thus cannot and does not need to carry out a "projection" as they conceive of it.

Dennett also holds that these alleged mental projections are misconceived. But he holds such a belief on a totally disastrous premise: there is no genuine unity of consciousness. Such a premise is a result of his totally self-destructive commitment to FUP: only spatially identifiable objects count, and thus mental qualia are "disqualified."

Hello, Mr. Stapp

According to Stapp, the full intrinsic description of the cognitive process of the brain in the classical framework is, if expressed in terms of physical facts instead of their digital representation, simply the conglomeration of its individual facts mutually separated by spatial locality. On the contrary, in an extrinsic description, the observer of the cognitive process can register the entire collection of these individual facts as a whole simultaneously. This distinction on the level of description is valid and significant. But what is equally important is that on the operational level, the possibility of the intrinsic description in the classical framework is impossible without the organizing function of the describer's constitutive mind on the extrinsic level. On the intrinsic level, each individual fact does not, according to the classical model, register any fact other than itself, despite its possible causal connection to each of those facts that are immediately next to it.

In other words, classically understood, at each point the event can affect the event at the next point *later* after a certain duration of time. Without such a duration, at each moment one event at a point is no more and no less than itself and thus does not affect any events at other points. For this reason, a detective can conclude that John did not beat David to death at 3 o'clock yesterday afternoon if it is evident that John was doing something else at that moment. By the same token, due to the temporal duration a causal transition has to take, a momentary mental state cannot, therefore, be derived from a transitory process of causal interaction. Instead, it must correspond to a simultaneous collection of facts apart from their causal interactions according to the classical understanding of causality. Consequently, one's mental state at any moment depends not on the causal connection of facts, but on the simultaneous conjunction of these facts.

Given this, an intrinsic description of the conglomeration of these facts is impossible, because totally separate facts cannot "conglomerate" themselves in a meaningful way. To each single state of affairs on one spot, all other states of affairs, far away or nearby, in the brain or outside the brain, are equally alien and irrelevant. Since at each moment no communication between these facts is possible according to the classical model, the perceived spatial relation of this fact to other facts at each moment must be imposed by the observing mind from the extrinsic level, and thus has no explanatory bearing on how this fact contributes to the target mental state being observed. This is so because in the classical framework, the mental state is understood as the mere collection of physical facts.

Einstein's Brain

By the same token, as Stapp suggests, the functional approach is futile, since any alleged functional entity would be subject to the same analysis if spatial locality of the classical model is still at work on this functional level. That is, if we claim that there is a function of the brain that unifies the discrete facts to reach the one-ness of consciousness, then we have this question of which part of the brain carries out the function. Then any alleged functional part of the brain will in turn need further explanation, and so on and so forth.

All those who believe either the neurophysiological or the computational model of the human mind assume that the apparent unity (or oneness) of consciousness can be explained by the interconnections among the components in their model. When they are engaged in the technical part of their research, they make intrinsic descriptions. But when they try to interpret their research in terms of its pertinence to the understanding of consciousness, they jump to the extrinsic level and project the unifying function of their own consciousness onto what they are describing and claim that the described is the same as consciousness itself. Such a projection is conspicuous when Hofstdater explains how Einstein's brain can be symbolized in a book and that book will be holistically equivalent to Einstein's conscious mind.

Clearly, if we allow such a projection, the necessity of understanding temporality in understanding consciousness will be concealed, and consciousness as such will forever escape our adequate explanation. In that case, we would mistakenly believe those manipulators of symbols and signals when they claim that they are master minds of all newly created minds that are equivalent to the human minds.

Intelligence versus Consciousness

Apart from FUP, there is a more straightforward way of seeing some Strong AI advocates' confusion: they seem to equate consciousness with intelligence. They often talk in such a way that they have such an explicit conviction or implicit assumption: to re-create intelligence through computers is to re-create a conscious agent. Others think that a certain degree of complexity of the computational process will lead to the "emergence" of consciousness; that is, they strive to produce artificial consciousness by producing highly complex AI.

But apparently, if we believe that there is consciousness at all, by "consciousness" we cannot possibly just refer to intelligence alone. According to our common understanding of the word, a more intelligent person is by no means a more conscious person, and an unintelligent person by no means unconscious. To compare humans with computers as they are now, even Strong AI believers are not ready to claim that, for instance, the chess-playing computer Big Blue is more conscious than any of its human opponents, despite its triumph over the human champion. But such a triumph could be understood in a certain sense as an indication of Big Blue's superior intelligence over most of human beings with regard to chess playing. On the other hand, a normal three-year-old child is in a sense less intelligent than a scientific calculator with regard to computing, but nobody would claim that in any sense the child is less conscious than the calculator. It's therefore again very clear that by intelligence we do not refer to the same thing as consciousness.

As for the idea of emergence of consciousness out of complexity, it could be understood either at the symbolic level or at the hardware (or wetware?) level. At the symbolic level, we have already realized that complexity is in the eye of the beholder because anything can be interpreted as a mixture of many infinitely complex symbolic systems. But nobody would claim that a non-conscious state is the mixture of infinitely many conscious states. Besides, a calculator can solve very complex math problems while a normal small child cannot. But if by "consciousness" we refer to anything at all, we would rather bet that the child has consciousness and the calculator does not have it. So symbolically, complexity does not have a direct contribution to the formation of consciousness; that is, a book of the complete information of Einstein's very complex brain is not a conscious book, even though we could agree with Hofstdater that the book could turn out to be, in a sense, as intelligent as Einstein.

At the hardware level, it is also obvious that complexity does not correspond to consciousness. The complexity of the brain is the reference base for an understanding of any alleged connection between complexity and consciousness. But if one brain is complex enough to let a conscious mind emerge, many brains put together in an arbitrary manner would certainly be complex enough to maintain the same level of consciousness. But we know that the increased complexity of two arbitrarily combined brains will more likely destroy consciousness rather than maintain or increase it, if consciousness could be explained in terms of the brain process. Therefore, the complexity of the hardware has no correspondence to the state of consciousness.

Summary: The World Re-Created without Strong AI

Dennett and other Strong AI proponents attempt to convince us that a computer can become conscious because consciousness is not anything extra-symbolic to begin with. For them, a computer can replace the human mind. But our analysis of VR leads us in the opposite direction. What we can create through computer technology is not the mind, but what they call the material world. Yes, we can re-create the whole universe as empirically perceived: Gods 'R Us, after all. But we cannot make computers conscious by hard-wiring or symbolic programming. In other words, we could become co-creators of an electronically mediated new empirical world, but could not create more conscious creators by means of electronic manipulation. Strong AI is impossible: from the silicon chip and lines of code no mind can be produced. But from the mind's standpoint empirical contents in any specific sensory framework are optional.

4.3   The One-ness of Consciousness, Brain, and Quantum Mechanics

Emperor Penrose's Mind

Quantum mechanics is a possible alternative for explaining consciousness precisely because, as Penrose and Stapp point out, it no longer assumes the classical concept of spatio-temporal order. The one-ness or holism is intrinsically in the mathematical structure of the theory itself, and thus does not depend on a specific sensory framework of the observer. According to quantum mechanics, there is no independent, isolated point of space-time at which an event goes on by itself.

Given such a quantum mechanical starting point, we can hope to gain an immediate understanding of consciousness as rooted directly in the original one-ness of the universe, whereas the observed physical world *in* space filled with separate objects is only a sensory version of that ultimate one-ness. Here the logic of explanation is entirely reversed. The mind is not a "property" or "function" of the observed objects. Rather, the ultimate one-ness of the universe shows itself first through human self-consciousness, then objectifies itself through spatialization and individualization under the order of causality. In such a pre-spatial model of understanding, we can comprehend how on the highest level our personal identity remains unified across all possible sensory frameworks as shown in chapter 1, and on the psychological level we can have multiple versions of the self as excellently analyzed by Sherry Turkle in her *The Second Self*[12] and *Life on the Screen*.[13]

It is well known that wave functions in quantum mechanics expressed by Schroedinger's Equation require the observing act as an inseparable factor in formulating the observed event. Here no unity projection is possible because a projection requires a previous separation. Here the absence of an original separation is an indication that wave functions operate on the level where the division between the first-person perspective and the third-person perspective has not originated. This is why any descriptions of quantum-related phenomena based on the classical concept of spatial locality and (sense-dependent) common sense will necessarily lead to paradoxes such as EPR and Schroedinger's cat, among others.

Dare to Dream

If quantum mechanics indeed operates on the pre-sensory level, then it will remain valid no matter what sensory framework we happen to adopt. Thus in either the actual or virtual world, it will be effective regardless of any particular spatial configuration. Such a cross-sensory nature exactly matches our account of the mind and personal identity. It is no wonder that when we retreat from the third-person perspective to the inner world of the first-person consciousness while we are dreaming, meditating, or being hypnotized, we may experience some extraordinary events. These events defy a classical or commonsensical explanation, but coincide with possibilities allowed by quantum mechanics.

Mystic experiences of other kinds, if they do happen to a few, may not be readily available to everyone, but presumably everyone dreams. It is unfortunate that dreams have been studied only in the psychological sciences but not in physics simply because they are regarded, wrongly, as mere subjective phenomena, which have little bearing on the basic structure of the physical universe. Let me illustrate how dream phenomena are relevant to our understanding of the physical world by two examples. These dream phenomena actually challenge our classical and commonsense view of the basic causal structure of the world on the fundamental level.

I have heard reports of—and I myself have had on more than one occasion—the type of experience similar to the following case. Some morning, you may have been woken up by an alarm clock you had set. At the moment you became awake, you remembered that you had a dream right before you were woken up, and the story in the dream ended with the ringing of an alarm clock, the sound of which was exactly like the sound of the alarm that woke you up. Evidently, the sound of the alarm in your dream was actually caused by the same *real* clock. But the oddity is that in your dream there was a long story line logically leading to the ringing of the alarm clock *prior* to the ringing alarm in the dream.

On one occasion, I had such a dream. My dream had it that I returned from an art museum and discovered that my clock on the desk had stopped; then I picked it up and shook it violently and the alarm began to ring; and then I woke up. Assuming that the ringing in the dream and the ringing in the real world are simultaneous (because they are from the same real clock), how could there be a story line logically connected to the ringing of the alarm?

Back to the Future?

There are three possibilities if we still use a third-person classical conceptual framework in which events in a dream are regarded as unreal:

(1) In the dream I had an implicit precognition of the *real* future event of the alarm clock ringing. In such a case, I could use that precog-

nition to construct a story to be logically connected to that future event.

(2) In the *real* world causal connection can run backward viewed from a different frame of reference and my dream enables me to be in that frame of reference. If so, the ringing of the alarm clock as a future event caused the dreaming me backward to start a story (going to the art museum, etc.) that would merge with the causal order in the real world.

(3) I did not have a dream prior to the ringing alarm clock; instead, immediately after the alarm clock began to ring, a false memory was created in my *real* brain so I seemed to have had a dream that did not happen.

Possibilities 1 and 2 contradict the basic assumptions of classical mechanics. As for possibility 3, it challenges our concept of the objective world even more. If a false memory could be created at random but still be well connected to the *real* world, how can we believe that the so-called world as a memorized collection of stories is real at all? As Bertrand Russell suggested, I could as well believe that the whole world was created three minutes ago with our built-in memory, or even that the world does not exist and only memory does. Such a claim is obviously incompatible with any scientific realism based on the third-person perspective.

In quantum mechanics, however, the division between the objective and the subjective is not assumed, and neither is the ordinary conception of space and time. So all three possibilities are held within its theoretical scope.

The Split Self

The following example of an ordinary dream may also have very interesting implications for our understanding of the nature of consciousness. It suggests that our one-ness of consciousness might be a direct manifestation of the ultimate one-ness of the universe. Most of us, I take liberty to assume, have dreamed that we have had a conversation with another person. During the conversation, the other person utters well-composed intelligent sentences without our knowledge of the process of the composition. The other person can often say something to our total surprise. He or she may defeat us in an argument in an unexpected manner. But how could such an unexpected surprise be possible? Since there is only one dreaming person, which is me, all meaningful sentences must have been composed by me alone. There is only one mind involved, even though there are two characters in the dream. If so, how can the I in the dream *not* know what the other is going to say? How can my mind create a fake other mind in the dream that the I in the dream does not have an access to?

By comparison, the reader of a novel can be surprised by a conversation in the story because he is not the author and thus did not create the characters in the story. If the reader happens to be the author, then he can still be surprised if he has *forgotten* his own thought. But in the dream situation, there is no such separation between the author and the reader or between the author in the past and the author at present. The seemingly "fake" other mind is working simultaneously with the "I" in the dream, but operates independently. In order to explain such an apparent split of one mind into many, quantum mechanics might lead us to comprehend individual minds as manifestations of the ultimate one-ness of an unconscious mind, which is the ultimate origin of everything: the original "Tao" that is neither material nor spiritual and defies any categorization.

Why Care about Your Future Pain?

There is another fundamental mystery of the one-ness of consciousness that preconditions our everyday life. I know, as everybody seems to know, that anticipating my own pain (or any type of discomfort) at 8:00 A.M. tomorrow is categorically different from predicting a pain of another person at 8:00 A.M. tomorrow. My pain will hurt me and there is no way another person's pain can hurt me. But on what ground do I realize that the one pain will be mine so I should have a special concern about it while the other pain will be yours and only you should have that special concern about it?

An easy answer is that my pain will occur in my body and your pain in your body, and I can only feel the pain of my own body. But this begs the question of why I should have a special concern about this body (which I call mine) instead of any other body. That is, why the one sufferer tomorrow morning is the same me while the other sufferer at that time is not. The obvious answer is that the future suffering body that has a continuous causal connection with my present body is mine and the one that has not is not mine.

But now the question is, since the future pain in either body will not be able to affect the present me causally, why should the present me care more about the one than the other? If I can stop one body's pain at 8:00 a.m. tomorrow, why would I choose to stop the one in this body (which I call mine) instead of the one in the other body (which I call yours)? According to the classical model of causality, later events can in no way affect earlier events, so there is no causal ground for us to be concerned about any future events from the present point of view: No matter what will happen next, the present me is exactly the same. We would like to change certain past events so as to change our present situation, but it is impossible. We should not care about a future event, but that is the only thing we can hope to affect. So according to the causal understanding of the world, the human concern and anticipation of one's own future experience is pointless. But we know directly that it is *not* pointless. My future pain and your future pain do *not* relate to my present self in the same way. Such a concern on my part is not a mere psychological disorder like acrophobia. In a sense, my present self is affected, on deeper than the psychological level, by my future pain, but not by your pain. The "I" that anticipates and suffers must be a unified "I" on a level of one-ness not defined in the classical model of causality.

Here again, quantum mechanics seems to be an alternative theoretical framework for an adequate understanding of a person's anticipation of, and special concern about, his or her own future experience. This is so because quantum mechanics need not assume the validity of the separation between two points of time. A pain belongs to the individualized consciousness so it only affects one single person. But the one-ness of the present self and the future self is identified pre-consciously as super-temporal. That is, the separation between the present and the future might be interpreted as a result of the operation of the individualized conscious mind, which is a manifestation of the one-ness of the universal mind-matter on the quantum level.

Now that we have discussed the possibility of quantum mechanics as an alternative for explaining consciousness, what about other theories of modern physics? We have not discussed the possible role the theories of relativity might be able to play in a unified understanding of the mind and the material world yet. To conclude this chapter, I propose a conjecture that draws quantum mechanics and the Special Theory of Relativity together in a unique way that might lead to a true unified science-philosophy that describes mind and matter in a single equation.

4.4   A Conjecture: The Square Root of −1 as the Psy-Factor

Theoretical Physicists Are Invited

In Schroedinger's Equation, the square root of −1 involved in determining the probability amplitude seems to draw in the intervention of consciousness of the observer that leads to the "collapse" or "split" of the superposition. The square root of −1 here makes the classical notion of spatial locality and the related notion of causality paradoxical.

In Einstein's Special Theory of Relativity, Minkowski's four-dimensional space makes time one of the structurally equivalent coordinates of the continuum by introducing the square root of −1 to time. So time seems to be a dimension of space "occupied" by consciousness. Here, the square root of −1 seems to draw in consciousness that turns a spatial dimension into time. Moreover, in Minkowski's space, light does not ever travel across a distance, so our notion of locality is also invalidated just as in quantum theory.

So, in both cases, the square root of −1 turns what "is there by itself" into what appears to consciousness. My conjecture is that the square root of −1 is the consciousness factor or psy-factor in both theories.

Exploring such a possibility might lead to the unity between quantum mechanics, theories of relativity, the Theory of the Mind, and more. My suggestion is that we re-normalize the theories of relativity and quantum mechanics in such a way that the square root of −1 in both can be used as the joint that connects the two together, with the consciousness factor inherently built in.

When we start with something like the square root of −1 that breaks down the structure of locality in the classical model, then the dichotomy between the observer and the observed may also break down accordingly. The result might be that light does not travel across any distance, and the outer limit (the largest, cosmological) of observation and the Planck limit (the smallest) might turn out to be equivalent. The space is totally curled up. It is the consciousness that "unfolds" and objectifies the space with four dimensions, one of which is still anchored in consciousness and is thus perceived as time. So a theory of physics that does not include the consciousness in it will result in a square root of −1, which is quasi-spatial but seems to dig a hole in the vacuum of the space.

This may require new mathematical tools developed out of the current theory of complex numbers, plus a kind of logic that deals with the self-propelling paradoxes with a manageable closure. Or maybe our experience with VR in cyberspace will inspire us to develop such mathematical tools. We don't know unless we try it.

Verifying Claims Made by Mystics

Claims about alleged mystic experiences are usually rejected by the scientific community on the basis of their unverifiability. One of the reasons they are not verifiable is that the alleged experiences are supposed to go beyond the constraint of spatiality. Scientific verification requires repeatability at different times and in different places by different people, which means that the repeatable events are totally independent of time, space, and observer. But alleged events observed or experienced by a mystic are mystical precisely because they involve the alteration of the relationship among time, space, the observer, and the described event. That is why mysticism seems to be incompatible with traditional hardcore science.

Modern physics, however, has gone way beyond the traditional conception of time, space, and observation as we have discussed. Traditional concepts based on a given spatial-temporal framework, when applied to interpret equations in new physics, lead to unresolvable paradoxes. Against such a background, physicists such as Fritjof Capra and David Bohm have tried to find a possible connection between ancient mysticism and modern physics. But such an attempt has been too speculative to be absorbed into the mainstream physical science. Its lack of empirically observable implications and predictive power is still the major drawback.

But new physics such as quantum mechanics, the theories of relativity, and superstring theory also have many unobservable implications about the structure of the world at the level deeper than space and time or in broader scope than spatio-temporal dimensionality. These theories are hyperspace theories. Can we find a way to bring a mystic and a hyperspace physicist together so that they can verify one another's statements about the unobservable?

Since the described is unobservable, there is no way we can use the empiricist criterion for its verification. However, now that empirical description of the world based on our given sensory framework has been shown to be optional in our analysis of VR, I suggest a non-empirical way of verification, which I call "convergent verification." What follows is a possible procedure.

1. Let the hyperspace physicist derive from his theory some qualitative and quantitative statements about what, in hyperspace, is possible on the one hand, and what is impossible on the other; the validity of these statements should have no apparent relation to our commonsense understanding of the world.
2. Mix these statements of possibility and impossibility at random in a questionnaire, without indicating which is possible and which impossible.
3. Let the mystic determine which is possible and which is impossible according to his alleged mystic insight.
4. A third person, the judge, checks to see if the number of the agreed items is significantly greater than pure chance allows. If yes, repeat (1) to (3) in a different environment.

After going through such a process, if the overall result confirms a better-than-chance match between the physicist's theoretical derivations and the mystic's choices with regard to what is possible and what is impossible, the physicist's theory and the mystic's insight are both convergently verified to a certain degree. But there is no way to conduct convergent falsification. Contrary to an empirical procedure, a total mismatch here does not falsify anything of either side.

5

The Meaning of Life and Virtual Reality

In a world of
  the colorful
    She settles behind the veil
      Confronting the dazzling sunlight
     She annihilates whatever
      is fundamentally real

Celebrating the sublime of
  the home-coming
    She shrinks to the nil
      Merging herself deep
     into the dark
      She embraces them all

"Shadow," Z. Zhai, 1993

5.1 Recapitulation and Anticipation

Reciprocity

In chapter 1, we did two things at the same time. On the one hand, we established the Principle of Reciprocity of Alternative Sensory Frameworks, or PR for short. From a vantage point that goes beyond either actual or virtual reality, we demonstrated, through thought experiments or free fancy variations, that the sensory framework of a virtual world has a parallel, instead of a derivative, relationship with that of the actual world. Our biological sense organs are no less signal-transmitters and signal-transformers than the goggles and bodysuit we would wear for the immersive experience of VR. On the other hand, we also demonstrated that no matter how the sensory framework changes from one to another, the self-identity of the person who witnesses such a change remains intact. Therefore the change of a person's sensory framework shatters only

119

the coherence of an outside observer's sense of that person's identity, not the person's self-identity. Logically, only if we have an unchanging point of reference can we understand the change of sensory framework; this unchanging point of reference is anchored in the given structure of the person's unified perceptual experience.

Virtually Do It All

In chapter 2, following PR established in chapter 1, we reinforced our understanding of reciprocity by demonstrating how all the functionality of the actual world can also be implemented in the virtual world. In such a context, we left behind the idea of the person's unchanging self-identity temporarily. In so doing, we found the concept of causal connection essential to understanding the foundational part of VR experience that enables us to tele-operate the natural process in the actual world. This kind of inside-out control is necessary for our subsistence.

We used the word "physical" to designate causal processes, which are prior to any sensory framework. Since a spatial relation depends on a particular sensory framework, our concept of causality here is independent of notions of distance, continuity, locality, and so on. Our talk about the inside-out control was, therefore, only a metaphor, since there is no "in" or "out" if these words are understood spatially. But if by "out" we mean the physical regularity "outside" the entire space, then our metaphor would seem to be more adequate.

In order to show that the virtual is *totally* equivalent to the actual in its functionality for human life, we demonstrated how cybersex for the sake of human reproduction is possible. Since we were still taking a standpoint from the actual world, we examined how interaction between two sexual partners in the virtual world can bring about the sexual-reproductive process in the actual world as we understand it before we enter the virtual world.

If VR were merely able to serve our basic economy of production and reproduction, that is, if it only had the foundational part, then it would not have such significant implications for the entire civilization as we purported. It is therefore the unlimited possibilities of the expansive part that will be able to make us creators of our own brand-new civilization. If by "ontological" we refer to what we call "real," then it is our ability to create our own meaningful experience in the expansive part *in addition to* our ability to alter our sensory connection to the natural process in the foundational part that entitles us to claim an ontological authorship.

Really Illusory

Then, in chapter 3, we first ventured into a progressive formulation of tentative rules we would implicitly use to distinguish the real from the illusory as assumed, but all those rules ended up being finally deconstructed. That further demonstrated how the virtual and the actual can also be reversed in regard to which is real and which illusory, as another exemplification of PR.

We also showed that even the concepts of physicality and causality, which were reserved in chapter 2 as belonging to the realm of a higher-level causal connection, could be applied to the virtual world for its own regularity as much as they could be applied to the actual world. That is, if we can understand physicality and causality in the ordinary sense as part of the actual world, we can equally take it as part of the virtual world. Vertically, if we are tempted to interpret the virtual as derived from the actual, then the actual has to be in turn derived from a world of still higher-order, and so on and so forth, ad infinitum. In so doing, we would again end up with some kind of transcendental determination as free from any sensory framework, even from space and time.

Then we analyzed how our ultimate concerns would be the same in both the actual and virtual worlds; we would ask the same types of philosophical questions without changing their basic meaning, and thus all philosophical propositions contained in works from Plato's *Republic* all the way down to this book would, if they are purely philosophical, have the same validity or invalidity in either world.

Ontology of the Mind

In chapter 4 we demonstrated that no matter how we shift from one sensory framework to another, the unity of the mind always maintains itself on the deepest level, despite the possibility of multiple versions of the empirical self. We demonstrated how John Searle and Daniel Dennett and many others who advocate either a classical neurophysiological or computational model of the mind have committed a Fallacy of Unity Projection.

Strong AI believers hold that consciousness is no more than intelligence, and intelligence can be realized in a digital computer. But our analysis of VR had shown the opposite: we cannot re-create consciousness, but we can re-create the whole empirical world. Consciousness is in fact not the same as intelligence. The mind as such cannot be explained in terms of brain science that presupposes a given sensory framework.

However, if we adopt a theory like quantum mechanics, which does not depend on a specific sensory framework, then we can avoid the Fallacy of Unity Projection and hopefully begin to establish a unified theory of mind-matter. Possibly, I suggested, the square root of –1 is the psy-factor in both quantum theory and the Special Theory of Relativity, and a re-interpretation of it might lead to a true breakthrough at the root of scientific enquiry.

Now we are at the beginning of chapter 5. What are we going to do next? So far we have only discussed what VR is and what it could be, utilizing concepts such as the virtual and the actual, the physical and the causal, the real and the illusory, the sensory and the perceptual, the experiential and the phenomenological. We have hardly touched upon normative issues that we must answer before we decide how far we should go along this fascinating but ominous-looking path of ontological transgression. What does it mean for us to enter cyberspace and plunge into VR? *Ought* we welcome VR? If so, then to what extent?

5.2   Meaning as Different from Happiness: Brave New World?

Orgy-Porgy

If you have read Aldous Huxley's *Brave New World*, you might won-der whether VR is just a digital fulfillment of that Dystopia. When we talked about human reproduction through robotic mediation, we may well be reminded of the way people are "decanted" from bottles in that "brave new world." Therefore, we may ask, if what Huxley presented has been justifiably viewed as the worst nightmare, why should we not view VR in the same way?

What Huxley envisaged is best summarized by his own retrospective words: "The completely organized society, the scientific caste system, the abolition of free will by methodical conditioning, the servitude made ac-ceptable by regular doses of chemically induced happiness, the orthodox-ies drummed in by nightly courses of sleep-teaching."[1] Such a picture appears horrible for a couple of reasons, but the major one is that in such a centralized hierarchical society, human beings are turned into zombie-like creatures who are artificially flooded with feelings but deprived of the ability to think creatively as free agents. In other words, everyone is turned into a happy slave in such a society:

> "Going to the Feelies this evening, Henry?" enquired the Assistant Predestinator. "I hear the new one at the Alhambra is first-rate. There's a love scene on a bearskin rug; they say it's marvelous. Every hair of the bear reproduced. The most amazing tactual effects."[2]

So they seem to be *predestined* to go to a first-rate entertainment center called "Feelies," where they are almost immersed in a fully geared-up environment of "orgy-porgy" sensory stimulations. Satisfied with their sensational life, they complain: "Old men in the bad old days used to renounce, retire, take to religion, spend their time reading, thinking— *thinking!*"[3] Since they are not critical thinkers, they can never extend their vision beyond their immediate circumstance, and thus all people "decanted" into any of the castes (Alpha, Beta, Gamma, etc.) are happy and grateful that they are a member of that particular caste and not of another. Therefore there is no discontent about the inequality of social status.

Does this sound like virtual reality? "Feelies"? "Orgy-porgy"? And you also read this: "Take a holiday from reality whenever you like, and come back without so much as a headache or a mythology."[4] If you view this only as a matter of *how much* impact technology makes on human life, you will see VR as we have discussed here go far beyond Huxley's imagination. But the real issue is not "how much" but is rather what kind of, and in what way, technology is used. Huxley's concern is whether we can remain the master of our powerful technological creation on the *individual* level, in contrast to a totally organized society where "neo-Pavlovian conditioning" is a substitute for moral education and chemical interference a substitute for moral virtues: "Anybody can be virtuous now. You can carry at least half your morality about in a bottle. Christianity without tears—that's what *soma* is."[5]

The Right to Be Unhappy

For Huxley, the biggest danger is the combination of a totalitarian government and a kind of technology that unambiguously enhances the government's centralization in the name of social stability. At his time, "applied science" was almost synonymous with "machinery and medicine," which were more enslaving than liberating if controlled by a power-hungry state authority. So he called for decentralization of power in order to produce "a race of free individuals" who are not paralyzed by sensory pleasure (or "happiness") and do not give up pursuing *meaning* in their creative participation.

Adopting the traditional assumption that God is the source of meaning, Huxley poured these words upon us through the Controller's mouth:

> "Call it the fault of civilization. God isn't compatible with machinery and scientific medicine and universal happiness. You must make your choice. Our civilization has chosen machinery and medicine and happiness. That's why I have to keep these books locked up in the safe."[6]

Ironically, when the Savage leads those Deltas in the hospital to rebel against the order of the "universal happiness," the pre-programmed Synthetic Anti-Riot Speech Number Two ejaculates the following rhetorical question: "What is the *meaning* of this? Why aren't you all being happy and good together?"[7] Here, "meaning" is presumably understood as subordinate to happiness and social order. But Huxley did not accept such an ideology, so he let his hero, the Savage, have the following conversation with the Controller:

> "But I don't want comfort. I want God, I want poetry, I want real danger, I want freedom, I want goodness. I want sin."
>
> "In fact," said Mustapha Mond, "you're claiming the right to be unhappy."
>
> "All right then," said the Savage definitely, "I'm claiming the right to be unhappy."[8]

So it seems that "the right to be unhappy" is a necessary part of a meaningful human life, insofar as art, poetry, wisdom, freedom, and many other meaning-rich goodies are not always part of happiness.

Now it's time for us to go back to VR again: Would VR do the same thing as the traditional machinery and chemicals would do to human race in the way Huxley predicted? Can VR be used as a tool for a centralized control that will retard human creativity by means of standardized "happiness"?

Optimism from the Frontier

Despite their disagreement on other aspects of the prospective electronic revolution, many commentators concur that VR and cyberspace would do exactly the opposite: it will promote human creativity and decentralize social power unlike anything we have ever had.

For some commentators on the Internet, which is understood as a primitive form of cyberspace, cyberspace's social consequences will work out in the direction set by our use of the telephone, which is opposite to that by our use of television. Television casts its centrally controlled messages to a passive and isolated audience. On the contrary, the Internet depends upon its users to supply and share content; they act cooperatively to disperse self-brewed multimedia messages. Since resource-sharing and mutual exchange are well-recognized traits of successful social participation, some advocates argue, cyberspace may help resume a wanted social dynamism that has been badly damaged by television.

They also celebrate the Internet as the harbinger of a more substantial form of free speech. Since the network allows everyone to become a publisher, it seems to offer a potent instrument for setting public discourse free from the control of private newspaper companies and broadcasters. According to these commentators, the digital technology of cyberspace clearly has a positive influence on human life, in contrast to Huxley's prediction about what the traditional types of technology would have.

Again, the VR guru Jaron Lanier has the following to say:

> When a person chooses to spend that much time watching television, it's equivalent to death as far as society is concerned. They cease to function as responsible or social persons during the time that they're simply perceiving media. Now Virtual Reality is just the opposite. First of all, it's a network like the telephone where there's no central point of origin of information. But, much more importantly, since nothing is made of physical matter, since it's all just made of computer information, no one has any advantage over anyone else in their ability to create any particular thing within it. So there's no need for a studio. There might be occasional needs for one, if somebody has a bigger computer to generate a certain kind of effect, or certainly if somebody's assembled people of a certain talent or reputation. But in general there's no built-in difference from one person to another in terms of ability to create.[9]

The Lawnmower Man

But there has not been a shortage of opposite opinions. The 1992 movie *The Lawnmower Man* and its sequel, *Lawnmower Man II: Beyond Cyberspace* (1996), take VR as a new kind of Frankenstein's creation that threatens to enslave its master. In the movie, the dumb lawnmower man Jobe functions as the meeting place of mind-altering drugs and sense-altering VR. As a consequence of such a sense-mind alteration, Jobe becomes almost all-knowing, all-powerful, and immortal. But as he attempts to extend these God-like features to all by bringing them into VR, they see it as an ultimate attack on them, and they have Dr. Angelo lead them to stop it.

This defensive attitude is, in the movies, based on the understanding that to dwell in VR is to become a mindless video-addicted zombie. But the irony is that VR is understood at the same time by the same group of people as a sphere in which humans can become both immaterial all-knowing mind-spirits (like Jobe) on the one hand, and immobilized mindless zombies on the other. How could such diametrically opposed views be descriptive of the one and the same VR or cyberspace?

Zombie or Pure Spirit?

On the surface, we can see the source of the opposition. For those who have not entered into VR, VR is just a video game that totally consumes the "player" who is turned into a "zombie." For those who are already in VR, VR is an immaterial world of pure perception and meaning in and by itself, and the hardware in the actual world is just a conglomerate of meaningless material objects.

But philosophically, we are not satisfied with such opposing points of view. We must find a neutral standpoint and base our understanding on something valid independently of either partisan perspective. As we have already seen in the last chapter, phenomenological descriptions are not made from either perspective and thus enable us to see the unity between the virtual and the actual. In addition, Huxley's implicit distinction between meaning and happiness has already pointed to the direction for our deeper understanding.

We should be careful not to follow those optimistic advocates blindly because they have only touched the surface of the issue insofar as their understanding remains at the social-cultural level. It has yet to be clarified: How can this kind of optimism about VR be extended to the ontological level when we take VR as the whole or part of life itself? How can Huxley's thesis about the opposition between happiness and the meaningfulness of human life be addressed in the context of VR as the Ultimate Re-Creation? In order to shed light on these fundamental issues, we return now to the question of whether God is the possible source of meaning of life as a step-stone for a thorough investigation.

5.3   Meaning and the Creator

Is God's Life Meaningless?

When Nietzsche claimed that "God is dead," he meant, among other things, that divinity was no longer viewed in Continental Europe as the ground for moral values. But if God is not the final source of values, on what are values grounded? The general public could not but think that values are groundless in every sense because they had not learned to make sense of moral values without God as a legislator behind the scenes of everyday life. For them, if religion did not provide the meaning of life, then life was meaningless. Thus these people became nihilists. This type of nihilism has been very well phrased by the Russian novelist Dostoevsky: "If God is dead, everything is permitted."

Nietzsche himself, however, did not think that God's "death" would necessarily lead to an irreversible destruction of values and meaning in general. He would rather let his "Über-mensch" take over the value-creating position so that human beings can reach the pinnacle by an assertion of their own creative power, intellectually as well as physically.

So he tried to construct a brand-new "table of values" that would function as a guideline for the adventurers who generate meaning by asserting his "will to power."

Regardless of our opinion about Nietzsche's attitude toward God, we can reflect on the relationship between the concept of God and the condition of the meaningfulness of life along the same line. To be sure, if anybody believes that the existence of God makes human life meaningful, then he or she must also believe that God's life is more meaningful than, or at least as meaningful as, human life. Such a belief is, however, also often accompanied by another belief, which says that the meaningfulness of our life is based on the alleged fact that we are creatures of God, the Creator, whose divine plan defines the purpose of our mundane life; only if, it is said, our life serves that purpose will it be meaningful, otherwise it will be meaningless. But the belief that the Creator's life is more meaningful than ours and the belief that a meaningful life depends on being a creature of the Creator are incompatible.

By logical necessity, if being created is a necessary condition for leading a meaningful life, then the Creator, who is un-created, would lead a meaningless life. Alternatively, if serving an externally given purpose is a condition of meaningfulness, then God as the sole purpose-giver would lead a meaningless life. But apparently, all believers in God will agree that God's life is more meaningful than, or at least as meaningful as, human life. Consequently, they cannot possibly base the meaningfulness of life on the status of being a creature that serves a God-given purpose.

If we were merely God's creatures, to serve God's purpose alone, then we would be on a par with all other things in the world such as rocks and dirt, because they are also part of God's plan. But if we believe that rocks and dirt do not live a meaningful life, even though they are part of God's creation, why should we assign any meaning to our own life for the sole reason that we are God's creatures?

Gods 'R Us, Again

On the contrary, a believer in God can make perfect sense if he or she understands meaningfulness of life in terms of creativity itself. Such an understanding will allow us to find meaning in both God's life and human life. God is the greatest creator, so He leads the most meaningful life. We are minor creators, so our life is not as meaningful as God's, but still meaningful to a lesser degree. It might be true that we live our life to serve God's purpose on the highest level, but on a lower level we produce and project our own purposes as well.

Therefore, if God exists as a super-creator and purpose-giver, how meaningful our life is will depend on how much we resemble God in that respect. If God does *not* exist, then God's nonexistence will still not undermine the meaningfulness of our lives, insofar as we are more or less creators and purpose-givers regardless. So whether God exists or not, our life remains meaningful if creativity and purpose are the source of the meaning.

To Believe or Not to Believe

In sum, since a believer in God must believe that God's life is more meaningful than human life, the meaning of life cannot be based on the believer's alleged status as a being of God's creation. A logically consistent believer in God must base his or her meaning of life on his or her resemblance to God. That is, true believers must understand the meaning of their own lives as derived from their own creative power. Meaning consists in purpose-giving, not in serving an imposed purpose. As for non-believers, they can simply understand the meaning of life as a function of their purposive creativity without referring to God.

It might be argued that the meaning of life has to be based on something that transcends the material perishability of our physical existence, and a belief in God gives us a hope for such a transcendence. This argument assumes that a permanent existence itself is the meaning. But if so, we don't need to hope for anything beyond, because we know that the physical components of our body will exist forever, and we can simply equate ourselves with these components.

Obviously all of those who derive their hope from an alleged divine plan will reject such an equation. Therefore, what they hope for must be some special kind of permanency, not the kind based on the physical law of conservation. So material perishability may not be the real issue here. As we know, this special kind of permanency is usually called "eternity" and requires *immortality* of the soul. But why should the permanent existence of physical "materials" not count as eternity while the immortality of the soul does? Or put it in another way, what makes the permanent existence of the soul meaningful but the permanent existence of the physical components meaningless? In order to see whether such an understanding of meaningfulness on the basis of immaterial eternity is justified, we must again go back to the concepts of creativity and purposiveness. Let us see why and how.

5.4   Significant Difference versus Real Difference

Fake Mona Lisa

In human life, things do not have to make a *real* difference, in the sense to be clarified, in a person's experience in order to be meaningful. If a difference is *significant* to the person, in the sense to be clarified, even if not really experienced, it will contribute to the meaning of the person's life in a positive or negative manner. In fact, such a notion of significant difference is essential to understanding all concepts, such as success, ownership, moral responsibility, and others, that are applicable exclusively to human life. The following situations will be used to demonstrate this point.

Suppose Mike, a best friend of mine, loved his cat and, knowing he was going to die of cancer soon, asked me to take care of his cat after his death. I promised him that I would. Then, last week Mike died. Regardless of my ethical and religious beliefs about promise-keeping or the possibility of afterlife, or any considerations of the well-being of the cat or my own like or dislike of the cat, does it make any difference *to Mike*, who is now dead, whether or not I keep the promise and take care of his cat?

Many tourists go to the Louvre to see Leonardo da Vinci's original *Mona Lisa*. Suppose that the original is destroyed by an accident, a fact the public does not know and has little chance of finding out, and that the museum has secretly kept a replica which is so well made that nobody can visually tell its difference from the original. If the replica were to be exhibited as if it were the original while the public remains ignorant of the truth about the replacement, would it make any difference to the tourists who travel there from afar for the sole purpose of seeing the original?

Jennifer believes that Sam had saved her from a rapist some years ago and she married him largely for that reason. Yesterday their house caught fire and in saving Sam's life, Jennifer was fatally burned. Jennifer is now dying but she feels good because she believes that she has done the right thing in the life of Sam, who helped her at a critical moment before. But Sam is actually the very one who had attempted to rape her; the one who had helped her was murdered by Sam shortly afterward. Sam played a trick on her, making her believe wrongly that he was the hero and goading her into marrying him. Nevertheless, after the marriage, Sam performed well as a husband. Now if Jennifer dies happily without knowing the truth, does this deception add a defect to Jennifer's life compared to the possible case that Sam was indeed the hero? That is, is there any positive or negative difference to Jennifer's life between the two possibilities?

Jeff and Tina are husband and wife; so are Henry and Heidi. Jeff and Henry are very good friends. Tina loves her husband Jeff so much that the very thought of her having sex with another man would make her sick. But Jeff and Henry are sexually attracted to the other's wife so one day they discuss the possibility of switching wives for sex sometime.

Knowing that Tina (and perhaps Heidi too) could not even bear hearing such an idea, they begin to practice each other's way of lovemaking in order to deceive Tina and Heidi one night in the dark. After weeks of practice, they finally take the risk and succeed. The next morning after the switched sexual intercourse, Tina says that she actually enjoyed last night's sex more than ever before and feels she loves Jeff even more because of her wonderful sexual experience of the night. Is Tina violated by Jeff and Henry if she will never learn about the conspiracy? In other words, apart from its possible effects on society at large, does it make any difference whether Jeff or Henry gives Tina sexual pleasure that night *only for Tina's sake?*

Suppose a dictator loves political power and is proud to show off his power. He abolishes the whole system of legislation and declares a new law, in addition to other necessary laws, for the sole purpose of showing his ability to exercise his power arbitrarily. He does it by writing, "Citizens shall not _____, and violators are subject to any punishment as the ruler wishes," and then, broadcast live on TV, drawing a card arbitrarily from a deck of cards on which certain clauses had been written beforehand. Whatever the drawn card says will fill the blank to complete the statement as a law. By sheer chance, the law ends up stating: "Citizens shall not kiss their own noses, and violators are subject to any punishment as the ruler wishes." Assuming nobody can possibly kiss his or her own nose, does it make, apart from its possible effects on legislation in the future, any difference to the citizens' political liberty with or without that law?

Another Sense of the Real

To any of the questions in these five examples about whether there is a difference, the answer is the same: there is no real difference but there is a significant difference. The key is the contrast between the *significant* and the *real*. But keep in mind, our use of the word "real" here has nothing to do with the contrast we made between the real and the illusory in chapter 3. Having finished discussing the ontological issues of VR, we need now to return to the way we used the word "real" before we heard of VR in order to make sense of the normative issues that now concern us. Then what do I mean by the real as opposed to the significant in this new context?

Of course, by "no real difference" I do not mean that there is no difference between the two events in their physical processes, because obviously I have in each case implied a contrast between what has happened and what could have otherwise happened. What I actually mean is that no real experiential contents occur in the person (or persons), or that the experiential contents are no more and no less objectionable than those in the alternative possibility. Put differently, by "real" I mean the experientially real.

So whether or not I take care of Mike's cat does not make any real difference in Mike's experiential contents because a dead Mike cannot experience anything. The fake *Mona Lisa* in my example does not arouse any less aesthetic response, as a real mental event, in the tourists. Real experiential differences are just a special type of real differences in general in the world of natural order.

Real differences can be found anywhere in the natural world as well as in human life, but purely significant differences belong exclusively to human life. A real difference may or may not be significant, and conversely, a significant difference may or may not be real. They do overlap, though.[10] Which difference is more essential to human life? It is the significant one. If a real difference is not significant, we are *indifferent* to which path things take; but if a significant difference is not real, we still value one more than the other.

In each of the previous five examples, we definitely desire one situation over the other, even though it does not make a real difference. It does make a significant difference to Mike whether I take care of his cat as I promised *to him*. Our dignity would definitely be offended if we were cheated by the museum in showing us a fake *Mona Lisa*, even though we do not know or feel that we are offended and have seen nothing less beautiful and experienced nothing less pleasant. Jennifer would have led a more fulfilling life if she did not marry Sam, the would-be rapist, but rather married her true hero killed by Sam. Jeff and Henry's conspiracy does add a big defect to Tina's life despite the absence of a consequential negative experience on Tina's part. The citizens' political liberty is definitely violated by the dictator who makes the law arbitrarily, even though nobody can possibly violate the law and suffer a real consequence.

Real but Irrelevant

On the contrary, we know that the authentic art work *Mona Lisa* we want to see is in reality different from the one da Vinci painted in his time; the real difference is due to the physical and chemical changes that have occurred during a few hundred years of history. But since it is not significant, we are, as a da Vinci admirer, *indifferent* to that kind of real difference. By the same token, Tina in my example knows very well that every day her husband Jeff's body undergoes some physical change. But she is indifferent to the change (or at least some of the change) as a lover and wife.

Therefore we can see that a significant difference is not a psychological or mental difference that belongs to the category of the real. In all but one (the dictator's law) of the given examples, no relevant psychological difference is introduced in reality despite its potential possibility. But it might be argued that it is such a possibility of psychological effects that makes the difference significant. If, with complete information given to all those involved, there could not be any relevant psychological difference as a consequence, then there would be indeed no significant difference.

Such an argument, however, puts the cart before the horse. It is because something is significant that we are psychologically affected, not the other way around; otherwise we would not be able to distinguish a legitimate (or "normal") psychological response to an event from an illegitimate (or "abnormal") one. If Tina goes crazy whenever she sees her husband drinking ice water, based on no medical reason, Tina would be correctly regarded as a psychotic because the difference between drinking ice water and, say, iced tea, is insignificant. But if Tina gets hurt psychologically when she knows the conspiracy of her husband and Henry, she wouldn't be regarded as psychotic since the conspiracy *is indeed* negatively significant in her marriage and love life. This is so *prior to*, and independently of, her knowledge about, and psychological response to, the conspiracy.

The Meaningful as the Central Concern

Clearly what matters in human life is primarily based not on what is experientially real but rather on what is meaningful.[11] Since this kind of meaningfulness is separable from anything empirically real, including psychological events, it is not equivalent to anyone's actual experience. We can lead a very pleasant yet meaningless life, or a very meaningful yet unpleasant life.

But if meaning is not based on reality, on what is it based? As a counterpart to "reality," we will call, after Husserl, the basis of meaning "ideality," which we will discuss more thoroughly in the rest of the book.

In fact, all concepts that are applicable to human life exclusively are to a certain extent related to such a notion of significant difference. Let us now examine just three fundamental concepts that pertain only to human life—success versus failure, ownership, and moral responsibility—to see how significant differences, in contrast to real differences, are a major factor that makes them applicable only to the type of life we regard as exclusively human.

An Unsuccessful Rich Man

What is a success or a failure? A person's total success is the realization of a goal set by the same person voluntarily as a result of an effort no greater than he or she intended to make to reach that goal. A person's total failure is the lack of the realization of that goal after the intended effort. Between the two extremes, a person can partially succeed or partially fail. A person's success or failure does not depend on other people's opinions about the matter, nor does it depend on a goal set or recognized by others. If everyone else wanted to become a millionaire and set that as the goal of life, but I alone set it as my goal to become a published poet, then the only measure of my success is whether I have published at least one poem. Suppose it ends up that everybody else has published a poem but none of them has become a millionaire despite all of their effort, but I have happened to make a few millions yet published not a single poem despite all my effort, neither I nor anyone else has succeeded, despite the possible deepest mutual envy between us.

But things get tricky when we consider the possibility that anyone can have a wrong belief about their own success or failure since whether a person has actually achieved something or not is not always correctly judged by the same person. Some magazine might have published my poems as a result of my effort without my knowledge of it, or my psychological disorder might lead me to believe that I have published poems while in fact I have published none; or the stocks I am holding might have gone up drastically but my broker has mistakenly told me the opposite and I believe him. Moreover, I might die before I get to know the fact, or I can live forever with a false belief.

Thus assuming that I intended to achieve X and set that as the goal of my life, we can use a table (see Table 5.1) to show the complex relationship between my belief and the actual state of affairs with regard to my success or failure.

Since belief is a real state of mind, there should be a distinct item of experience corresponding to each belief. If a belief of success gives you pleasure and a belief of failure does not give you pleasure (perhaps gives you pain?), then we have Table 5.2 to show such a modified relationship.

In Tables 5.1 and 5.2, we can see clearly that whether I am successful

TABLE 5.1
Intention and Success

The one intending to achieve X:	did not achieve X	did achieve X
believes X is not achieved	Failure	Success
believes X is achieved	Success	Failure

TABLE 5.2
Experiencing Pleasure and Success

One who intended to achieve X:	did not achieve X	did achieve X
experiences no pleasure of achieving X	Failure	Success
experiences the pleasure of achieving X	Failure	Success

depends on whether the goal is actually reached, but not on whether I know it or experience a psychological response to it. Therefore success or failure is primarily a matter of meaning, and the difference it makes to the person is significant, but not necessarily real. You might believe and feel that you are a failure but actually be a success, or vice versa.

He Is Happy but He Has Failed

There might be an objection to my argument. Perhaps my definition of success or failure is incomplete, or else people would not care about whether they succeed or not so long as it does not have a necessary connection to their experiential contents. They may therefore understand success implicitly as the achievement of the intended goal *plus* the knowledge and the feeling of the achievement, and failure as the lack thereof. Thus, it may be argued, between success and failure there must be a real, instead of significant, difference to the person involved. Since whether or not my definition of success or failure is complete is a matter of linguistics, we do not have to be concerned more with that. But the assertion that people care only about real differences and not significant ones does not hold for the following reasons.

It would certainly be perfect if we can reach the goal *and* feel the euphoria of the achievement. It is self-evident that if due to some misinformation we feel the same amount of euphoria but have not reached the goal, it would be *less than* perfect. This already shows that there is a significant difference in addition to the real difference. But is the real experiential difference or the significant difference more important in such a context?

For the sake of further argument, let us assume that we can only have one but not both. That is, due to misinformation or psychological disorder, I can either reach the goal but not feel the pleasure, or not reach the goal but still feel the pleasure. Suppose I want to become a published poet. If now I can either (1) become published but not know it (and thus not be able to feel the pleasure of knowing it), or (2) publish nothing but feel the pleasure as if I were published, which situation would you like me to be in only for *my* sake?

Indeed, there is something imperfect in option 1, but at least what I intended to make happen has happened, and that is in concert with my intention. But does option (2) contribute any positive value to my life? I can be led to believe and feel that I have achieved many things I did not achieve if I am a madman or get brainwashed or just become totally drunk. If only the experiential contents count, then the most desirable life would be a certain kind of insanity that lets you believe and feel whatever you wish. So I assume you would like me to be in the first situation rather than the second for the sake of my goodness. Or at least, if you choose the second and let me have the feeling, you would certainly consider my lack of actual achievement, that is, the actual publication of poems as desired, a serious defect despite my sincere belief and strong feeling that I am published. Perhaps given the actual condition that I have not reached my goal, the experienced feeling of achievement makes me even more miserable than no feeling at all; it might even be worse than a feeling of frustration based on a correct understanding of the fact. Therefore, a significant difference does matter apart from an experiential (real) difference. Nay, it may even matter a great deal.

A Homeless Millionaire

Now let's discuss ownership. The concept of ownership seems to be the most down-to-earth of concepts that apply exclusively to human life: it sounds so materialistic. But whether you own something or not is nevertheless primarily a difference of significance rather than that of real experience on the possible owner's part.

In our earlier discussion of the concept of success, we already realized that we might be millionaires but have no idea that we are and feel totally broke due to the misinformation we received. In such a case, no matter what I believe and feel, or what anybody else in the world believes or feels, insofar as I am holding the stocks that have gone up explosively so that my total asset has reached a million dollars, then I am literally a millionaire. Or, the stocks I am holding might become worthless and I have actually "lost my shirt" overnight while I am honeymooning in Jamaica, believing and acting as if I were the richest man in the world. Therefore how much I own does not depend on anybody's experiential contents. It depends solely on the institutional stipulation about ownership.

A natural disaster or an unexpected accident could also create a huge mismatch between what you own and what you believe you own. And, of course, insanity would do it as well. The point is that you could live with that mismatch and nobody else might know about it all along before you reach the end of your life. Here, you do not get a chance to experience the real difference, but the significant difference with regard to ownership has been there nonetheless.

In What Way Am I Morally Responsible?

Finally, we examine the concept of moral responsibility. I am morally responsible for what I have done. If I did something morally wrong *in the past*, I am *now* morally culpable. Suppose yesterday I killed an innocent child, I should be punished now solely for certain moral reasons. Why so? It is certainly not merely because I *caused* the child's death; otherwise the gun I used to kill, which is no less part of the cause, would be as wrong, and thus as guilty, as I am. It may be argued that my past behavior of killing suggests a higher probability of my doing the same sort of thing again now and in the future, while there is no similar consideration with regard to the gun. But such a consideration of probability has nothing to do with moral responsibility, since we do not attribute moral responsibility to life-threatening animals to whom the consideration of probability may apply as well. Thus construed, the concept of moral responsibility is not directly pointed to any empirically describable elements of human behavior.

The answer might be that I *intended* the killing and *knew* the consequence, while the gun did not, and thus I am the agent of the act of killing whereas the gun is merely a passive tool. If such an answer is certainly on the right track, then we are left with the question of why the present "I" is responsible for the intention of the past "I." To be sure, the fact that yesterday I intended to kill does not entail that I still intend to now or will in the future. Also, my present intention cannot possibly have any influence on my previous intention. Thus, if my intention is what makes me morally responsible, then certainly the punishment I deserve is not imposed on me for the sake of making a real difference on the part of the victim. So if my intention is understood only as a cause of the child's death without a further account of how the punishment, which cannot undo what has already happened, is morally justifiable, apart from the practical consideration of deterrence, our concept of moral responsibility remains a riddle.

But if we view the punishment as a way of making a significant difference rather than a real difference in relation to what I intended and what I did under that intention, the riddle disappears right away. Since a significant difference does not belong to the natural order of causality as a real difference, we can safely say that I am morally responsible for not only what I did before but also for what I will do in the future, because my past, present, and future actions belong altogether to one and the same agent in relation to which these actions are significant. Nobody has yet blamed me for what I have yet to do because nobody knows what I will do, but I am *now* morally responsible for whatever I will do in the future, because what path I will travel makes a significant difference to me now. The temporal order is here unessential just as in my earlier example of Mike, Mike's cat, and me: what I do to Mike's cat after Mike's death makes a significant difference to Mike alive.

Try More by Yourself

You can, along the same line, further analyze concepts such as dignity, respect, honesty, integrity, citizenship, and so forth, to see how they are primarily based on a notion of significant difference. In fact, all concepts essential to understanding human individuals or human society must pertain to the concept of significant difference, and this is what the five examples given at the beginning of this section were intended to demonstrate. Therefore, anybody who denies the central role of this kind of non-experiential significance will in effect believe that these concepts are meaningless. But these concepts are certainly meaningful, so such a denial is totally wrong.

We usually only take the humans as possible candidates for success or failure, ownership, moral responsibility, and so forth. If we do sometimes apply these concepts to alien beings other than human, we then regard them as the same type of beings as us humans according to a certain criterion. But what is this criterion? It is exactly their apparent ability to make sense of a *significant* difference. In other words, their lives are not only real, but also *meaningful*. For that reason, they are not zombies, but persons.

Meaning of Life Right Under Your Eyelashes

A significant difference is just a manifestation of meaningfulness in the context of a contrast between two or more alternatives. Having understood that the notion of the meaningful is central to all fundamental concepts of human life, we need now to see what the root of these concepts is, on the phenomenological level, so we can find the key to the understanding of the uniqueness of humanity. This is the basis for a valid answer to the question of the meaning of life as different from happiness as Huxley raised.

The complexity of the question is that even though a significant difference is separate from the real experiential difference, the significance does depend on a real difference in the actual world. In my examples, whether I succeed *does* depend on what the value of stocks really is, or whether any publisher has really published my poems, even though it does not depend on how I or anybody really feels experientially. So what is exactly the relationship between the real and the meaningful? This question brings us back to the Husserlian understanding of the nature of human subjectivity based on the concept of *intentional* nature of consciousness.

5.5   Three Modes of Subjectivity and Intentionality

Subjective but Fair

In the empiricist camp of philosophy, the term *subjective,* when used in the theory of knowledge, has negative connotations similar to those in everyday language. In fact, the former is the categorized form of the latter. Empiricist epistemology embraces the correspondence theory of truth: a belief on the side of the subject is true if and only if it corresponds to a fact on the side of the object. The subject is the knower, and the object the known. Since there is supposedly only one sphere of objects to be known, but a multiplicity of isolated knowing subjects, the correspondence, if there is one, must be determined by the known object rather than by the knowing subject in order for truth to be univocal. That is to say, the anchor of truth is the object. Given such an interpretation, we can readily understand how, in everyday language, being "objective" is being "unbiased," "impartial," "fair," and "agreeable," and is how we want to be when making a judgment, while being "subjective" is being "prejudiced" and "partial," and so on.

But when we stop to reflect, we may ask ourselves: How can a person *not* be subjective if he or she *is* the subject that "opens up" the field of perception for the object to show up as we witnessed in chapter 1 when we discussed PR? Here we are using the word "subjective" in a different sense: not as opposed to objectivity but as what makes objectivity possible to begin with. Thus phenomenologically, anything understood from the first-person perspective can be regarded as subjective. The assumption that observation from the third-person perspective is possible without the first-person perspective is what makes the ordinary sense of "subjective" problematic. It is now time for us to understand subjectivity in the phenomenological sense in its relation to objectivity.

Logical Positivism and Its Discontent

The principle of verifiability as a criterion for the meaningfulness of empirical statements was the most celebrated position the logical positivists took. Here the verification of a statement consists in the agreement between what is stated and what is observed.

Since a scientific theory is a conceptually organized body of ideas that does not describe an event by itself, we cannot compare it with our observations directly. Thus its verifiability depends on its ability to generate statements that allow for such a comparison. Since observation is an immediate result of our experience of the external world through our senses, the principle of verifiability is claimed to be in line with traditional empiricism.

There have been many discussions of the impossibility of presupposition-free observations. For that reason, along with the reason given by Thomas Kuhn in his account of scientific revolutions as a shift from one "paradigm" to another, people even began to talk about the universal presence of subjectivity and to blur the line between a project of ideological propaganda and that of scientific research. This is a dangerous move, of course, and I am certainly willing to show how such a move is without a solid ground when it is called for. But I am not now in a position to attack such a move. The point I want to make here is rather as follows. It is true that no judgments and statements can be made without an involvement of subjectivity, but we need to distinguish three modes of subjectivity from one another so that we will know which mode of subjectivity is a precondition of objectivity and thus does not at all bring in personal biases, whereas other modes may indeed be the source of preconceptions or misperceptions.

Be Proud of Subjectivity

Subjectivity is that which makes human beings a subject. A subject, qua its subjectivity, observes but cannot be observed, perceives but cannot be perceived. This was clearly demonstrated when we discussed the case of Adam and Bob in a cross-communication situation in chapter 1. When a word stands for that which is inherent in the notion of humanity but cannot, in principle, be observed and located in a physical place, then it refers to a component, or the totality, of subjectivity. Thus, words such as "idea," "concept," "emotion," "consciousness" are a few examples of them, since, by definition, anything that is empirically observable cannot be what these words stand for. For example, if you open somebody's brain, you may see many things and be unsure of what they are, but one thing for sure is that you will never see a concept or an idea as an object in the brain. Instead, that which each of these words is meant to stand for is exclusively attributed to a subject. Our understanding of the meaning of these words, therefore, is not based on the operation of our sense organs, but on our self-reflections.

Does a Hole Exist?

But one may ask, if the referents of these words are not empirically accessible, how can we know they actually exist? My response is that the word "existence" is among the most ambiguous items in our language. Besides the presence of physical objects, which certainly exemplifies a possible case of existence, we are not so sure what else we can claim to exist or not to exist. Does a hole, which is an absence among masses that exist, itself exist? Does a number exist? Does the equality between three plus three and six exist? Does a headache exist? If our answers to these questions are affirmative, there is no sufficient reason I can think of why we cannot say that ideas, emotion, and consciousness, and so forth do exist. But the meaning of the concept of existence is not our major concern at the moment. We can just suspend the seemingly important question of whether subjective items exist or not, and turn now to the question of the structure of subjectivity in the sense I just specified.

The Trinity of Subjectivity

Subjectivity has its three modes, namely, constitutive, communicative, and conative modes. For the sake of convenience, I will simply call them constitutive subjectivity, communicative subjectivity, and conative subjectivity, respectively, even though they are merely three modes of the same subjectivity.

As we noted, the empiricist use of the word "subjective" is not much different from the ordinary sense of the word, in which "subjective" never means anything desirable. In contrast to "objectivity," which always implies rationality and sound judgment, "subjectivity" is regarded as a weakness of the human mind that leads us to prejudices and errors which we should try to avoid by all means. "Subjectivity" here means pertaining merely to the particular subject who holds that opinion, such that the opinion is merely "personal" and therefore cannot be taken as necessarily correct. Such an understanding of subjectivity is, as I said earlier, the basis for the epistemology of the empiricist philosophers since John Locke.

The Conative Mode

This kind of subjectivity is, in our sense, conative subjectivity, because it affects our judgments as a result of our conative mental activities such as desires, wants, wishes, whims, feelings, impulses, and the like, which are often considered the sources of personal preferences or tastes or "values," as some people tend to call them. All of these are supposedly subject matter for experimental psychology, and thus their expressions, though not themselves, are open to empirical description in a certain way, perhaps due to their affinity to our bodily functions or our physiological structure. Since in this mode of subjectivity what happens in one person cannot be shared with any other persons, it is intersubjectively separate.

Actually, insofar as partisan interests are derived from this mode of subjectivity, mutual isolatedness often results in external exclusiveness. Therefore conative subjectivity is something we should prevent from getting into our process of observation when we try to verify an empirical statement, and most of the ideological conflicts in our political life probably have much to do with this mode of subjectivity. Also, when we accuse somebody of being irrational in making a judgment, we probably mean that there is too much conative subjectivity involved when he or she makes that judgment. If anybody believes that such a prevention is not possible because our sense organs are always influenced by our conative subjectivity, then he or she will consequently believe that the distinction between science and ideology is not a matter of kinds but merely a matter of degrees, and thus will fall into cognitive relativism.

The Communicative Mode

The second mode of subjectivity is what I call communicative subjectivity. Here the word "communicative" is largely understood in the framework of Habermas's theory of communicative action or communicative rationality. According to his usage of the word, to communicate is not merely to convey a message but rather to make propositional claims and to argue for their validity. Therefore, it involves conceptualizing our preconceptual experience, defining words, making judgments, formulating propositions, stating the propositions, theorizing, defending argumentatively, etc.—all those things we usually call cognitive activities.

Therefore, according to this theory, rules of formal logic are rules for effective communication. The external world does not break itself into many separate objects, but in order to organize our own experience and communicate with others, we use concepts to break it into many items. When we use our words to catch those items, ideally we need a one-to-one correspondence between our words and those items and stick to that correspondence consistently. Therefore we have a rule of non-contradiction in formal logic. All other rules of logic can be understood basically in the same way. What is a theory then? A theory is an organizing framework in which to arrange concepts and propositions consistently.

But how is observation related to this mode of subjectivity? In recent years people's talk about how observation is impossible without an involvement of previous concepts and a pre-established theory, and how our instruments are built on the basis of previous convictions, etc., can be understood in terms of the necessary involvement of communicative subjectivity. Because there is more than one possible framework on the same level in which to organize our concepts and propositions, there can be more than one theory competing for their merits in efficacy. Because framing can be carried out on different levels, a new theory can cover a broader area than the old one and acquire a stronger organizing power and thus replace the old one. And also because observation is itself a conceptually organized and theoretically guided activity, there is no such thing as a "pure objective" observation. Thomas Kuhn's idea of paradigm and its shift may be adequately understood at this point.

But now it is clear that the mode of subjectivity involved here is not the same as the first mode, that is, the conative mode of subjectivity that brings in arbitrary biases due to one's wishes, whims, desires, etc. Communicative subjectivity is intersubjectively transparent, so we can see the merits of one concept, or theory, or argument in comparison with the alternative ones by executing our communicative rationality. Thus a competition between different positions or theories, either in fields of natural science or social science or philosophy, is not at all the same as an ideological conflict. It will, in an ideal situation, lead to a consensus through rational argumentation, rather than an involuntary submission of all parties to one authority, the Almighty. So a belief in the necessity of communicative subjectivity need not lead us to cognitive relativism of the kind that tends to equate science with ideology.

Schlick's Concern

But admitting communicative subjectivity has already threatened traditional empiricism, which claims that the only source of knowledge is sense perception. In the Vienna Circle, Neurath adopted a holistic view of scientific truth. According to this view, no single statement, even on the protocol level, can be verified independently, but only the whole theory is to be verified according to a regulative principle such as the principle of economy. Schlick sensed immediately a danger of a rationalistic departure from empiricism in this view, and thus introduced a concept of affirmation in place of Carnap's protocol statement. In so doing, Schlick thought, he could save the empiricalistic character of their logical positivism. But how?

There is an epistemological discrepancy between a statement and an observation. An observation is not by itself a statement with a linguistic structure. In order to verify or falsify a statement derived from a theory, we must formulate it in such a way that it represents the pure fact obtained from our senses on the one hand, and is also to be verbally stated and thus conceptually understood on the other. Such a statement is called by Carnap, for the first time, a "protocol statement."

In a protocol statement, physical objects and events may be depicted. But to claim that one has observed a physical object already involves a fallible assumption as a result of synthesizing one's sense-data, which are not themselves objects or events. For this reason, Schlick developed a new concept: Konstatierungen or "affirmations" in English. In his affirmation, only the un-processed phenomena, and nothing else, are to be recorded. An affirmation will take a form like: "Here now blue." Obviously, such a statement is not a statement in a regular sense, not only because of its lack of a complete grammatical structure but also, more importantly, because of its sheer private and momentary character and its separation from a general spatio-temporal framework.

But our certainty about the validity of such a statement will evaporate immediately after the moment of verification. According to Schlick, this is the price we pay for the absolute certainty of that moment. Such an absolute certainty is obtained because the affirmation is entirely empirical, that is, the only thing that comes into play is our observation through our sense organs. Therefore, a statement that refers to invisible objects such as an atom and a quark can never be verified, even though it is verifiable in the sense that we can make predictions such as "Here now blue" deductively from that statement.

What Schlick fails to recognize is that even such a quasi-statement as "Here now blue," if intelligible at all, has already been idealized. An observation takes place only if the observer understands what is observed, and thus only meaningful phenomena can be formulated in an observation statement. In other words, the observed must be experienced *as* something *meaningful*. At this level, the concept of blue, for example, is no less associated with the non-blue part of the world than the concept of an invisible atom with the concept of the visible even at the very moment of verification. The meaning of either "here" or "now" as experienced at the moment also implies an infinitely large spatio-temporal configuration wherein "here now" is a point.

The Constitutive Mode

Actually, I am already talking about the third mode of subjectivity, namely, constitutive subjectivity. What the term "constitutive subjectivity" designates is subjectivity on its highest level, which *constitutes* the physical objectivity and objectivity in general in the spatio-temporal continuum of the world. In other words, constitutive subjectivity is the *precondition* for us to perceive anything as a material entity when our sensations meet the criteria for the physically *real* as discussed in chapter

3. It does so by filling in the absent to the present and enables us to go beyond what is immediately received by our sense organs. Without such a preconceptual operation of constitution, no meaningful experience whatsoever is possible at the very beginning. Such a concept of constitutive subjectivity has, as we know, mainly been developed by the founding father of phenomenology, Edmund Husserl, in his basic writings.

The point I want to emphasize is that the involvement of constitutive subjectivity not only introduces no personal biases, but furthermore functions as a precondition of any kind of objectivity we can possibly comprehend. It is intersubjectively transcendent because it is at work with any possible subject but nobody voluntarily puts it into or out of operation.

When I observe any object, say, a tree, what is presented to me is one side of the tree, and nobody can, in principle, see the whole tree in its totality. But the *concept* of a tree, even in its purely physical sense, already embraces the infinitely many possibilities of perspective from which to observe it. So at the moment of observation when I identify a tree, or simply one side of the tree, I have already brought in a horizon of the un-perceived aspects of the tree to constitute the objectivity of the object we call a "tree."

Even the objectivity of the world, or of the universe, when we use the word to refer to it, is already a product of the constitutive operation of the mind. Who has ever perceived the whole universe as a physical object? Nobody. But we do believe, even after our discussion of the parallelism between the actual and the virtual worlds, that the universe is there by itself. We are destined to have such a belief thanks to the operation of constitutive subjectivity. This kind of operation does not have anything to do with arbitrariness. The way it works is *determined* beyond anybody's preferences and tastes. But we know that it is still subjectivity, true subjectivity in the sense that it makes us a human subject, a knower, a perceiver.

The dimensionality of space and time is the precondition of any physicality and objectivity. According to Husserl's analysis, the experience of such a dimensionality is impossible without the intentionality of constitutive Subjectivity. In the case of perceiving a spatial object, the absent part of the object is added to the present part through a process he calls adumbration. In the case of time-consciousness, as we touched upon previously, the present moment is experienced as a point in a continuous time flow from the past to the future through retention and protention, which are different from recollection and anticipation. Otherwise, a momentary "now" would be impossible to comprehend. In sum, without a constitutive operation of subjectivity, even Schlick's simplest affirmations such as "Here now blue" would be meaningless, not to speak of their verification or falsification.

Back to Virtual Reality

So far, I have tried to show sketchily how objective observation is inseparable from constitutive subjectivity. But in the case of virtual reality, the constituted objectivity does not maintain its solidity when we retreat back to the reflective mode of thinking, even though the whole constitutive operation works as usual at each moment of our un-reflective act of perceiving. It is so because as soon as we get out of the process of immediate response to the constituted object, a process of *deconstruction* is activated by the mind's unavoidable intentional reference to our pre-learned knowledge that the stimuli are digitally generated.

After a series of thought experiments or free fancy variations conducted in chapter 1, we have seen that inside a coherent system of simulations we cannot know that anything in it is a simulation. Therefore, if we suspend our naturalistic attitude about what exists and what does not in a Husserlian phenomenological reduction, we arrive at the plane where both the "real" and the "virtual" are at stake equally. The three modes of subjectivity will work in the same way in either case. As we saw in chapter 3, the regularity of the virtual events will enable the constitutive mode of subjectivity to constitute causality and physicality behind the virtual world and form the concept of objectivity. It is so because the infrastructure is given as an external necessity, at least at each moment of the immediate virtual experience.

Intentionality, not Cultural Relativity

At the core of all the three modes of subjectivity is the self-transcending *intentionality* that projects personal goals to be achieved in the conative mode, proposes and redeems impersonal theoretical validity to be justified in the communicative mode, and constitutes objectivity in the constitutive mode. Three modes of subjectivity are given with necessity *prior to* any social-cultural relativity of the specific contents of life.

Now we can see clearly how the meaningful is different from but definitely related to the real in our analysis of the concepts of success, ownership, and moral responsibility. Since a significant difference pertains primarily to the initial intention with regard to what real changes (a real difference) the chosen *part of* the objective world (the constitutive) should undergo (the conative), it does not have to include anybody's experience as a component of that part. The concept of success versus failure pertains initially to the individual's intention, the concept of ownership to the collectively institutionalized intentions of all individual participants, and the concept of moral responsibility to the interaction between each individual's intention and the collectively institutionalized intentions. Since the intentional structure is the precondition of the natural order in a spatial-temporal framework, but not itself in the framework, a significant difference is not limited by the temporal order of past–now–future in its meaningfulness. So we can be morally responsible *now* for what we did in the past and what we will do in the future.

The Meaning of "Meaning"

There are, as I discussed in my first book, many theories of meaning in the analytical tradition, and among them the best known are the denotation (Russell), picture (early Wittgenstein), verification (Schlick), and use (later Wittgenstein) theories. Despite great differences among these theories, they all take the meaning to be an attribute of *words* and do not concern its final source in the three modes of subjectivity. This is to a certain extent legitimate because by "meaning" we do *mean* something separable from what we mean. But these theories are destined to be inadequate as an ultimate interpretation of meaning because they do not trace the root back to intentionality as the origin.

If we notice the fact that the noun "meaning" is derived from the verb "to mean," then we will not try to reduce meaning in general to anything separate from subjectivity. While the meaning of "cat," for example, may mean what it denotes (the bearer), to exemplify Russell's theory, the meaning of "if" may very well mean the way it is used in a sentence, to exemplify later Wittgenstein's. But why do we say that in one case the meaning is the bearer but in another case the meaning is the use? If we take all these different theories as indeed theories of meaning, we already presuppose that there is a sense of meaning that covers all these theories. That is, at least the meaning of the word "meaning" should be a constant. Therefore, there must be something that unifies the meaning as bearer and the meaning as use in common independently of any bearer or use in order for us to claim that the bearer *and* the use are both the meaning of a word in different cases. This unifying denominator lies, as we have shown, in the intentionality of the one who *means*, that is, in subjectivity in our sense.

Whether or not our intended state of affairs come true does depend on how things turn out in the objective world. This is so because constitutive subjectivity does not belong to one's capability of choice. It is different from conative subjectivity precisely due to its involuntary operation constrained by an external necessity. The itemized manifestations of that external necessity are laws of nature studied in natural science, laws of society in social science, and laws of behavior and mental process in psychology. Therefore the objective world is constituted but not constructed because we have no choice what laws it has to follow. Thus whether we succeed or fail, for example, does not always match what we perceive it to be after we initiated the process, as we saw earlier. A recognition of subjectivity does not, therefore, support cognitive relativism.

5.6   Meaning, Ideality, and Humanitude

Humanitude versus Human Nature

In my book *The Radical Choice and Moral Theory*,[12] I developed the concept of "humanitude" to counter the naturalistic notion of human nature. As I remark in that book, if human nature is supposed to refer to something that distinguishes humans from non-humans and that cannot be changed as long as we are humans, then a naturalistic description of what we observe empirically will never do the job. In the Aristotelian language, since human nature is the unchangeable essence of the human species, but the attributes empirically described about humans are accidental and therefore always subject to change, an inductive procedure would never lead us to understand what make us uniquely human. Moreover, an attempt to characterize humanity in terms of the law of nature would fail to explain the autonomy of a human agent, because a law of nature is by definition imposed upon us as an external necessity. There I concluded:

> The concept of human nature is unfulfillable because of its inherent inconsistency concerning the ideas of immutability vs. empirical contingency, and self-determination vs. the heteronomy of natural laws.[13]

Humanitude, on the contrary, is a notion that goes against the current fashion of (anti-?) philosophical enquiries that try to naturalize everything. The concept of humanitude is based on the position we reached earlier, when we distinguished a significant difference from a real difference, that all those concepts applicable to human life exclusively pertain primarily to the meaningful but not to the empirical. So humanitude characterizes what is uniquely human instead of the empirical "nature" of *Homo sapiens* in the biological sense, and we can make a contrast (Table 5.3) between the intentional and the empirical orders.

Obviously, except for the last row, all items in the left column of the table pertain only to human life, whereas items on the right pertain to everything in the empirical world (including humans as observed *Homo sapiens*). The current trend of various kinds of naturalizing (or socializing) philosophy can be understood as attempts to reduce, explicitly or implicitly, items in the left column to those in the right, that is, to reduce the intentional to the empirical. But we have shown that to be impossi-

TABLE 5.3
A Contrast Between the Two Orders

The Intentional	The Empirical
subjective	objective
ideality	reality
meaning	event
meaning-complex	state of affairs
concepts	words
propositions	sentences
logical	causal
projection	continuation
autonomy	heteronomy
humanitude	human nature

ble.[14] Therefore, the last item on the right, human nature, is, if intended as a concept that designates unique features of humanity, destined to be self-defeating and thus needs to be replaced by the one on the left, that is, humanitude. Clearly, the contrast between humanitude and human nature is based on the distinction between reality and ideality. So let us turn now to a discussion of that distinction.

How Can We Understand Each Other?

Whenever we are engaged in an effort to understand others and to make ourselves understood, ideality is in effect. When I try to understand somebody, say, *A*, I am not trying, in the first place, to discover the physical or psychological process of his speech, but to follow his train of thought as composed of complexes of meaning. These complexes of meaning are understandable in distinction from natural processes as explained in physico-psychological terms. In order to understand what *A* means, *A*'s physical properties are not logically relevant, so we can follow *A*'s thought without any knowledge of *A*'s physico-psychological constitution. Let us see how this must be so.

If you are having a conversation face to face with *A* and really trying to understand *A*, you must listen to *A*. But when you are listening, you cannot possibly be primarily concerned with the physical quality of the sound emanated from *A*'s voice, because you cannot and are not supposed to know this physical quality through listening. If you were concerned with the physical quality of *A*'s voice, you would have to use a certain type of instrument and concentrate on the data collected with the help of that instrument. But in so doing you would have to ignore the meaning the sound may carry, and this means that the meaning of *A*'s speech does not consist of the atmospheric vibrations that *A*'s voice apparatus produces.

We may say that the source of that meaning lies in the person, and that one's personhood is beyond, or at least more than, one's physical qualities. Indeed, the physical process in which meanings are conveyed is so unessential to the process of understanding that different physical processes can carry exactly the same meaning. You can listen to a tape of *A*'s speech or read an article he has written without directly conversing with him, and still understand the same meaning. Here we see the involvement of ideality, because ideality is that which makes something meaningful independently of natural processes that carry meanings.

Leave Human Nature and Go Home

Put away "reality," which is contingent upon the sensory framework we happen to be trapped in, and we also distance ourselves from the notion of human nature. The three modes of subjectivity that relate to each other in a meaning-complex are the basic components of our personhood, and it is this kind of personhood that distinguishes us from the contingent objects we usually call "real" or "physical." If in this sense we identify ourselves as humans, then we do not have human nature. Instead, we use the word *humanitude* to designate the totality of the features that make us uniquely human.

The concept of humanitude therefore drives us back home for our authentic self-understanding from a mis-oriented realm of heteronomy. We can lose our sense of what is "real" when we realize that we can shift from one framework to another, but our sense of ideality which is inherent in humanitude will never leave us because it is un-mediated by any contingent framework. Conversely, once we have returned to the realm of ideality, we can re-establish our sense of the "real" or "objective" or "causal" since we realize that the alleged primary ontological status of materiality attached to these concepts was not well established in the first place. We can simply accept notions of immaterial reality, objectivity, and causality in relation to the notion of constitutive subjectivity, at home.

At home, we become a true creator in a limited sense and lead a kind of life the meaning of which only a creator is entitled to, as we have argued. After a thorough discussion of the intentional structure of the three modes of subjectivity, we have now understood how the non-experiential meaning as exemplified in a significant difference is inherent in the concept of humanitude.

The understanding of the three modes of subjectivity also leads to a more systematic account of the relationship between the meaning of life and creativity as we raised earlier. Creativity on the individual level is possible only if both the constitutive and conative modes (on the social level plus the communicative mode) of subjectivity are at work. Constitutive subjectivity alone gives us a sense of the world of external necessity but does not enable us to project upon open possibilities. Conative subjectivity alone allows us only to wish or desire but does not tell us what to work on and how to make things come true. Thus, to create is to strive to make the constituted world of objects proceed toward the goal projected by conative subjectivity as the external necessity allows. Accordingly, to lead a creative and thus meaningful life does not depend on any pre-determined sensory framework, nor on the alleged ontological status of materiality of the "physically real."

Materiality Discredited Again

We may interpret the notion of the material as equivalent to the notion of substance understood as the bearer of properties in the rationalist tradition. In such a case, whether we are in the actual world or in the virtual world, our senses do not have access to this kind of putative material regardless.

Causality, as shown previously, does not hinge upon materiality either. If we still want to keep the concept of the material and attribute materiality to the actual world, then we can attribute the same to the foundational part of the virtual world as well. What the objects in the expansive part are to those in the foundational part in the virtual world is what the objects of visual art are to the natural objects in the actual world. About movies and virtuality, Theodore Nelson puts it nicely:

> The *reality* of a movie includes how the scenery was painted and where the actors were repositioned between shots, but who cares? The *virtuality* of the movie is *what seems to be in it*. The *reality* of an interactive system includes its data structure and what language it's programmed in—but again, who cares? The important concern is, *what does it seem to be?*[15]

Nelson does not discuss the ontological foundation of the distinction between what is "real" and what it "seems" to be. But clearly he implies that what it seems to be is more meaningful than "reality" in a movie.

Why? Because what it seems to be is what we *intended* it to be when we started to make a movie.

5.7   Virtual Reality: The Way Home

Ethics of Intentional Reality

As we recall, Jaron Lanier suggests that a better name for VR might be *intentional* reality. But by "intentional" he emphasizes the total fluidity of the VR environment under the influence of our whims and wishes at any moment. The problem is that when this kind of fluidity is pushed to the extreme, constitutive subjectivity will be taken over by conative subjectivity and our sense of reality will be totally lost according to our phenomenological analysis. In that case, what we perceive as "objects" would be merely immediate images of our own ideas; ideas and images of ideas and objects would become indistinguishable or simply identical. Then our creative activity would be rendered impossible since there would be no gap between *things* we want to put *effort* to create on the one hand, and our projected ideas on the other. As we have shown, creativity presupposes objectivity constituted under *external necessity*, which separates objects from ideas.

Lanier, as a programmer himself, should not, of course, be ignorant of the constraints the underlying software must put on the way we construct objects in his "intentional reality." But programming is no less creative than constructing virtual objects, only on a different level. His Virtual Programming Language (VPL) will even make programming itself a special kind of virtual construction inside the same virtual world.

Thus, for the foundational part of our VR experience, we are dealing with the same type of external necessity that pertains to the *causal* connection. But since our conative (goal-projecting in the design process) and communicative (information-sharing and justification of the design) modes of subjectivity get involved *in addition to* the constitutive mode in the act of lawfully altering the sensory framework, objects become more *meaningful* than those perceived in the given framework. Apart from the experiential difference they bring about, there is a significant difference being added to the meaning-complex as part of the content of our humanitude. Thus concepts such as success, ownership, and moral responsibility discussed earlier will apply here in exactly the same way as before.

On the other hand, the expansive part of our VR experience consists of the eventualized ideality. By "eventualizing" I mean turning non-experiential meaning-complexes into spatio-temporal events that we can experience in cyberspace. Taken as a whole that includes both the creative programming for the software and the creative construction of virtual objects, our intentional projection on both collective and individual levels becomes perceived events free from external necessity or cross-level causality.

There are also, as we see, two levels of creativity involved here: the act of programming, and the act of constructing virtual objects according to the program. On the first level, the creation can be carried out either individually or collectively, as in the case of teamwork for producing huge programs. On the second, however, it's entirely up to the individual since an individual does not have a chance to interact with any other individuals who are not mere simulations. Remember, in this expansive part of our virtual experience, we only confront purely digital simulations of live or lifeless objects. To be sure, a simulated storm is not a storm and a simulated woman won't have orgasms, despite different opinions expressed by reductionists such as Daniel Dennett and Douglas Hofstadter. Here, we can use building blocks offered to us by the program to create our personal favorite environment in which to get immersed.

It's worth noticing that when we talk about the foundational and the expansive as "two parts," we do not mean that the two need to be separated in cyberspace; they are two parts only in terms of their different relationship to the world of causality. Therefore, we can and should mix the two types of objects together to enrich our experience and invite our friends to join us if they want.

The Merging of the Experiential and the Meaningful

On the expansive part, concepts such as success, ownership, and moral responsibility retain their meaning partially insofar as there remains a contrast between the collective and the individual levels of operation. But since the objectivity derived from the external necessity of natural causality has been mitigated, the possible gap between the experiential and the meaningful as we uncovered earlier is reduced to the minimum. The experienced happiness and the non-experiential meaningfulness, which are implicitly distinguished by Huxley in his *Brave New World* as we saw in the beginning of the chapter, converge in our perpetual creative engagement. Therefore, VR enriches both experience and meaning, and brings them closer to one another harmoniously in the eventualized meaning-complexes perceived by us, their very *creator*.

The Good and the Virtual

So is life in the virtual world a better life? In Western philosophical tradition since the Greeks, the goodness in life has been classified into the intrinsic and the non-intrinsic, or the good in and of itself and the good that serves an intrinsic good. Since a non-intrinsic good is valuable only in terms of its relationship to an intrinsic good, its contents depend entirely on what consequences they may lead to in serving the intrinsic good. So non-intrinsic goods are a matter of practical efficacy which does not concern us here.

Intrinsic goods, which are our true concern, have rarely been understood as anything beyond experiential happiness or transcendent meaningfulness. So let's see how VR fares with respect to both experiential happiness and transcendent meaningfulness.

Central to the conception of happiness is pleasure against pain or suffering, if meaningfulness is separately understood. In order to be happy, a person avoids pain and seeks pleasure. Does VR enriches our happiness on the experiential level? Yes. As we know, intentional objects in the expansive part of VR are created and experienced by one and the same person. If a person always avoids pain and seeks pleasure, then those objects must bring the person more pleasure than pain if the person knows what she wants.

On the other hand, the notion of transcendent meaningfulness is always based on an understanding of what human beings are supposed to be. On this score, our concept of humanitude incorporates the idea of meaningfulness and that of the uniqueness of humanity at a single stroke. Our VR experience as eventualized meaning-complexes is therefore intrinsically good if the good is non-experientially understood.

Therefore VR experience is intrinsically good in both experiential and transcendent senses. Since the intrinsic good in either sense does not depend on the materiality of the objective world, there is no way VR can deprive human life of intrinsic values. On the contrary, VR enriches these values in a revolutionary way. It brings us from the falsely concocted world of materiality back to the world of the meaningful, the home of humanitude. Can we say that the Hegelian absolute Geist is returning home from an alienated and temporarily objectified world of materiality?

Huxley's worry that individual freedom will be replaced with a total control by an authoritarian government in a "scientific caste system" is therefore finally eased in the virtual world. If the authority does not return to the physical world and threaten to inflict physical harm on individuals, the control won't be able to go beyond the necessary minimum.

Should We Erase the Boundary?

Should we therefore erase the experiential boundary between the physical and the virtual so we will never be able to tell which world we are in? Of course not. The reason is simple after we discussed the relationship between a significant difference and a real difference. If there is a difference between the two levels of sensory perception but we are not able to tell the difference, the meaning of our life is negatively affected. On the other hand, if we give up the distinction, we would have let go a fundamental option on the ontological level, and thus jeopardize our freedom of choice at the very bottom. By the same token, an actual migration to VR is not the best choice either: Why should we abandon one for the other if they are reciprocal ontologically?

Should we then claim that there is no danger in our acceptance of VR and cyberspace? No, there is indeed a danger, which we will discuss in the next chapter. After that, we will explicate further implications of the concept of humanitude for understanding VR as a possible vehicle of eternal meaning. In the discussion, we will also realize how our understanding of personal identity from the first-person perspective as the unified reference for all possible sensory frameworks is essential to a correct evaluation of VR.

6

VR and the Destiny of Humankind

Steer your passion out of the little nest
Inhale the whole space into your chest
Stage your final ontological protest
Let the eternal light unfold all the rest

"New Genesis," Z. Zhai, 1997

6.1   The Fragility of Technological Civilization

The "Dark Side" of Cyberspace

So what is the most dangerous aspect of VR or the "dark side" of cyberspace? It is the Reality Engine breakdown, of course. This could happen on both the hardware and software levels. As a result, we could have an accident of virtual reality annihilation or cyberspace collapse, comparable to a collision of the earth with another planet in the actual world!

The fragility of our technological civilization has been a major topic of reflection in the critical tradition of philosophy for decades. Our dependence on an interlocked technological system designed by our fallible fellow beings makes us vulnerable at least in two senses. The first is that we are always susceptible to the strike by our hidden "not-know-what" wrapped in every case of know-how. A typical example is that no matter how much new information we have accumulated by analyzing the black boxes of crashed airplanes, airplanes continue to crash due to unexpected causes. In a computer program, there is no way for us to be sure that there are no more bugs there despite our endless effort to debug it. Sooner or later, bugs will attack us when we expect them the least.

The second source of our vulnerability is our own misconduct. Because we are the designers of the technological system, we know how to control it; and by controlling it, anyone can command a tremendous amount of

Chapter Six

energy for many purposes in a split of a second. If a person happens to have the access and also happens to have a desire to destroy a great part of the civilization, he or she can do it simply by, perhaps, pushing a button.

Without exception, VR, as a result of the most sophisticated technology, harbors these two sources of danger. A bug in the software, or a person's destructive conduct in shutting down the Super Reality Engine would be enough to cause a total disaster. For this reason, we definitely need a backup system. For such a purpose, we can certainly build a few extra Reality Engines, but the final haven should be the actual world itself, which we did not create and of which we do not know where the "Engine" is or how it works.

Don't Abandon This World!

This is why we *should not* abandon the actual world even though we could move to the virtual world permanently. So the key issue is how to keep going back and forth between the virtual and actual worlds so that we can always live comfortably in either world without forgetting the basic skills for survival in the other world. After all, why should we keep only one option if we can have two? We may choose to spend most of our lifetime in VR for its unlimited possibilities of creative interface, but we should never close the door back to the actual world.

Here we seem to see a breakdown of the reciprocity between the virtual and actual worlds. In fact, the ontological reciprocity still holds here since in the actual world, we also face the same type of uncertainty. There is no guarantee of safety in the actual world as the final haven. All accidents in our life and all large-scale natural disasters in the actual world can be understood as manifestations of the malfunction of the hidden Reality Engine. It's possible that one day the whole universe will simply stop running due to an accidental system breakdown.

No Hero in the Wife's Eye

But why do we feel safer in the actual world? Because as the creator of VR we know how its infrastructure is imperfect. But the actual world is given to us without our knowledge of its infrastructure. In our scientific exploration we simply assume its lawfulness and in our religious faith we simply assume its perfection. At the present, VR based on the kind of computation machine and the kind of robot we can envisage seems to be far less elastic than the actual world we have been used to.

Can we therefore conclude that the actual world must be safer than the virtual world forever? No. There is nothing that can, in principle, prevent us from improving the elasticity of our VR infrastructure. Someday our Reality Engine of VR might become more reliable than the hidden engine of the actual world. It is possible because our Reality Engine can be based upon the more reliable part of nature on the one hand, and teleoperation will enable us to avoid direct contact with the destructive part of the natural world on the other.

We do not feel that we are re-creating the empirical world anew because we know who the co-authors are and how they are doing it in general terms. We are like the hero's wife who knows her man too well to regard him as a hero. On the contrary, we have no clue how the natural world came about, and do not know why dinosaurs were wiped out and HIV invaded us, for example. So we revere whatever agent, if any, is behind the scene as the Super-Being. Consequently, we tend to regard the totality of the universe as perfect even though it appears to us as imperfect.

Nothing Is Thick

VR seems to be illusory because it cuts through the thickness of materiality between the external necessity and the vividness of our perceptual experience. Our notion of reality seems to require that kind of materialistic thickness. But our analysis all along has shown that such a sense of thickness itself is no more than our own construct. In modern physics, the thickness of elementary particles is replaced by the interactive events of the pervasive field. Light is understood as the limiting instance of materiality because its thickness is infinitely approximate to zero. The speed of light, therefore, is the upper limit of possible speed. Light does not depend on anything else to propagate; instead, it appears to be the final "stuff" of all other stuff. In the Special Theory of Relativity, the speed of light, as a constant, functions as the ultimate measuring stick for physical distance, which is the condition of the notion of thickness. But light itself is massless and never stays anywhere. It is like the Tao of the cosmos, from which come and to which return all the material and immaterial things and non-things.

But all the coming-from and returning-to still seems to take a path of detour through that thickness of materiality in the actual world as long as our perception of the world depends on a burdensome conception of the masses. In the expansive part of VR, however, this kind of mandatory burden is overcome once and for all. Light becomes the only "stuff" we need to deal with. Our perceptual experience is now in an immediate contact with light; the speed of our interaction with the environment is the same as the speed of the digital interface. We have returned to the Tao of everything!

Biologically Mortal

In order to continue our worldly life, however, we need to postpone such an ultimate return. Our perceptual experience depends on the biological processes of our body. If we want to maintain such biological processes, we need to work in the foundational part of VR now and then to submit ourselves to the mandatory causal order. In such a causal order, we are, unfortunately, deemed to be mortal beings: each of us, as an individual, will die sooner or later. Immortality in the experiential sense is beyond us.

However, VR is not only a place of perceptual experience, but also a place of meaning-complexes. Since our personhood is anchored in, but goes beyond, the experiential contents through the operation of constitutive and conative subjectivity, as we discussed in the last chapter, humanitude will perpetuate in the realm of ideality. Insofar as VR enables us to become unprecedentedly creative, it enhances our ability to project our intentionality to form much richer meaning-complexes in the realm of ideality. In the first place, our personhood as individualized humanitude transcends experiential contents and is thus already immortal in a mitigated sense. Insofar as VR or cyberspace is an arena of our interactive creation, it will certainly enrich our immortal personhood in this sense. So let us further examine this concept of non-experiential immortality.

6.2   The Question of Death

Meaningfully Immortal

Looking back to ancient Greece, we recall that Plato dealt with the question of death in his reflection on the question of mortality. For Plato, only the immortal soul is to live the life of "truths," which consists in a proximity to the eternal "Forms." If we replace his Forms with meaning-complexes, then our concept of immortality will hinge upon the notion of ideality. To be sure, what Plato had in mind is the conviction that our mundane life in the realm of becoming is an imitation of the divine life in the realm of being, and that the ultimate source of the meaning of life is to be found only in the realm of being. For us, the non-experiential personhood is anchored in life but it does not need to "live" forever in order to be eternally meaningful.

For many contemporary philosophers, the concept of immortality does not need to be based on a metaphysical doctrine of eternal Forms or divinity. When the existentialist philosopher Jean-Paul Sartre claims that human life is a continuous striving toward being God, he means, like Plato, that we are destined to desire immortality. But unlike Plato, he does not mean that God as an immortal being is a thing-in-itself-for-itself *by* itself. For Sartre, God is assumed to be such-and-such only as a guiding principle that defines the existential condition of human life. That is, a notion of the immortal God is held by some people because they want to make reality and ideality one and the same.

Death Never Experienced

Martin Heidegger is among the few philosophers of modern times who are deeply concerned with, and have given a full account of, the problem of death. In *Being and Time*, human life is characterized as, among other things, Being-towards-death. Heidegger says that death

> is not something to which Dasein ultimately comes only in its demise. In Dasein, as being towards its death, its own uttermost "not-yet" has already been included.[1]

Such a claim seems to suggest that even when we are in the best of health we are nonetheless in fact dying. If so the claim would be either a trivial truism or a plain falsity depending upon how we define the term "dying": trivial if "dying" means approaching the temporal endpoint of organic life, false if it means, as it does in ordinary language, being fatally ill.

When Heidegger claims that the question of death is inherently connected with the question of the wholeness of life, he seems to touch upon the question of the limit or boundary of life. Although Heidegger's jargon is confusing and subject to various interpretations by both his admirers and critics, we, fortunately, do not have to be involved in controversies about his thought. It suffices for us to see how the question of death is essential to understanding the human desire to transcend the destiny of mortality.

At any self-conscious moment of the life process, one can always pose the question of "to-be-or-not-to-be." If one is not under the control of an alien power, one can always be confronted with the choice between continuing to exist and committing suicide. In other words, to live implies a possibility of self-negation. But how is the awareness of this possibility essential to making us value-creating beings?

Heidegger calls the possibility of death Dasein's "ownmost possibility." If this is understood as meaning that death is a human being's most intimate experience of all, as some interpreters believe, then it will certainly be false. Nobody can "experience" one's own death, because in its very sense death is the end of the experiencing subject. This holds even when there is an immortal soul that survives physical death, because insofar as the soul does not die, there is no possibility for it to experience *its* own death. Or, if the soul does experience death, this soul must be something other than the human being who dies. How can we make sense of death as the most intimate experience at all?

One might tend to think of "death" as equivalent to "dying"—as the process of getting closer to the end of life when fatally ill. But there is no evidence that there is any essential difference between the experience of a fatal illness and that of a curable one. On the contrary, our common practice is based on the belief that the patient is in no better a position than anyone else to know (through private experience) whether or not he is going to die. Thus, if we believe that there is a difference here, we have to refrain from treating some patients the way we have been treating them in order to be performatively consistent.

Obviously, Heidegger is not concerned with the physical process of dying—he is supposed to be dealing with the ontological questions of Being instead of the "ontic" questions of beings. But here we are concerned with the contrast between the finite experiential contents of human life and the infinite radiation of meaning from these contents of life. We need to explicate the connection between our implicit understanding of death and the initial condition for normative claims about the meaning of life in general.

Death is the negation of life, and this is why the notion of death is a delimiting concept for understanding the totality of life. On the empirical level, in order for an assertion to be cognitively meaningful, as some analytic philosophers have correctly pointed out, both the assertion and the negation of it must cover logically possible states of affairs. Thus, from an external observer's point of view, the contrast between the life and the death of *others* is the basis for our grasp of the referential meaning of "life." Therefore, an understanding of death may be a vantage point that connects the subjective experience of an ego to an intersubjective life-world experience.

I can experience my own pleasure, pain, anxiety, etc., which are not experiencible by anyone else in the same way. In fact, if my pleasure and pain ever occur, I *must* and cannot fail to experience them, since my experiencing them and their being present are one and the same process. But in the case of death, no such kind of identity holds. On the contrary, the presence of experience in me shows that I am not yet dead. What I have been experiencing may be anything, the fear of death, an illusion of ascending to heaven, the nightmare of witnessing my body being burned, or something else, but not my death as such. So regardless of whether there is an afterlife, it is safe to say that nobody, as a human being, can possibly experience his or her own death.

Nobody else can tell me about the experience of death either, because he or she is in no better a position to experience death than I since he or she is still alive. If neither experience of my own death nor knowledge of death from others is possible, then death as my own destiny must be understood negatively as the negation of my ongoing life as a whole. In that case, we do not experience death itself, but the anticipation of death as the possibility and eventuality of no longer being. We confront death intentionally but not actually.

Thus, we have an alternative way to interpret Heidegger's thesis: we do not actually experience death, but understand the meaning of death as intrinsically linked to the experience of the "wholeness" of life. By "wholeness" we refer to the apprehension of death not only as the temporal end of life but also as the logical counterpart of life that makes intelligible our life experience as the originator of a unified meaning-complex that goes beyond life. If an intentional confrontation with death is not *the* way, it is certainly *a* way to an adequate grasp of the meaning of life in its relation to Being as such. Our understanding of the meaning of death leads us to see what is beyond death in terms of eternal ideality.

6.3 Transcendence of Personhood and Immortality

Little Anthony's Dying Wish

From: Cibotti Ron
Sent: Thursday, November 14, 1996 6:20 AM
To: DiTomaso, Lisa; Markou, Mike; Nedder, Carol; Snelling, Richard;
  Dunne, Susan
Subject: FW: Fwd: pls forward this one :)

This little boy at the Mayo Clinic is very sick and he knows that he will die. Well you know how they have those "Make a Wish Foundations" that give terminally ill kids a dying wish, well this is kind of like that. He likes computers and his wish is to live forever by having his chain letter be eternally passed on the Internet. This is not some joke. And for those of you who care please send this to as many people as possible so his wish can be granted. (THIS IS NOT A CHAIN LETTER JUST DO SOMETHING NICE FOR ONCE!) It is all the way down at the bottom.

[names of dozens of forwarders and their sympathetic comments deleted here by Zhai]
———————————— Forwarded message begins here ————————————

From: Anthony Parkin
<Parkin@MayoHospital.health.com
Date: Wed, 17 Apr 1996 12:46:46 +080 To: Amy E Nygaard [e-mail address here erased by Zhai]
Subject: My dying wish

   My name is Anthony Parkin, and you don't know me. I'm 7 years old, and I have leukemia. I found your name using gopher, and I would like for you to carry out my dying wish of starting chain letter. Please send this letter to five people you know so I can live forever.

Thank You very much

What you have just read is a piece of e-mail I actually received on 3 January 1997. What do you think about little Anthony? Is his wish total nonsense or does he make some sense, or strong sense, on the matter of immortality? Why did the forwarders of his e-letter feel some kind of obligation to help fulfill his wish even though they usually hate to participate in a chain-letter campaign? Suppose Anthony dies before he gets to know of their support—does it make any difference to Anthony whether this letter is being distributed continuously or not?

The Little Boy's Immortal Personhood

After our discussion of a significant difference versus a real difference in the last chapter, we know that the answer is that there is no *real* difference but there is a *significant* difference to Anthony even though he can in no way experience the difference. What we do after his death matters to him in a significant way.

In *The Radical Choice and Moral Theory*,[2] I discussed the transcendence of ideality at length. But I did not show its tight connection to the notion of immortality. Here, I will reiterate my argument in a similar way, but in a new context.

As we established in the last chapter, we understand personhood in terms of the meaning complex that constitutes a person's identity, and personhood thus transcends the person's physical existence. Even though one's personhood is inseparable from one's status as an acting agent, the scope of one's personhood extends beyond one's capacity for action. Personhood also transcends one's physical death, even though one's concrete life in the world is the anchor of the meaning complex of which one's personhood consists. This meaning complex is not the same as an *idea* of a person. We can even speak of the Being of personhood, if such a use of the word does not commit us to a metaphysics of person-substance. The point is that even though we are not sure whether we can say that personhood *exists*, we have nevertheless shown that our language pertaining to human life does assume its underlying function. As we recall, concepts such as success, ownership, and morality assume non-experiential significance apart from anybody's opinion or knowledge of the relevant facts.

What is said above can easily be interpreted to mean something we are already familiar with, namely, that a human being is the being who is aware of the meaning of his or her actions. But this presupposes that our being is logically separable from the meaning complex, and such an assumption of the separability is exactly what makes all traditional accounts of personal identity problematic. What we insist upon here is that the meaning complex, which is neither the same as our awareness of meanings nor as any one single isolated meaning, is exactly what we take as essential when we speak of personhood. Personhood thus understood transcends space and time, and nobody can possibly terminate it. It is necessarily immortal. But personhood is also anchored in one's experiential life by one's desires.

My desires are an important component of my life and I cannot have any desire without actually living in the world. My ability to have desires evidences my possession of conative subjectivity. But the satisfaction of my desires goes beyond my life. Let me use the same two examples I used in the other book to show how.

My Great-Grandchildren and Beth's Stepfather

Suppose I desire that one of my great-grandchildren becomes a great musician. This may or may not be satisfied after my death. If one of my great-grandchildren does become a great musician, then my desire is satisfied; if not, then it is not. Thus what happens after my death affects the fulfillment of my life, not by causing actual effects, but by entering into my personhood through its concord or discord with my expectation or my projected *telos*, and thus enters into the meaning complex around my life. Thus construed, the satisfaction of my desire does not necessarily require that I actually experience the satisfaction.

Suppose now that Beth regards knowing who her true parents are as one of the most important parts of her life. But she has lived and died with confidence that the one she called "father" was indeed her father, when in fact he was not. Has she lost that important part of her life according to her own criterion? In a very important sense, she has, even though she never actually realized the fact and was therefore never psychologically disillusioned before her death. That is to say, her personhood is affected by the distorted meaning complex pertaining to her life, which is independent of her actual life-experience.

A Pleasing yet Worthless Life

In both examples above, the satisfaction of a desire is not a psychological event in the sense of achieving the aim of the desire, quieting that same desire and resting the conation; to put it another way, the desire is not satisfied *experientially*. Since desires, as a mode of conative subjectivity, are intentional, their object need not be limited in the span of one's lifetime and thus be realized therein actually. But a desire must in principle be satisfiable. Thus if I desire X, where X's actual accomplishment is beyond my life experience, my desire of X is satisfiable *transcendently*.

Because the transcendent satisfaction of one's desires is of utmost importance, a life full of experiential satisfaction based on, for example, an overall deception, is psychologically pleasing but not very much worth living. To be sure, here we do mean the life itself, not the concept of a life. In this case we see that even though all the experience in someone's life is positive and full in that person's or anybody else's eyes, it can still be a life unfulfilled in its authenticity. This again shows that the meaning complex that identifies a particular person and that can develop differently than that person or anybody may have intended or may even know is essential to human life.

In this sense, the formation of our personhood goes far beyond our life, even if we do not believe in an afterlife or human soul. In a similar way, what we have said about one's desires and their satisfaction also applies to other intentional activities and their transcendent counterparts. One's prediction, which is also intentional, may be verified or falsified after one's death, and the outcome contributes to the shaping of the meaning complex in one's personhood.

Suppose a historian who died five hundred years ago predicted that World War III would break out in the year 2005. If in 1997 we saw the danger and worked hard to prevent the predicted war, what we do will contribute a great deal to the making of the historian's personhood with regard to the meaning complex involved in the intelligible relation between the war and the prediction. This is so even if, keep in mind, nobody ever knows about the historian's prediction and there is no record thereof, because the connection between meanings does not depend on any empirical interactions. Thus whenever we read Plato's *Republic* and interpret or misinterpret it, we are re-shaping Plato's personhood, even though Plato had no way to experience anything about it. But such a trans-empirical connection is anchored in Plato's experiential life through his act of writing that book.

In any event, as an essential feature of subjectivity, conative projection connects our life-experience to the trans-empirical constitutive subjectivity. Inasmuch as the meaningfulness of life-experience is based on the meaning-complexes of one's personhood, it acquires the same non-empirical character of transcendental subjectivity in spite of its direct connection to the experiential aspect of human life.

Human Soul Refurbished

In fact, our concept of personhood is a substitute for the popular concept of the human soul. The difficulty in the concept of a soul is that it tries to combine two incompatible ideas in one. On the one hand, a soul, as the continuation of a person's meaningful experience, is supposed to take no physical space and have no sensations. On the other hand, a soul is also supposed to be able to move around like a spatial entity and to experience the sensible world like a corporeal being. The personhood of a person, however, captures all the meaningful elements of a person's being while leaving out the idea of entitative existence apart from worldly existence.

Now, even though meaning intrinsically relates to an intentional subject either actually or potentially, the actual awareness of a particular meaning by a person, any person, is not a necessary condition for that meaning to enter into the meaning complex of a person's personhood. It is nevertheless anchored in the person's real life through conative projection. Thus, insofar as that meaning is the one in which the person participates by the operation of subjectivity which is intentional and always transcends itself, what happens in the world after that person ceases to exist can still pertain to that person by entering into his or her personhood. Just as subjectivity is not a separable and independent entity that "exists," personhood need not be a ghost-like quasi-entity either; nay, it must not be.

In fact, in the Chinese tradition there has been a similar notion of immortality separate from a belief in immortal souls. This Chinese understanding of immortality prescribes three ways a person may become immortal: by doing great deeds (*li-gong*), setting great moral examples (*li-de*), or uttering great words (*li-yan*). Evidently, none of the three has anything to do with a soul; all of them pertain, however, to the origin of the meaning-complex that follows: how much can you leave behind as a contribution to the overall meaning of humanity after you kiss this world goodbye?

Humanitude Revisited

But as we see, this transcendency of personhood is logically correlative to the experiential contents of a person's life. Only a living human being can have desires, make predictions, and the like. And it is the having of desires or making of predictions or the like that makes one's either experiential or transcendent fulfillment possible.

In principle, when we talk about anything that transcends, we must at the same time suppose an empirically identifiable counterpart above and across which something can transcend. In this respect, transcendent personhood retains its affinity to transcendental ideality. When we say that ideality is logically *prior* to objectivity, what we mean is that whenever we understand the empirical world, we understand it within a dimension of ideality—the dimension of meaning, which is transcendentally conditioned. This is true as well when we try to understand ideality itself, that is, we understand it within the dimension of ideality. But this does not mean that in our understanding we can make sense of ideality without the empirical. To be sure, that which is transcendent and ideal must transcend something other than itself. This shows how and to what extent transcendent personhood pertains to transcendental subjectivity. Consequently, how humanitude as discussed in the previous chapter transcends empirical objectivity becomes evident, because personhood is simply the content of humanitude anchored in an individual person.

Therefore, personhood designates the unique sphere of meaningfulness that distinguishes one person from another. A human being's personhood is interwoven with every other's personhood and thus we have a common sphere of personhood-interconnectedness. This is so because we not only interact in the actual world so as to share a common ground for anchoring points, but also enter into each other's meaning complexes in the world of ideality.

This does not mean, however, that we can share the same personhood. The uniqueness of the configuration of each complex of anchoring points guarantees the uniqueness of each unit of meaning complexes of the personhood. It is from one's unique personhood that purposes emanate that lead a person to act upon the actual world. In principle, nobody's personhood is the same as any other's. Like subjectivity, therefore, the personhood of a human being transcends the natural order of the world, and thus makes us immortal in a mitigated, non-experiential sense. Now we can understand why little Anthony makes a lot of sense in connecting his desire of living forever to the unlimited possibilities of cyberspace.

6.4   What Could Happen Soon

No Hype

This is not a book of futuristic predictions of VR technology, so we have not been concerned with the possible timetable of VR development in the near future. In fact, the validity of the positions argued in this book does not depend on whether VR will flourish or diminish in the future. We are stretching the *idea* of VR to its logical extreme so as to see its ontological implications for human life and the entire civilization if we take the path.

But after this intense and intriguing process of philosophical struggle, we might want to relax a little bit and try to see what could happen in our daily life before we die, if you are, like me, in your late thirties. Such an estimate does not depend on the force of logic, which is the strength of this book; it is rather based on crude extrapolations from the latest reports.

Entertainment could be the first public area in which VR will prevail. People speculate that sooner or later VR will replace television and movies. That is, instead of watching, you will participate in a story. Here the expansive part of VR will develop much sooner than the foundational part. In such a case, we will at first still be able to make sense in calling the VR experience "illusory."

How soon and to what extent VR will actually replace other types of entertainment is contingent upon many factors, including the technological, social/political, economical, ideological, and psychological, and so forth, about which I do not know much more than anybody else. But it is fairly reasonable to assume that things comparable, in complexity, to the following scenario will be available before long.

Take a Virtual Shower

You go to an amusement park and buy a ticket for a "virtual shower." When it's your turn, you enter a locker room and take off your clothes. A laser scanner then scans your body while a scale takes your weight. You then enter a closet that encloses you like a peanut inside the shell, and the only difference is that the complex structure of the shell allows your limbs to be separately enclosed. The shell is made of heavy material but the surface in touch with your skin is planted with micro-sensors and stimulators that give you continuously changing tactile and thermal sensations all over your body. The shell is driven by sophisticated motors that are controlled by a computer, which receives signals from the sensors on the shell. Under your feet is a treadmill that allows you to walk without leaving the shell. The motion of the treadmill generated by your walk will also, of course, be detected by the computer. Right in front of your eyes is a 3-D display and next to your ears are stereophones. In such a setting, you can move your limbs and your whole body freely but the shell will also be able to let you feel changing pressure, temperature, heaviness of objects, and so forth, through those stimulators.

As soon as the system is turned on, you are immersed in a 3-D environment as if you were in the tub, unclothed and ready to take a shower. You bend over and push the knob to turn on the water. You feel hot water running from the fountain head all over your body; you see and hear everything exactly like what you see and hear in a real shower!

Such a "virtual shower" is relatively easy to implement because the feeling of hot running water over the body is repetitive; so is the image of the running water. We do not have to coordinate the tactile feeling with the image in a strict manner. For that reason, the tactile feeling and the visual image can be largely pre-programmed or pre-recorded if we have a tactile recording system. Also, the motion-tracking need not be very complicated either since taking a shower does not involve very complicated body movement and the player is confined in a narrow area. So a "virtual shower" does not take an awful lot of computational power, while the effect on the player could be extremely impressive.

Shopping on the Web

One of the major problems of online shopping today is that customers cannot see and touch the merchandise before they pay for it. Since the launching of VRML language, many 3-D Web sites have been constructed. But this is still far away from a Web-based cyberspace as we discussed in chapter 2.

In the foreseeable future, some halfway VR with partial tactile stimulation will be available and affordable. You won't wear a bodysuit nor walk on a treadmill. You will only have a helmet and a pair of gloves, but you can still pick up a teddy bear and turn it over, then squeeze it and hear an "Ouch!" from it. You can also fetch a tape recorder and push its play button to hear it playing. Of course, these items are only virtual items as a means of advertisement. In order to be able to test the item you want delivered to your home, a very sophisticated system of teleoperation has to be built. But that is unlikely to happen soon in the area of online shopping.

VR Conferencing

Multimedia conferencing is already gaining popularity each day. But VR conferencing requires more than multimedia. It has to be immersive and at least involve partial sense of touch in addition to the stereo video-audio coordination. At a VR conference, participants should be able to shake hands with each other, and pass documents around and write on them. Such a real-time coordination requires, perhaps, much more computational power than the "virtual shower," but is within our reach soon.

Making Love while Continents Apart

When we discussed cybersex and human reproduction in chapter 2, we took it as an integral part of the possible virtual world, which is ontologically equivalent to the actual world. That could be achieved through a seamless total combination of digital simulation, sensory immersion, and functional teleoperation. In the near future, however, we can have simpler versions of cybersex without the concern of procreation.

We don't have to follow the paradigm of the CD-ROM striptease, though. It could happen between, perhaps, a husband and his wife when one is on a business trip. In a setting similar to what was described in chapter 2, the genital motion of both partners here would not have to be real-time coordinated. But we could add more fun to it by changing the view of the love scene—so both partners could zoom in and zoom out so as to see themselves from different angles and distances at will. They could also change their looks and body sizes or shapes and thus experience richer variations. Or the two partners could exchange their perspectives during the foreplay and thus experience something like an erotic spiritual union. This kind of exchange of perspective is structurally equivalent to Adam and Bob in CCS as discussed in chapter 1.

Walk through . . .

Medical applications of VR are among the first practical fields of research in which Jaron Lanier got involved. These applications belong to the so-called augmented reality. An immersive field of vision enhanced by electronic or mechanical devices will enable your doctor to walk through internal organs as we recall. By VR walkthrough, architects and their customers can inspect and have a feel inside a finished house before the house is built. Actually, some VRML 3-D Web sites already have non-immersive versions of that.

Educational VR and Virtual Art

Probably HITL at the University of Washington is currently at the forefront of the educational applications of VR. Students will "enter into" the structure of a molecule, for example. As for VR art, it's not hard to imagine what it will be like to be a sculptor in a virtual environment. Lanier as a musician has been very active in VR music. In fact, the whole expansive part of VR is nothing but an immersive type of art. It is precisely because of the artistic nature of virtual experience that we celebrate it as a habitat of humanitude that allows us to be extremely creative and lead a meaning-rich life.

Of course, there will be more, expected and unexpected. Disney World alone will bring us more and more VR excitement in their studios and theaters, I bet. And the Japanese will also surprise us time and again in the coming decades.

No matter what may happen next, we do not want to limit our vision in the immediate future. Keep in mind, our major concern is the ontological implications of VR in terms of its ultimate possibility.

6.5 Virtual Reality and the Ontological Re-Creation

Let's Swim in the Sea of Meaning

Now that personhood is transcendent and anchored in a person's experiential life through the act of the person's conative subjectivity, the structure that makes possible the transcendent personhood must be what makes us human. That is, humanitude must consist in experientially anchored transcendent personhood.

Cyberspace, as we have demonstrated, is a collectively built platform on which human experiential contents are generated through digital-perceptual interface by our own creative power. On this platform, the unity of constitutive subjectivity, intersubjectivity, and objectivity is shown in an unambiguous concreteness. We can say that, in a sense, VR is a series of eventualized meaning complexes, or perceptualized ideality.

VR is fluid. This kind of fluidity not only facilitates our self-affirming act of creation, but also mobilizes our self-transcending act of re-creation. It enables us to appreciate the mitigated immortality with a playful spirit. The spirit that is returning from a materially objectified alien world has to be, by its destiny, seriously playful. Such a playful spirit navigating in cyberspace is beginning to learn to swim in the ontologically "decoded flow," to use French philosopher Gilles Deleuze's words.

One may argue that, by rendering our action in cyberspace non-consequential, VR deprives human life of the ethical contents necessary for a meaningful life. After our discussion in the previous chapter, we are now ready to see why such an argument is misconceived. On the one hand, it puts the cart before the horse. How good a human life is depends on how meaningful that life is, and morality is about the responsibility for such goodness. The meaningfulness is therefore more fundamental than morality in human life, not the other way around. On the other hand, our teleoperation in the foundational part of VR remains as consequential as our act in the actual world. Therefore, morality there retains its consequentialist relevance, or even more so if it increases our ability to control the natural process: isn't our moral responsibility for a consequence proportional to the degree of our creative contribution to that consequence?

The Media That Shape Our Being

Marshall McLuhan has made us aware of the visible and invisible power the media have upon us in the formation of our self-identity on the social-psychological level, and Sherry Turkle is shifting our attention from the television screen to the computer screen on that matter. But VR or cyberspace, as we are dealing with them here, unfolds the structure of our self-identity on the metaphysical level. Since the purpose of ethics is to serve our social life, we cannot justify our inclination to take the consequentialist consideration in the actual world as a universal measure of values. Unless we trace back to the source of the ultimate meaning as the foundation of morality, we cannot do justice to any attempt to universalize our pre-conceived moral precepts beyond the scope of immediate evidence. Listen to what our visionary Michael Heim has to say:

> VR is bringing about something new in our relationship to technology in general. . . . After all, is not VR the world reborn in artificial form? . . . we are positioning ourselves to create whole worlds in which we will pass part of our lives.[3]

Yes, we will pass "part of our lives" rather than our entire lives, as a matter of choice. Maybe it's too early, but we can still celebrate the debut of VR and sing a meaning-rich, sexy cyber-song:

The Metaphysical Maturity of Civilization

Civilizations have envisioned reality by combining beliefs, rituals, customs, institutions, habits, arts, arguments, myths, and so on. Since such a combination is not made on the basis of crystallized evidence of the harmonious interaction among these component parts, an explicit clarification has always been in demand. But attempts at such a clarification produce their own problem of coherence, now manifest on the symbolic level. Since we cannot but use concepts to clarify, we have been led to a hopeless struggle between our drive for comprehensive synthesis on the one hand and our propensity for depending on the separating function of words on the other. We postulate an intangible world of "realities" in terms of tangible features without knowing the necessarily self-defeating nature of such a postulate: how can the intangible be understood as tangible without a self-contradiction?

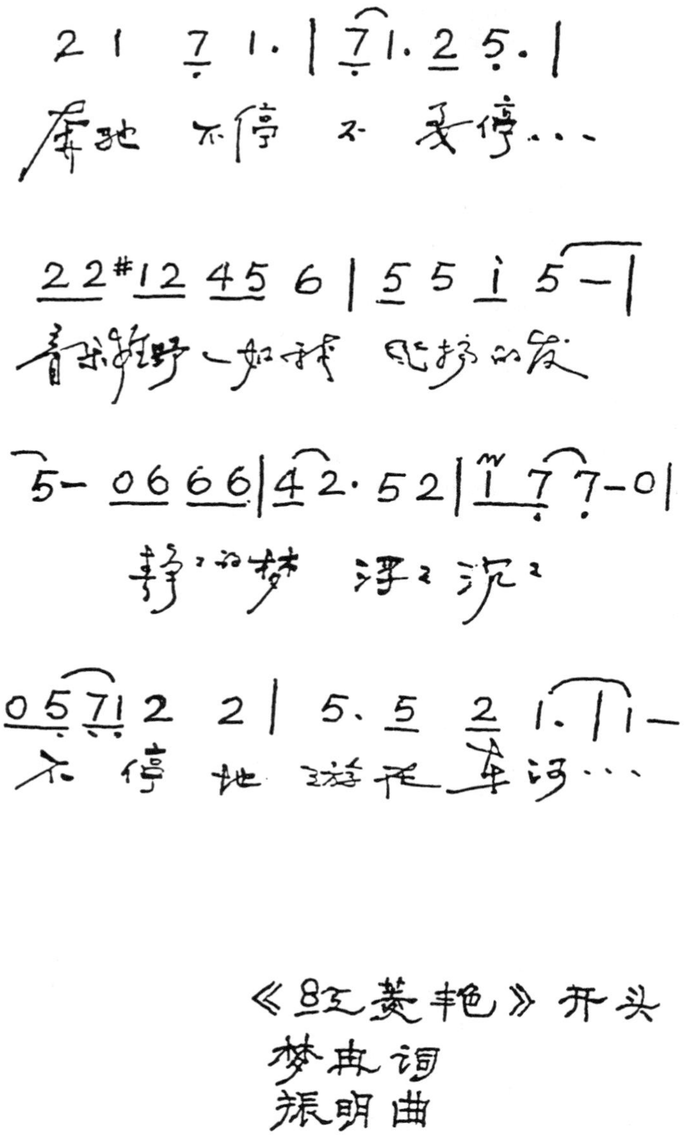

Figure 6.1 The beginning of a song in numerical notation and Chinese words.

With the invention of VR we are beginning to reach a stage of metaphysical maturity such that we can see through, without destructive disillusionment, the trick of the alleged materialistic thickness. We welcome it as an occasion for our participation in the Ultimate Re-Creation.

Appendix

Jaron Lanier's Virtual Reality Debut Interview

A Vintage Virtual Reality Interview[1]

This interview captures some of the wild bliss I exuded in my twenties as I told the world about Virtual Reality for the first time. It was first published in 1988 or so in *Whole Earth Review*, but was conducted a few years earlier. It was reprinted many times in many languages.

Adam Heilbrun: The word 'virtual' is computer jargon. Could you clarify it for those unfamiliar with the concept?

Jaron Lanier: Maybe we should go over what Virtual Reality is. We are speaking about a technology that uses computerized clothing to synthesize shared reality. It recreates our relationship with the physical world in a new plane, no more, no less. It doesn't affect the subjective world; it doesn't have anything to do directly with what's going on inside your brain. It only has to do with what your sense organs perceive. The physical world, the thing on the other side of your sense organs, is received through these five holes, the eyes, and the ears, and the nose, and the mouth, and the skin. They're not holes, actually, and there are many more senses than five but that's the old model, so we'll just stick with it for now.

Before you enter the Virtual Reality you'll see a pile of clothing that you have to put on in order to perceive a different world than the physical world. The clothing consists of mostly a pair of glasses and a pair of gloves. Exactly what clothing there will be it's too early to say because there are a lot of different variations that are possible and it's really too early to predict which will be the most popular ones. A minimal kind of Virtual Reality outfit would have a pair of glasses and a glove that you put on. The glasses allow you to perceive the visual world of Virtual Reality. Instead of having transparent lenses, they have visual displays that are rather like small three-dimensional televisions. They're much more sophisticated than small televisions, of course, because they have

175

to present a three-dimensional world to you that's convincing, and there's some technology involved in accomplishing that, but that's a good metaphor.

When you put them on you suddenly see a world that surrounds you—you see the virtual world. It's fully three-dimensional and it surrounds you, and as you move your head to look around, the images that you see inside the eyeglasses are shifted in such a way that an illusion is created that while you're moving around the virtual world is standing still. The images come from a very powerful special computer which I like to call the Home Reality Engine. It will be sitting there in your room and will plug into the phone outlet. I'll say some more words about the Home Reality Engine in a second, but let's stay with the glasses for now.

There's another thing that the glasses do. At the end of the stems they have little headphone speakers very much like a Walkman, which allow you to hear the sounds of the virtual world. There's nothing too unusual there; they're just exactly like your everyday Walkman speakers. The sounds you hear on them are a little bit unusual in that they're processed to have three-dimensional quality; they come from certain directions. The glasses do one other thing too; they have sensors in them that can sense your facial expression. This is very important because you are a part of the Virtual Reality and the clothing that you wear has to sense as much as it can about your body. It uses that information to control the virtual version of your body, which both you and other people perceive as being you in the Virtual Reality. So, for instance, you might choose to become a cat in Virtual Reality, or really anything. If you're a cat you might very well be wired, so to speak, so that when you smile in the real world the cat that you are in Virtual Reality smiles. As your eyes dart around looking, the eyes of the cat dart around as well. And so the eye glasses also have a function in sensing your face.

The headset, the eyeglasses—they're sometimes called eyephones—you have to remember that we're witnessing the birth of a culture here, so a lot of terms aren't really settled down into being a particular way just yet. I think we have to give the community of people working in Virtual Reality a chance to jostle about these different possibilities before we decide definitely what things are called and exactly what they'll do. But this is a very plausible setup here that I'm describing. You wear gloves on your hands. These allow you to reach out and feel things that aren't really there. The inside of the surface of the glove has tactile stimulators so that when the Home Reality Engine can tell that your hand is touching a virtual object (even though there's no object there) you'll actually feel the object. The second function of the gloves is that they actually allow you to interact with objects. You can pick up an object and do things with it, just like you would with a real object. You can pick up a virtual baseball and throw it. So it allows you to do things to the world. It does more than that; the glove also measures how your hand is moving. This is very important so that in the virtual world you can see a version of your hand to see your movements. It's important that you wear clothing that not only transfers sensations to you but measures what your body is doing.

The computer that's running the Virtual Reality will use your body's movements to control whatever body you choose to have in Virtual Reality, which might be human or might be something quite different. You might very well be a mountain range or a galaxy or a pebble on the floor. A piano . . . I've considered being a piano. I'm interested in being musical instruments quite a lot. Also, you can have musical instruments that play reality in all kinds of ways aside from making sound in Virtual Reality. That's another way of describing arbitrary physics. With a saxophone you'll be able to play cities and dancing lights, and you'll be able to play the herding of buffalo's plains made of crystal, and you'll be able to play your own body and change yourself as you play the saxophone. You could become a comet in the sky one moment and then gradually unfold into a spider that's bigger than the planet that looks down at all your friends from high above.

Then, of course, there's the Home Reality Engine. The Home Reality Engine is a computer that by 1989 standards is a very powerful computer but in the future will just be a regular computer. It has a lot of jobs to do. It has to be repainting the graphics that your eyes see, and calculating the sounds that your ears hear, and calculating the textures that your skin feels, all the time quickly enough so that the world is realistic. That's a very big task. It has to communicate with other Home Reality Engines in other people's houses so that you can share realities with other people, and that's a very big task. It's quite a special computer and it makes a Macintosh look like a little speck.

AH: When you first put on your clothing and become aware of the Home Reality Engine, are you presented with something analogous to the Macintosh desktop, that is to say a work space with tools in it?

JL: Once again this is a cultural question. The point is that in Virtual Reality there's no need for a single metaphor, whereas there is a need for a single design metaphor in a computer. We are used to switching contexts in real life. It's normal to be in your living room in which you behave one way and in which you do certain things, and then go to work, say, and you do something totally different, you go to the beach and you're in an utterly different state of mind, and you go into a temple and you're in a still different state of mind. All those places are really different streams of life that we associate with an overall environment. There's simply no need for one unified paradigm for experiencing the physical world, and there's no need for one in Virtual Reality either.

Virtual Reality is not like the next way computers will be; it's much, much broader than the idea of a computer. A computer is a specific tool. Virtual Reality is an alternate reality and you shouldn't carry over into Virtual Reality the limitations that are necessary for computers to make sense. It's an absurd limitation. Because what we're synthesizing here is reality itself and not just a particular isolated machine; there are a lot more possibilities than with the Macintosh.

What will probably happen is that the Home Reality Engine will have a capability to scan the room that it's in and so will your glasses. The very first thing that you'll see when you put on Virtual Reality clothing for the first time will simply be an alternate version of the physical room that you started out in. So, for instance, if you are in your living room and you put on Virtual Reality clothing—let's suppose that your living room has a couch, and it has a set of shelves, and it has a window, it has two doorways, it has a chair; it has all these things and it has certain dimensions (walls and ceiling). When you put on your glasses the first thing you'll see is an alternate version of your living room with the same dimensions. Wherever there is a thing in the living room there will be something in the Virtual world. Where there's a chair in the living room there will be a something in the Virtual world. It probably won't be a chair—it very well might be a chair, though. The Home Reality Engine will just do a substitution. The reason for this is that it will prevent you from bumping into anything. It will have some early tools that you can use. For instance, it will have the equivalent of directories in computers, but they won't look like directories, of course. There may be giant trellises, trellises a million miles across, that are perfectly lightweight, that you can pull yourself through, that carry with them all sorts of different objects, a veritable museum of different objects that you might explore. You might have one of those that shows up in your room. You might very well have a whole bunch of little buckets, and whenever you put one of those buckets on your head you find yourself inside another world, another universe. There will be things like that.

AH: Will these buckets be things that you've created yourself or will they come as a software package?

JL: There will be some starter ones. They would have been created over time communally by the community of users. They would have been started by some of us. You'll certainly make your own after a while. But the thing that you have to remember is that Virtual Reality is a much broader idea than, say, the Macintosh. Its purpose will be general communication with other people, not so much getting sorts of work done. The Macintosh was conceived as a way of automating desk-type of work, so they used the desktop metaphor. It was quite appropriate and obviously it's been very successful; it was a cultural match. Virtual Reality is conceived of as an expansion of reality, the provision of alternate realities for people in mass in which to share experiences, and so the types of metaphors that come up are things like cars, travel, different countries, different cultures.

For instance, you might very well have a virtual car that you ride around even though physically you're in one place. It would go through different territories in Virtual Reality so that you could get around them—or transporter booths, perhaps. So you could have geographical metaphors. There might very well evolve a new geography, let's say—a fictitious planet with new continents that you can dive into to find new realities. In the early Virtual Realities you'll only be able to see the Virtual Reality when you're in it. Later, there will be more sophisticated ones where you can blend Virtual objects and physical objects so that you can live in a mixed reality for a while and be able to see your physical environment as if you were wearing sunglasses but also have nonphysical objects mixed in it. That will be a later stage. We're already developing technology to do that but it's an order of magnitude more complex to pull off.

In Virtual Reality any tool is possible and there will be some wonderful tools. In Virtual Reality your memory can be externalized. Because your experience is computer-generated, you can simply save it, and so you can play back your old experience anytime from your own perspective. Given that, you can organize your experience and use your experience, use your externalized memory in itself, as the basis for what you would call the "Finder" in the Macintosh. That will be quite a different thing. You can keep whole universes in your pocket or behind your ear and pull them out and look through them any time.

AH: Mechanically, how do you go about playing back your memory?

JL: What would you actually do? See, that's a very personal decision. You have to understand that in the Virtual Reality, each person might have very personal idiosyncratic tools that might even be invisible to others, but it's the shared reality that you affect by using your tools that counts. That's what's the most important thing. And it's nice to see each other's tools too; it's kind of intimate but it will be fun. My way of having my memories might be . . . I think I'll keep them behind my ear. I imagine reaching behind my ear and pulling them out in front of my eyes and then I'll suddenly find myself wearing bifocals where I wasn't before. In the lower half of the bifocals I see the virtual world as it is shared and in the upper half I'm looking into my memories of the past. These aren't real bifocals, of course. From now on whenever I refer to anything, I'm talking about virtual things, not physical things. There will be a machine that looks like that machine at the optometrist's where you can flick little lenses into place; there will be this machine that's floating out in front of me, and each of the lenses I can flick into place filters out different aspects of my history. One will say, "Well, filter out everything that wasn't in this room." Another will say, "Filter out anything that wasn't with this other person." And another will say, "Filter out anything that didn't involve music," and so forth. When I flick all these filters into place, I have a narrower and narrower view of my history, so I'm looking at less and less of it.

Another filter I might flick into place will order it in different ways. I might want to order it chronologically as I experienced it, or I might want to have it play back sorted according to its geographical distance in the virtual geographic space. Then I have a little device, a knob that I can turn to go forwards and backwards through my memories and flick filters at the same time. The filters might also change the ways the filters look. For instance, one object might make only certain kinds of things bigger and brighter. Like if I only want to find musical instruments from the past, I might go forwards and backwards through my history and the instruments will be particularly easy to see because they'll be bigger and brighter but they'll still be in their context, so I can still rely on my internal memories, which remember things in context. Of course, I'm somewhat simplifying things because I'm only using the visual metaphor now. I'll have the same thing for tactile and sonic memories. Then, if I see something I want to bring into the present reality, or if I see an old memory that I want to relive in a different way with the people that I'm currently with, we can either pull something out of it (simply reach into that memory and pull it out into the current circumstance) or we can all climb into the memory—either way. It doesn't matter.

AH: How did all of these memories get from your mind into the Virtual Reality?

JL: They never were in my mind. You see, they're memories of external reality. Let's say you're experiencing a few moments in Virtual Reality and perhaps you're sitting on the rings of Saturn—whatever turns you on. Now what's happened is that in order for you to perceive everything you perceived, in order to perceive that you were looking out into the vastness of space and that if you looked behind you there was this huge planet Saturn and so forth, in order to perceive that, the Home Reality Engine was generating those sensations. It was generating the images you saw in your glasses. It was generating the sounds you heard in your earphones. It was generating the textures you felt inside the glove. It can simply store these like any other computer information. There they are. You can play back exactly what you experienced. Experience becomes something you can store in a computer file.

I know that might sound rather cold. I'm the first one to criticize this horrible substitution of information for human experience. I think information in itself is a dreadful concept. It robs us of the richness of life. It robs us of the act of the joy of each moment and the mystery of the next. But it is simply true that the external experience, not the internal experience, but the external experience of Virtual Reality, is a computer file. And it's that simple. Now the reason that the whole thing works is that your brain spends a great deal of its efforts on making you believe that you're in a consistent reality in the first place. What you are able to perceive of the physical world is actually very fragmentary and a lot of what your nervous system accomplishes is covering up the gaps in your perception. In Virtual Reality this natural tendency of the brain works in our favor and as soon as there's a threshold, the brain will tend to think of either the physical world or the virtual world as being the reality you're inside of. But as soon as the brain thinks the virtual world is the reality you are inside of, all of a sudden it's as if all the technology works better. All variety of perceptual illusions come into play to cover up the flaws in the technology. All of a sudden the world becomes much more vivid than it should be. You perceive things that aren't there. You perceive the resistance of objects that actually have no mass as you try to push on them, and things of that kind.

Absolute Physics

AH: For interface shouldn't you be able to talk within your environment? Current voice recognition technology isn't very impressive.

JL: Well you should be able to and it would be a nice thing but it's not central at all. In fact, it's pretty superfluous, at least the way I think about Virtual Reality. I'm pretty sure that it will turn out to be a not very important aspect of it. It would take a while to explain why, but I suppose I should! There are a few special things about Virtual Reality to keep in mind, the things that make it important. One is that it's a reality in which anything can be possible, provided it's part of the external world. It's a world without limitation, a world as unlimited as dreams. It's also a world that's shared, like the physical world. It's as shared and as objectively real as the physical world is, no more, no less. Exactly how shared or real that is, is open to question, but whatever the physical world has Virtual Reality has as well. The thing that's remarkably beautiful to me about Virtual Reality is that you can make up reality in Virtual Reality and share it with other people. It's like having a collaborative lucid dream. It's like having shared hallucinations, except that you can compose them like works of art; you can compose the external world in any way at all as an act of communication.

The question is: well, given that you have a world where you can change it, how do you change it? Do you just talk to it and does it become the way you say it should be? Or do you do something else? Now, there are real limits to how you can change the world by talking. For instance, imagine that you were trying to teach a robot to fix a car engine and you tell the robot, "Okay now, connect this piece to that piece, turn this bolt and so forth." Well, you can do that to a degree but you can't really do that with a person. You have to show them. You can't run the world with language. Language is very limited. Language is a very, very narrow stream through the plain of reality. It leaves out a great deal. It's not so much it leaves things out as that language comes as a stream of little discrete symbols and the world is made of continuity and gesture. Language can suggest things about the world, but no painting could ever be fully described by words, nor can reality. The way that you can probe the reality is with a special kind of physics that can only exist in Virtual Reality. It's what I call Absolute Physics. For some time now I've been working on software that will be able to make Absolute Physics work in Virtual Reality. Coming back to the physical world for a second, there are only a very few things in the physical world that you can change fast enough to use as forms of communication. Mostly it's your tongue, and to a lesser degree the rest of your body. Your body is basically the extent of the physical world that you can communicate with in real time, but you can communicate with it as fast as you think. That's the way the body is. But then, beyond that you can change the physical world but you need tools. You can suddenly change a room from being dark to light by turning the switch because the switch is there. Technology in the physical world mostly functions to extend the human body one way or another so that it can be used as a medium for human action. The problem is that the kinds of tools that you can have are very limited. You can't have a light switch that turns day to night or a knob that makes the room suddenly grow or shrink in size. You can have tools that can color your face, but you can't have tools that can change you from one species to another. Basically, all that absolute physics is, is a physics that has any kind of causality at all, so you can have all these tools. Once you have all these tools, you can start, using whatever body you choose to have in

Virtual Reality, to use the tools to change the world very quickly in all kinds of ways. Then, you have this idea of being able to improvise reality. That's the thing that excites me the most about it.

AH: What does the interface look like? If I wanted to turn this cup green, what would I do to make it green?

JL: Okay, here's the deal. There's no one way. There would be a million ways to change the cup green. You could make up new ones and you could change that one over there. See, the tools that you use to change reality are somewhat private. It's the result of the change in reality that's the more social thing. People will be somewhat idiosyncratic about that and that will be an aspect of someone's personality. You have to understand what these tools are. In Virtual Reality . . . . well, things are vastly different. You would be able to have all kinds of tools with you all the time. In fact, memory in Virtual Reality is external. You have a movie of your life that's there all the time that you can pull out. It has in it all the tools you've ever used. You can find them quickly. You'll have all kinds of tools. Now the way you turn the cup green would probably be with some kind of little coloring device. The kind of coloring device that I'm going to have is a little wand thing, a little prism that I pick up. I turn it and it reflects the rainbow of my eyes. Whenever the color looks right I'll squeeze it and whatever it's pointed at will turn into that color. That will be my personal one; you might want something completely different.

Broadcast Media vs. Social Media

AH: We are witnessing a breakup of consensus reality in the external world right now and the political repercussions seem rather frightening as large segments of society have no common ground, no shared assumptions about reality. Will Virtual Reality not further undermine consensus reality?

JL: It's a complicated question with many, many angles to it. Let me just cover a few. One is that it's important to understand that notions of consensus reality are of a different order than what Virtual Reality is. Consensus reality involves a series of subjective realities and Virtual Reality only addresses objective reality, that is, the shared reality that is external to the senses. But there is interaction between the two on many levels. Another angle is that idealistically, I might hope that Virtual Reality will provide an experience of comfort with multiple realities for a lot of people in western civilization, an experience which is otherwise rejected. Most societies on earth have some method by which people experience life through radically different realities at different times, through ritual, through different things. Western civilization has tended to reject them but, because it's a gadget, I do not think that Virtual Reality will be rejected. It's the ultimate gadget. It's the culmination of gadgetry in many ways. I think that it will bring back into western experience something that has been lost.

Why that is so is a big topic. It will bring back a sense of the shared mystical altered sense of reality that is so important in basically every other civilization and culture prior to big patriarchal power. I hope that that might lead to some sense of tolerance and understanding. But there's more to it than that. I often worry about whether it's a good technology or a bad technology. I have a little benchmark I use for that. I believe that if a technology increases human power or even human intelligence and that's its sole effect, then it's simply an evil technology at birth. We're already both powerful enough and smart enough to accomplish a great deal. All of our problems are self-brought at this point. If the technology, on the other hand, has a tendency to increase human communication, human sharing, then I think it's a good one overall, even though there might be many ways it could be used badly. My chronic examples of these are that the television is bad but that the telephone is good. I could go on about that forever.

I do hope that Virtual Reality will provide more meeting between people. It has a tendency to bring up empathy and reduce violence, although there's certainly no panacea ultimately. People simply have to grow up and that could take a long time, too long. There are some other levels of interaction, too. You see, Virtual Reality starts out as a medium just like television or computers or written language, but once it gets to be used to a certain degree, it ceases to be a medium and simply becomes another reality that we can inhabit. When it crosses over that boundary it becomes another reality. I think of it as acting like a sponge where it absorbs human activity from the physical reality plane into the Virtual reality planes. To the degree that that happens there is a very beneficial asymmetry that comes into play. When Virtual Reality sponges up good energy from the physical plane, then what you get in Virtual Reality is beautiful art, beautiful dance, beautiful creativity, beautiful dreams to share, beautiful adventures. When Virtual Reality soaks up bad energy from the physical plane, what we get is some decrease, however small, in violence and hurt on the physical plane in exchange for events on the virtual plane which, while they might be uglier, are of no consequence whatsoever because they're virtual.

Barbara Stack: Unless they're syndicated, in which case they are educational propaganda. And don't they have consequences in that they further brutalize the participants?

JL: Well, physical reality is tragic in that it's mandatory. Virtual Reality is multiple-channel. People can choose and switch which Virtual Reality plane they're on. They can also simply take off their clothing if they want to get out of it. It's easy to take the physical world for granted and forget that you're inside it. (Well, that's a hard comment to explain.) It's harder to forget that you're inside of Virtual Reality and therefore it's harder to suffer it. You can simply take the clothing off.

AH: One of the images that haunts me is growing up watching Tom and Jerry cartoons, where in an alternative reality you can see somebody squashed by a steamroller and then pop up and be whole again. I think having absorbed so much of that king of imagery has numbed us; we have become a generation that is unaware of the pain of others.

JL: Virtual Reality is a very different situation than movies or television. I'm going to say something roundabout but it comes back to exactly the point you're bringing up. Movies and television are, first of all, broadcast media, so one facility has to generate the material that you see. Furthermore, it's very expensive to generate this material so very few people are in a position to do it. Therefore, the material becomes supernaturally remote and universal. It has a numbing effect on people and it reduces empathy. Television ultimately reduces empathy because people live in a world in which they can't act or have responsibility or meet each other. The shocking statistics about the number of hours that people in the United States spend watching television explain, I think, all too much about our actions in the world and our lack of empathy. When a person chooses to spend that much time watching television, it's equivalent to death as far as society is concerned. They cease to function as a responsible or social persons during the time that they're simply perceiving media.

Now Virtual Reality is just the opposite. First of all, it's a network like the telephone where there's no central point of origin of information. But, much more importantly, since nothing is made of physical matter, since it's all just made of computer information, no one has any advantage over anyone else in their ability to create any particular thing within it. So there's no need for a studio. There might be occasional needs for one, if somebody has a bigger computer to generate a certain kind of effect, or certainly if somebody's assembled people of a certain talent or reputation. But in general there's no built-in difference from one person to another in terms of ability to create. This means that there's going to be such a profusion of different forms. There will be movie studios that get involved in making Virtual Realities, but I think more there will be little entrepreneurs who will be like Reality Troubadours who will travel about spinning realities, if anything. What'll happen is that there will be such an enormous variety of form that "things" will become cheap. Basically, in a Virtual Reality everything is in infinite supply, except for one mysterious thing called creativity. And time, certainly, and health, and other things that are really still inside your body. But in terms of external things, they're infinite and wonderful and abundant and ever-varied and all equally valuable because they all can be made as easily. So what really is of value, what really will stand out as a foreground against a background in Virtual Reality is quite different than what stands out in the physical world. In the physical world mere excess or novelty will often make something stand out. A thousand dollar bill will stand out in the physical world. In the Virtual world there is absolutely no difference between a thousand dollar bill and a one dollar bill; they are simply two different graphic designs and they are both as plentiful as you can make them. Other people are the life of the party in Virtual Reality. Other people are the unique things that will animate Virtual Reality and make it astonishingly unpredictable and amazing. Personality will be accentuated since form will be so cheap; since form will be so non-precious, personality will be quite accentuated.

A good experiment to do is to observe somebody watching television. They look like a zombie. Then watch somebody using the telephone and they look animated. The difference is that one is a social medium and the other is a broadcast medium. In the social medium they're interacting with people. Virtual Reality is like that, more so than any medium ever has been, including, I believe, things like spoken language. And so you'll see people activated and animated. When people get social and see each other, especially in a context that will be so, let's say, 'illuminating' in the sense . . . . Virtual Reality is the ultimate lack of class or race distinctions or any other form of pretense since all form is variable. When people's personalities meet, freed of all pretense of that kind in the virtual plane, I think that will be an extraordinary tool for increasing communication and empathy. In that sense it might have a good effect on politics. You can't really ask what the purpose of Virtual Reality is because it's just too big. You can ask what the purpose of a chair is because it's a small enough thing to have a purpose. Some things are just so big that they become the context, or they become the problem.

AH: That is what we mean by a paradigm shift.

JL: I think Virtual Reality will have an effect of enhancing and, in a sense, completing the culture. My view is that our culture has been abnormally distorted by being incredibly molded by technology, but when technology was astonishingly young. I mean, television is a weird anomaly that will be remembered as a bizarre technology in the twentieth century, and

Ronald Reagan could only exist in television. We have to remember that we're living in a very peculiar bubble. Virtual Reality, by creating a technology that's general enough to be rather like reality was before there was technology, sort of completes a cycle. I think the reasons for having Virtual Reality are everything. There's recreation, there's education, there's expression, there's just pure work, there's therapy—all of those things. All of the same things that you'd find in language or physical reality or any other very large human pursuit.

AH: There's been a lot of loose talk over the past few years about Gaia, about our planet being an organism. What kind of vision can we have of Virtual Reality becoming an externalized consciousness of that organism?

JL: It's an interesting question. Virtual Reality represents a new mystery on the order of the mystery that nature presents us. It's a mystery that's entirely human-made in that it's the intersection of people in Virtual Reality that creates the mystery, that creates the chaos that will make it into a full-scale reality that's worthy of being experienced. I don't view machines as becoming conscious myself. It's not that I'm opposed to the notion; it's simply that I think that it's the wrong question to ask. But I do think that there will be a new emergent social consciousness that can only exist through the medium of Virtual Reality. Virtual Reality is the first medium that's large enough not to limit human nature. It's the first medium that's broad enough to express us as natural beings. It's the first medium within which we can express our nature and the whole of nature to each other. Actually, that's all rather vague, so let me just say that when we can make nature ourselves, we can empathize with the nature that there is and appreciate it fully.

We've split ourselves off in this culture of ours from nature. Our egos are very important to us and we really separate ourselves off from environment and from the overall flow of life. What'll happen is that in Virtual Reality we'll recreate the flow. The flow anywhere is the same flow, so the flow that we create in Virtual Reality will be a new flow but it's also a part of the same eternal flow and we'll become all of a sudden. . . . See, now there's an opposition. Our power in the world, our power of action, has always involved doing things to physical matter. It's very slow to do things to physical matter, so in order to be powerful we have to limit ourselves. Now in Virtual Reality, all of a sudden we become powerful in terms of: we can have action without that limitation. It allows us to not wish we could behave like gods but actually to behave like gods, albeit in a simulation. But that really doesn't matter because the simulation recreates exactly the same role that the physical world has to us (it's an external shared reality). It will reunite us with the flow of nature. Because ultimately, a new flow we create is just the same old flow of nature popping up in a new place. We'll just be paying attention to it since we'll be able to feel powerful in relation to it, which we can't with the physical one. We can do it a little bit with the atomic bomb every once in a while, but that's about it. It's actually very limited and I think it frustrates us terribly. I think we all feel like we did when we were just born; we want so much but we can do so little. All we can do is scream and then eventually we learn to talk, and maybe we learn some technology and can do a little more to the world, but we never overcome that horrible frustration at not being able to make the world around us that we share with other people as fluid as our imagination. It's so frustrating! We are of the world, we act in the world, and yet we're limited in it.

Now of course, Virtual Reality only gives us a temporary limitlessness. We still live in our physical bodies and we're still mortal. It might highlight our mortality to a degree that will make it harder to ignore than it is currently. People imagine Virtual Reality as being an escapist thing where people will be ever more removed from the real world and ever more insensitive. I think it's exactly the opposite; it will make us intensely aware of what it is to be human in the physical world, which we take for granted now because we're so immersed in it.

The Hardware

AH: Are these going to be linked up by phone lines?

JL: Absolutely. Obviously we're not talking about the current phone lines but about future phone lines, so this whole project is not something that's going to happen next year. It's going to wait until the placement of fiber optic phone lines into American homes. But that's already beginning; there's quite a few in place already. I should point out, just for the technologically oriented readers, that the bandwidth required for Virtual Reality is actually rather low because you're only communicating the changes in a database; you don't actually have to send images or sounds over the phone lines. So it's actually quite a low bandwidth communication. It's almost conceivable to do it with current phone lines. In fact, it probably is, if you just have a few of them instead of one. You can probably do crude ones. So it's not a major bottleneck in getting the technology working.

AH: Could you give us some idea of the state of current prototypes and how far down the road until I'll have a virtual reality device in my own home?

JL: Well, it's very early right now. We're in the same stage with Virtual Reality that computer science was in the very earliest days. We're about in the same place computer science was back in 1958 or 1960, perhaps. The systems being built were rather large and special purpose. Only institutions could afford them. But that will be changing, and it will be changing much faster than it did with computers. The first headset, the eyeglasses, were invented in 1969 by Ivan Sutherland, who was also the founder of computer graphics. Actually, Marvin Minsky, the founder of artificial intelligence, did make a pair in 1965, but the person who really got the whole thing going was Ivan Sutherland. The glove was originally invented by Tom Zimmerman. The current glove was designed by Young Harvel. Both of those people are from VPL. Right now, all of the basic components I've described exist, although in rather crude forms. The overall system works, although in a rather crude form. The best ones are behind locked doors in defense contracting companies and probably have no bearing to any real conversation about the subject. The most fun one that's working as a complete system is the one at NASA Ames, which is called the View Lab. It was put together by Mike McGreevy and Scott Fisher.

VPL has some wonderful surprises in store, but part of the fun is not telling just yet. You'll start to be able to experience Virtual Reality within a few years. There will be Virtual Reality rooms at universities that students can do projects in. I think there will be rather spectacular amusement park rides that will be tacky and not really worth bothering with. I've toyed with the idea of opening a Virtual Reality Parlour that would be a little bit more civilized. It would be sort of like a salon scene where people could have Virtual Reality conversations and have wild experiences, but they would be collaborative. It wouldn't be like an amusement park, some dumb experience designed to get you to drink a certain soft drink and see a certain movie and buy certain clothes, but rather would be a Virtual Salon. I think that would be very nice. Perhaps we'll see something like that in a few years. I hope so. I think so. A few years is a little bit vague, but I have to be because there are so many unknowns. But in three to five years, let's say, these things will be around. They'll be too expensive to have in your home, but a lot of people will be able to experience them through those institutions and businesses. On the other hand, Mattel has licensed the data glove from VPL and is marketing an inexpensive version as a Nintendo controller. In terms of actually having them in your home, I see it as being roughly around the turn of the century when that will start to happen. It won't be so much that you buy a set of reality clothing as that it will be through the phone company. They'll own the clothing itself or they'll own parts of it and you'll own other parts. Right now it's rather expensive, but at the turn of the century

I don't think it will be. You'll pay for the time that you use it in very much the same way the telephone was introduced. I see the telephone, from a business point of view, as being an extremely analogous kind of technology. Now telephones are so cheap that you go ahead and buy them. Originally, the telephone company continued to own the equipment and made the money off of your phone bill.

In a few years we will see medical Virtual Realities, where handicapped people can experience full motion interaction with others, where people with movement disabilities or paralysis will be able to experience a complete body. Another medical use is having surgery simulators so surgeons can enjoy the same benefits that pilots do and learn without putting lives at risk. Of course, surgeons can do that with cadavers, but it's not the same thing. A cadaver isn't the same thing as a body that really reacts, that can really bleed. You can't really make mistakes on a cadaver. There are people that are actively pursuing this. There's Dr. Joe Rosen at Stanford and Dr. Robert Chase, who are both looking at the problem from different angles. Joe Rosen might also be familiar to some people as the inventor of the nerve chip, but that's another story.

Another area is having miniature robots that could enter the human body. They would have microcameras and tiny hands. You would transfer your actions to the robot and the robot would transfer its perceptions to you so that you'd have the sensation of being inside the patient's body performing microsurgery. There are actually people now working on this technology. I'm sure none of the current projects will be the ones that work, but it is already something that people are attempting to do, and I'm sure that we'll see that sometime. I think that it will be working by the end of the century.

BS: When I think about what kind of old age I want as well as what old age is going to be possible or feasible in a society that's going in the way it is going . . . if I'm going to be locked into a very small room, I want to be locked into that room with a lot of machines that I love. So in a way it will liven up our old age and in the process to be connected not with people who happen to be in that neighborhood rest home but, in fact, the people who we want to communicate with who are spread all over the world. But on the other hand, it will be a good justification for their locking us up because after all, we've got our machine. It will be a cheap way to deal with us. . . .

JL: Yeah, that's certainly a horrible thought. I tell you the most vivid experience of Virtual Reality is the experience of leaving it. Because after having been in the reality that is man-made, with all the limitations and relative lack of mystery inherent in that, to behold nature is directly beholding Aphrodite; it's directly beholding a beauty that's intense in a way that just could never have been perceived before we had something to compare physical reality to. And that's one of the biggest gifts that Virtual Reality gives us, a renewed appreciation of physical reality. And so, I'm not sure what to say. I'm sure bad things will happen with Virtual Reality; there will be some pain that it plays a part in because it will be a big thing and the world can be cruel. But I think overall it will actually have a tendency to enhance people's sensitivity towards nature, towards preserving the earth, because they'll have a point of comparison.

Post-symbolic Communication

AH: Will Virtual Reality have interface with a Xanadu-like database of the world's knowledge?

JL: Well, Virtual Reality raises the question: "What is knowledge and what is world?" As soon as the world itself becomes changeable, it becomes immediate, and in a sense description becomes obsolete. But this goes into another realm that might take a long time to describe. Very briefly, there's an idea that I'm very interested in called post-symbolic communication. This means that when you're able to improvise reality as you can in Virtual Reality and then that's shared with other people, you don't really need to describe the world anymore because you can simply make any contingency. You don't really need to describe an action because you can create any action. Yes, there will be Xanadu-like knowledge bases, but then, once again I think that the Xanadu conception still separates knowledge and the world. Xanadu is still a way of connecting together descriptions in a network; it is still very descriptionary. Virtual Reality really opens up a territory beyond description, that transcends the idea of description.

AH: It seems to me that having a vast knowledge base, the great ideas and images from history, would be a wealth of raw materials out of which to compose our Virtual Realities.

JL: Absolutely, absolutely. That will be wonderful.

AH: Only it's the stage setting. We have this legacy of sets and props and costumes.

JL: Yes. Virtual Reality is a very general thing and it can do a lot of things. You can make up a Virtual Macintosh that would act like a real Macintosh within it, or a book, or a library, or a Sanskrit tablet, or whatever. It does all those things and all of those structures within Virtual Reality that act like things in the physical world are very important because they serve as the bridge. I think they'll be essential. In fact, I'm going to be talking to the Xanadu people about interfacing, about what we're doing and what they're doing, so that we'll have the bridge going from the start. I don't know how they'll feel about this but I think that from the Virtual Reality point of view, Xanadu might end up as being a standard interface to the physical world because it will have the best descriptive universe in the physical world. Computers live by description. We shouldn't, though.

Let's suppose that you could have a time machine go back to the earliest creatures who developed language, our ancestors at some point, and gave them Virtual Reality clothing. Would they have ever developed language? I suspect not because as soon as you can change the world in any way, that is a mode of expression of utter power and eloquence; it makes description seem a little bit limited. I don't fully know what this means. I don't know what direct reality communication would be like, reality improvisation without symbols. I doubt if we'll ever leave symbols behind because our brains have grown to adapt to symbols; you know, there's a language cortex now and all that. All a symbol is, is something that we perceive that refers to something else. And so every symbol has at least a double nature, which is it in itself if you don't interpret it as a symbol and then, whatever it stands for. What happens is that in, say, a poem, there are both the thing referred to by the words as a collection and then there's also the inherent rhythm and typography and all of the other things that are the nonsymbolic aspects of it as an artifact. Even those things might also have symbolic aspects. For instance, a font might symbolize something but it also is a font in itself. It gets kind of complicated; it gives philosophers jobs. There's really no nonsymbolic way to communicate a lot of things and our lives are just built around symbols. By symbols I'm speaking pretty broadly, including gestures and pictures as well as words. Virtual Reality will inaugurate a whole new parallel stream of communication. I've been working on a whole description of what it might be like to communicate without symbols. It has a different rhythm. For instance, in symbolic communication, you have the notion of question and answer and this kind of repartee which defines the flow of communication. In Virtual Reality, since people are collaboratively changing a shared reality as a means of communication, what you'll have is nodes of relative static quality versus periods of very dynamic quality. There will be this rhythm between when the world is being changed quickly and when it sort of settles down. That rhythm is something like what a sentence is in language. In spoken language you have the phenomenon of finding the next world and going, "Um . . . um . . ." The same thing will happen in Virtual Reality where people will go through an interval of spacing out from the reality, preparing their next change to the shared world.

I can point to the direction of what it might be like in the general sense, but it's almost by definition impossible to make completely compelling examples. I'll give you a few, though. If we think of an experience where you're describing something to someone else—let's suppose you're describing what it's like to live in the East Coast in these grungy violent cities and how you have a completely different set of expectations versus living in what seems to be the rather safe and lovely but rather bland and aimless cities of California—now to describe those things . . . I just did that. I just came up with some brief symbolic descriptions of what cities in New York and California are like. In Virtual Reality there's the possibility of simply playing back one's memory with the other person inside it from the other city. When you directly have at your beck and call external reality to be played back, created, improvised at will, description is simply narrow. Now description is interesting because, in its narrowness it does bring in possibilities for poetry that probably don't exist in the fullness of post-symbolic communication where you can just create experience as a whole all the time. On the other hand, in creating experience as a whole all the time, you have this possibility of a kind of collaboration that you really can't have with symbols, where people can be simultaneously molding a shared reality. I realize these things are hard to describe and that's appropriate. What I'm trying to describe is communication that is itself beyond description. The idea might turn out to be wrong; it might turn out that communication without symbols and description is just a silly idea and a path wrongly taken. So it's really a grand experiment, and I think it will be a lot of fun.

Of course communication without symbols already happens constantly. First of all, the clearest example of receiving communication that is nonsymbolic is to commune with nature. The direct perception you have when nature communicates to you as you walk in the forest is simply prior to or beyond symbols. There's no need to prove that. Any linguist who would argue otherwise is beneath contempt. An example of communicating outwards without symbols is when one moves one's own body. You don't send a symbol to your arm or to your hand; you communicate prior to symbols to your own body. The most beautiful example that now exists of an intense sort of communicating outward without symbols is in lucid dreaming. When you dream lucidly you are aware that you're dreaming and you control the dream. It's rather like Virtual Reality except that it's not shared. The means by which you communicate to your dream is without symbols. There you are spinning the world, spinning anything in the world without symbols, simply making it be.

Now, of course, those are the purified examples, some purified examples of nonsymbolic communication that already exist. But, of course, all of life is deeply imbued with nonsymbolic communication. A book has its nonsymbolic aspects; I mean, a book is a book as an object prior to being a book that can be decoded as a bearer of symbols. Everything has symbolic and nonsymbolic aspects to it. A thing isn't a symbol; it's just that you can use anything as a symbol. The idea of symbol is a use for a thing, but everything is also a thing in and of itself; everything has a primary thingness. (Twisty sentences like that are part of what led me to the search for post-symbolic communication!)

AH: How does Virtual Reality relate to the images of cyberspace that we've had in so much recent science fiction?

JL: It's better. I mean, cyberspace is just another set on which to have adolescent fantasies unfold. In these novels, like True Names and Neuromancer and so forth, people don't do anything interesting with the artificial reality.

AH: It's like CB radio.

JL: That's right. Cyberspace is the CB radio of Virtual Reality. That's an excellent metaphor. It's a trivial use of it.

AH: Considering the freedom that people have to fantasize in D & D games, it's amazing how restricted the imagination is that's manifested.

JL: I agree completely. And I'm sure there will be mundanity in Virtual Reality as well, because mundanity is a part of humanity. But I'm not too worried about it. The whole 'economy' of Virtual Reality is set up to accentuate creativity since it is, as I said, the only thing in short supply. In a sense it's the only thing that really exists. Personality and creativity are perceivable and forms will be less and less noticed because they'll be so plentiful.

AH: Where does that leave those of us who collect "stuff"? What are the prospects of house cleaning now?

JL: Well, the stuff will seem more precious and the house more dirty because the physical world will appear amplified in comparison. I'm not anti-physical world and I'm not anti-symbolic communication at all. I mean, I love those things.

AH: Are there any historic images that come to mind that set the stage?

JL: Oh many, many. God, that's a huge question too. So many, so many. There are the lost memory arts, the memory palaces. Most of the western cultures relied on imagined Virtual Realities, these imagined palaces that people hung their memories in as artworks. People would memorize their palaces in order to have a way of remembering things, and before Gutenberg that was a very important thing. It was absolutely as primary as music or the arts of war to a particular culture. The memory arts sort of vanished because they were rendered obsolete. But they were remarkably like Virtual Reality. So many things come to mind about that. It's really too broad a question. Our attempts to change the physical world. We have raped the physical world because we don't have Virtual Reality. I mean, technology is just our attempt to use the physical world as a means of action. The physical world resists it and therefore we have the ugliness that we live with all the time. But Virtual Reality is the ideal medium for that type of action. Just architecture, technology in general, is really the strongest precedent, our attempts to modify the physical world as a means of human action. That's the strongest precedent. Oh, so much more. The very first time that somebody put on glasses that had imagery in them actually wasn't—I mean the glasses I mentioned that were done by Marvin Minsky and Ivan Sutherland were the first ones that had computer imagery. But some people had attached a stereo camera to a set of eyeglasses with stereo television sets as early as 1955. Some engineers from Philco had it rigged up in a periscope-like setup. There was a stereo camera on the top floor of a building. You could look out through it from inside the building. It had a limited degree of tracking, so you could have the feeling of looking over the side of the building. That was a big thrill back then. It probably still would be now.

AH: I can imagine what a thrill it was for the first people who looked through their stereopticons back at the turn of the century.

JL: Absolutely. There are so many precedents. I think Virtual Reality is a major node of culmination of culture. I think there are just enormous things that are fulfilled by it and an enormous number of things that can be seen as precedents.

Notes

Chapter 1. How to Go "behind" Physical Space

1. For those who are not familiar with thought experiments as an often-used philosophical method, a word of explanation may be necessary. A thought experiment is a hypothetical situation designed to test a theory about the logical relations among concepts or to grasp the essence of phenomena under a concept. It does not concern the practical implementation of the process involved in such a situation nor does it imply that such a process has actually existed in the world. It does, however, require the situation to be possible in principle.

In everyday life, we also often use a thought experiment to make a point. If somebody claims that, referring to a man's height, "the taller, the better," you may show him that such a claim is inadequate by a simple thought experiment. You may ask him, "If you were taller than any building in the world, would that be better than being just as tall as Michael Jordan?" He might realize that his claim "the taller, the better" is invalid after imagining himself taller than every building in the world in contrast to being as tall as Michael Jordan. Does he need to grow taller than every building in order to see the point? Of course not. Do we need to know how to make him that tall? We don't. In this simple thought experiment, the relationship between the two concepts, being tall and being good, is clarified.

In our discussions here, thought experiments are much more complex. We are trying to grasp the essential components of, and conceptual relations among, ideas of reality, sensory perception, personal identity, and so on. We need to be completely focused in order to follow the train of thought. "Why don't we use real-life examples that are easier to follow?" you may ask. The reason why usual examples do not work is this: When there is a conceptual confusion and thus there is a need for philosophical clarification, the confusion is usually caused exactly by the incompleteness of our experience in everyday life. Since (to continue on the same example) we may not have met a person tall enough to cause obvious inconvenience in everyday life, while we do know people who complain about being too short, we might get the impression that taller is always better. To shatter such a misconception, we have to go beyond the extraordinary. By the same token, thought experiments in philosophy often need to be very outlandish in order to shake people's fundamental yet unjustified beliefs.

2. Michael Heim, *The Metaphysics of Virtual Reality* (New York: Oxford University Press, 1993), 130.

3. In Einstein's Special Theory of Relativity, anything that travels at the speed of light is understood in the Minkowski's space-time continuum as non-traveling since the interval is always zero. Thus the radio waves involved in a CCS might be understood as intact and thus there is no "distance" between A1 and B2 or between B1 and A2. In a Minkowski framework, physical one-ness and the one-ness of the person might be equivalent. We will discuss this more later when we deal with the issue of consciousness.

4. When either one feels an itch on his face, for example, and raises his hand to scratch it, he will find that his hand is touching a face but his own face is not being touched and the itch remains. The other person will feel no itch (unless there is a coincidence) but is being scratched by a hand. It is so because there is still a discrepancy between the perception of two parts of the body.

5. This raises another fundamental question about the nature of light in understanding the relationship between the mental and the physical. Light doesn't travel "across" space but makes space possible, which starts the perceived division between the mental and the physical in terms of intentionality. This topic needs to be discussed fully in a separate project.

6. Quoted from Jaron Lanier's "A Vintage Virtual Reality Interview" on his web site available online in October 1996 at: http://www.well.com/user/jaron/vrint.html. It was first published in *Whole Earth Review*, titled: "Virtual Reality: An Interview with Jaron Lanier," Fall 1989, vol 64. The online version of this interview is included in this book as an appendix.

7. Lanier, "A Vintage Virtual Reality Interview."

8. See Hilary Putnam's *The Many Faces of Realism* (LaSalle: Open Court, 1987), 17.

Chapter 2. The Causal and the Digital under the Virtual

1. Actually, many interesting activities, apart from the sexual, could be a result of such a combination. The interaction between a surgeon and her patient is clearly one of the many examples.

2. See chapter 7 of Heim's *The Metaphysics of Virtual Reality*.

3. When we discuss Daniel Dennett's philosophy of consciousness in chapter 4, we will know why even smart people can make such a big mistake.

4. Heim, *The Metaphysics of Virtual Reality*, 114–15.

5. ?? Stewart, "Interview: Jaron Lanier," *Omni* 13 (January 1991): 45.

6. Stewart, "Interview: Jaron Lanier," 115–16.

7. Only temporal continuity or discontinuity is inherent in the sequence of the signals as a result of the consciousness's intentional projection. This will become clearer after we have discussed the one-ness of consciousness later in chapter 5.

8. Stewart, "Interview: Jaron Lanier," 113.

9. Nicole Stenger, "Mind Is a Leaking Rainbow," in *Cyberspace: First Steps*, ed. by Michael Benedikt (Cambridge: The MIT Press, 1994), 50.

10. Stewart, "Interview: Jaron Lanier," 114.

11. Michael Benedikt, "Cyberspace: Some Proposals," in *Cyberspace: First Steps*, ed. by Michael Benedikt (Cambridge: The MIT Press, 1994), 119–224.

12. Heim, *The Metaphysics of Virtual Reality*, 115–16.

Chapter 3. The Parallelism between the Virtual and the Actual

1. Myron W. Krueger, "An Easy Entry Artificial Reality," in *Virtual Reality: Applications and Explorations*, ed. by Alan Wexelblat (Boston: Academic Press Professional, 1993), 152.

2. Considering the distinction between primary and secondary qualities, sense of touch might have priority over other modalities in terms of whether there is something real out there. If you feel that you bump into something but you cannot see it (while you can see other things), hear a sound from it, you will have a stronger sense of confronting something real than, say, seeing or hearing something when your sense of touch tells you there is nothing there. But even your sense of touch needs an agreement by other modalities of sensation such as vision to establish your conviction of reality.

3. Zhenming Zhai (my original Chinese name), *The Radical Choice and Moral Theory: Through Communicative Argumentation to Phenomenological Subjectivity* (Dordrecht: Kluwer Academic Publishers, 1994), chap. 2.

Chapter 4. All Are Optional Except the Mind

1. I have a suggestion for the world scientific community to consider. Currently physical science is divided into different branches based on the division of our senses. For example, optics is based on our sense of vision, acoustics on our sense of hearing, and rigid body mechanics largely on our sense of touch. But we can now try to reduce all known laws of physics based on different modalities of sensation in these fields into laws based on only one modality of sensation. For example, we can try to reduce laws of optics into laws of acoustics, or vice versa; or to reduce laws of rigid body mechanics into laws of optics. This kind of reduction is based on creative use of mathematics and reductive imagination. We ask questions such as: "If we did not have a sense of vision but only a sense of hearing, how could we express those laws of optics, as we have known them up until now, without an idea of color?" or, equivalently, "If we use an analog device that transforms all regularities of the change of color into corresponding regularities of the change of sound, how can we reformulate our known laws of optics from a purely acoustic point of view?" Different groups of physical scientists can work in different directions, one trying to reduce everything into optics, the other into acoustics, and so forth. Such a cooperative effort will result in a greatly

expanded explanatory and predictive power of physical science, and hopefully in unexpected scientific discoveries.

2. John R. Searle, *The Rediscovery of the Mind* (Boston: The MIT Press, 1992), 63.

3. Searle, *The Rediscovery of the Mind*, 211.

4. He is right that some cognitive scientists commit such a fallacy when they believe that a physical process can be digital without being interpreted as digital. They implicitly assume that inside the human brain there is a human-like interpreter, but such an assumption will lead to an infinite regression.

5. Stewart, "Interview: Jaron Lanier," 115.

6. See chapter 5 of my *The Radical Choice and Moral Theory*.

7. Daniel Dennett, *Consciousness Explained* (Boston: Little, Brown and Company, 1991), 365.

8. Dennett, *Consciousness Explained*, 356.

9. Henry P. Stapp, "Why Classical Mechanics Cannot Naturally Accommodate Consciousness but Quantum Mechanics Can," *PSYCHE* 2 (1995).

10. Actually, the idea of looking for a small image of the object in the brain is a silly idea because an image like that would only show that there is a duplicate of the retina in the brain. A duplicate, of course, wouldn't help us understand anything more than we did by studying the eye itself, apart from the knowledge that there is a duplicate. By the same token, the question of why an upside down image on the retina does not cause an upside down perception is a false question because the information the brain processes has no "up" or "down" side since it is not an image. If it were still an image, then we would need to look further until we find something which is not an image in order to explain anything about visual perception. Geometrically, if everything were "upside down," there would be no frame of reference for anything to appear "upside down."

11. Stapp, "Why Classical Mechanics Cannot Naturally Accommodate Consciousness but Quantum Mechanics Can," 2.2.

12. Sherry Turkle, *The Second Self: Computers and the Human Spirit* (New York: Simon and Schuster, 1984).

13. Sherry Turkle, *Life on the Screen* (New York: Simon and Schuster, 1995).

Chapter 5. The Meaning of Life and Virtual Reality

1. Aldous Huxley, *Brave New World Revisited* (New York: Harper & Row, 1958), 1.

2. Aldous Huxley, *Brave New World* (New York: Harper & Row, 1958), 39.

3. Huxley, *Brave New World*, 66.

4. Huxley, *Brave New World*, 65.

5. Huxley, *Brave New World*, 285.

6. Huxley, *Brave New World*, 281.

7. Huxley, *Brave New World*, 257, italics mine.

8. Huxley, *Brave New World*, 288.

9. Jaron Lanier, "A Vintage Virtual Reality Interview."

10. A difference that is both real and significant is perhaps called an "authentic" difference in many circumstances. Correct me if I am wrong.

11. In everyday English, being significant is not totally equivalent to being meaningful; especially, meaningfulness seems always to be understood as positive. People would not usually say, "It's meaningful and it is also disastrous," if they are not expressing some kind of irony. Here, however, I use the word "meaningful" in a little bit different way that will become clearer as we proceed.

12. Zhai, *The Radical Choice and Moral Theory.*

13. Zhai, *The Radical Choice and Moral Theory*, 86.

14. It is unfortunate that most naturalistic philosophers do not understand or misunderstand Husserl's deadly attack on psychologism at the beginning of this century. Actually, a thorough analysis of mistake of the naturalistic reductionism can be developed to undermine all kinds of attempts to understand humanity in a naturalistic fashion. Hot philosophers, such as Richard Rorty, Daniel Dannett, Charles Taylor, Alesdair MacIntyre, Steven Fuller, and others, can be shown to be fatally wrong at the very bottom after such an analysis. Philosophical reflections on VR alone, on the other hand, will also challenge the very presuppositions of these philosophers' arguments. A full technical discussion of this requires, though, a separate project. For a phenomenological critique of naturalism in general, see chapter 4 of my book, *The Radical Choice and Moral Theory.*

15. Howard Rheingold, *Virtual Reality* (New York: Summit Books, 1991), 177.

Chapter 6. VR and the Destiny of Humankind

1. Martin Heidegger, *Being and Time*, trans. by John Macquarrie and Edward Robinson (New York/London: Harper & Row, 1962), 303.

2. Zhai, *The Radical Choice and Moral Theory*, chap. 5.

3. Heim, *The Metaphysics of Virtual Reality*, 143.

Appendix

1. This interview was originally published in the *Whole Earth Review*. It is protected by copyright, and the Web version is published here by Lanier's permission.

Glossary

Actual Reality
    The reality that is naturally given, as we are now accustomed to, opposed to virtual reality, which is artificially made.
Artificial Intelligence (AI)
    Alleged intelligence of man-made objects, such as a computer, a robot, etc.
Causal
    In this book, a causal (as opposed to subcausal) process is defined as a process of physical interaction which leads to another physical process, and is not carried out for the purpose of facilitating a parallel digital process.
CCS (see Cross-Communication Situation)
Communicative Mode of Subjectivity
    One of the three modes of subjectivity, characterized by its conceptual/theoretical and argumentative orientation; leading to an intersubjective consensus on the validity or invalidity, or the strength of a concept, a claim, or a theory.
Communicative Rationality
    The kind of rationality by which a consensus on the validity or invalidity of a claim is reached among members of a communication community through reasoned argumentation alone; the core of communicative rationality is the requirement of performative consistency, that is, a consistency between the claim being made and the act of making the claim, apart from the general requirement of formal logic.
Community of Interpersonal-Telepresence
    A community of mutual exchangeability of functioning sense organs by means of telecommunication; any member of the community can be present, without an actual trip to the place, in any location where one of the shared bodies is present.
Conative Mode of Subjectivity
    One of the three modes of subjectivity, characterized by its projective and volitional orientation; leading to the act that changes reality more or less in the direction as projected.
Constitutive Mode of Subjectivity
    One of the three modes of subjectivity, characterized by its a priori constitution of a world of objectivity in a given framework; leading to a cognitive separation of an objectified world of physical entities from consciousness.

Cross-Communication Situation

A situation involving two people, in which each person's brain communicates with the other person's lower-than-neck part of the body through telecommunication attachments.

Cross-Sensory Perception

For two modalities of sensation, typically vision and hearing, each is fed with artificially transformed signals originally received by the other; that is, light signals are transformed into sound signals and will be heard with ears, whereas sound signals into light signals and seen with eyes.

Cybersex

Sexual experience, including intercourse, through telepresence and teleoperation such that its experiential part is fulfilled in virtual reality while its procreative part is accomplished in actual reality.

Cyberspace

A totally coordinated system of stimuli of all senses tied to perceived objects in a dynamic 3-D field of vision; it is ontologically parallel to what we now call the "physical space" since we can interact with objects in it and thereby manipulate the physical processes effectively just as we can in the actual world.

Expansive Part of VR

The part of virtual reality furnished solely for the sake of expanding human creative experiences which are beyond our reach in actual reality. It does not have to involve teleoperation as in the foundational part.

Fallacy of Unity Projection

A fallacy that mistakes the unity attained in the inquirer's mind as a unity that occurs in the objectified brain, which is being studied in a model of classical mechanics.

Foundational Part of VR

The part of virtual reality in which our interaction with simulated objects causes a process in actual reality. As an intended result, teleoperation is carried out through robotic technology for purposes of maintaining necessary agricultural and industrial production.

Humanitude

The human uniqueness that separates human beings categorically from objects in the world. This is characterized by the intersubjective meaning-complexes generated through the interplay among the three modes of subjectivity.

Immersion Technology

The technology that generates totally coordinated system of stimuli to our sense organs that replaces, and thus isolates us from, the system of natural stimuli in the actual world.

Immersive

Totally surrounded by an artificial environment in one's experience and totally separated from perceptual experience in the natural environment.

Inside-Out Control

Teleoperation carried out by interacting with virtual reality from cyberspace so as to manipulate physical processes in the actual world.

Interpersonal-Telepresence

A cross-connection is established between one's brain and another person's lower-than-neck part of the body by means of telecommunication. A person can be present in the place where another person is willing to give up his/her presence in that place just by switching to a new state of connection.

Meaning-Complex

A non-causal interconnection among many items of meaning generated by each individual in the past, at present, or in the future, which is independent of any individual's recognition of it.

Metaphysics

A kind of philosophical inquiry that asks, discusses, and attempts to answer questions about that which is ontologically significant yet not accessible by sense perception.

Ontology

A kind of philosophical inquiry that asks, discusses, and attempts to answer the question of what is fundamentally real or not real and why so.

Personal Identity, The Question of

The philosophical question about what makes a person uniquely one and the same person despite ever-changing attributes.

Principle of Reciprocity (PR)

The Principle of Reciprocity between alternative sensory frameworks says that all possible sensory frameworks that support a certain degree of coherence and stability of perception have equal ontological status for organizing our experiences.

Psy-Factor

A factor in a law of physics that indicates the participation of consciousness in the process this law describes; in this book, the conjecture is that the square root of -1 in quantum mechanics and Special Theory of Relativity is the psy-factor.

Simulation

Reproducing the pattern of interaction of a certain natural process by creating and running certain computer programs with certain parameters.

Subcausal

A special term adopted in this book to designate a physical process (such as the electronic process in a computer chip) carried out for the sole purpose of supporting an intended digital process.

Subjectivity

Subjectivity is that which makes human beings a subject. A subject, qua its subjectivity, observes but cannot be observed, perceives but cannot be perceived, and is thus the precondition of objectivity and meaningful experiences.

Teleoperation

Manipulating a physical process from a remote place while the operator perceives it as an on-site operation as a result of utilizing telepresence technology.

Teleportation

Changing one's presence from one place to another without a continuous process of moving through the physical space between the two places.

Telepresence

An experience of being in one place while located physically in another place during one's normal state of consciousness.

Three Modes of Subjectivity

The constitutive, communicative, and conative modes of subjectivity (see).

Three Principles of Reflexivity

1) Whatever reasons we have for justifying the materiality of the actual world are equally valid or invalid for justifying the materiality of the virtual world.

2) Whatever reasons we have for calling the perceived objects in the virtual world illusory are equally applicable or inapplicable for calling those in the actual world illusory.

3) Whatever functions we need to perform in the actual world for our survival and prosperity we can also perform in the virtual world.

Virtual Reality (VR)

An artificial system of sensory perception that separates us from actual reality but allows us to manipulate physical processes and interact with other human beings equally well or better, while providing unprecedented possibilities for expanding our creative power.

Zombie

An object that looks and behaves like a human being but does not have consciousness or self-consciousness.

Bibliography

Benedikt, Michael. "Cyberspace: Some Proposals", in Michael Benedikt, ed. *Cyberspace: First Steps*. Cambridge/London: The MIT Press, 1994, pp. 119–224.

Dennett, Daniel C. *Consciousness Explained*. Boston: Little, Brown and Company, 1991.

Dertouzos, Michael L. *What Will Be: How the New World of Information Will Change Our Lives*. San Francisco: HarperEdge, 1997.

Gibson, William. *Neuromancer*. New York, Ace Books, 1984.

Heim, Michael. *The Metaphysics of Virtual Reality*. New York/Oxford: Oxford University Press, 1993.

Huxley, Aldous. *Brave New World*. 2nd ed. New York: Harper & Row, Publishers, 1946.

———. *Brave New World Revisited*. New York: Harper & Row, Publishers, 1958.

Lanier, Jaron. "A Vintage Virtual Reality Interview", on his web site at http://www.well.com/user/jaron/vrint.html, available on-line, Oct., 1996. First published in *Whole Earth Review* as "Virtual Reality: An Interview with Jaron Lanier," Fall 89 v n64.

Larijani, L. Casey. *The Virtual Reality Primer*. New York: McGraw-Hill, Inc., 1994.

Nelson, Theodore. "Interactive Systems and the Design of Virtuality." In *Creative Computing*, Nov.–Dec., 1980: 56–62.

Nozick, Robert. "Fiction." In *Ploughshares*, vol. 6, no. 3, 1980.

Pimentel, Ken, and Kevin Teixeira. *Virtual Reality: Through the New Looking Glass*. New York: Windcrest Books, 1993.

Putnam, Hilary. *The Many Faces of Realism*. LaSalle: Open Court, 1987.

Rheingold, Howard. *Virtual Reality*. New York: Summit Books, 1991.

Searle, John R. *The Rediscovery of the Mind*. Cambridge: The MIT Press, 1992.

Slouka, Mark. *War of the Worlds: Cyberspace and the High-Tech Assault on Reality*. New York: Basic Books, 1995.

Turkle, Sherry. *Life on the Screen: Identity in the Age of the Internet*. New York: Simon & Schuster, 1995.

Walker, John. *Through the Looking Glass*. Sausalito: Autodesk, Inc., 1988.

Wexelblat, Alan, ed. *Virtual Reality: Applications and Explorations*. Boston: Academic Press Professional, 1993.

Zhai, Zhenming. *The Radical Choice and Moral Theory: Through Communicative Argumentation to Phenomenological Subjectivity*. Dordrecht/Boston: Kluwer Academic Publishers, 1994.

Index

About the Author

Philip Zhai holds a bachelor's degree in engineering and a doctorate in philosophy. He is the author of the book *The Radical Choice and Moral Theory* and numerous articles. He also plays musical instruments and composes music. He is currently a professor at Muhlenberg College.